T0233829

Lecture Notes in Computer Science 9269

Commenced Publication in 1973
Founding and Former Series Editors:
Gerhard Goos, Juris Hartmanis, and Jan van Leeuwen

Editorial Board

David Hutchison
  Lancaster University, Lancaster, UK
Takeo Kanade
  Carnegie Mellon University, Pittsburgh, PA, USA
Josef Kittler
  University of Surrey, Guildford, UK
Jon M. Kleinberg
  Cornell University, Ithaca, NY, USA
Friedemann Mattern
  ETH Zurich, Zürich, Switzerland
John C. Mitchell
  Stanford University, Stanford, CA, USA
Moni Naor
  Weizmann Institute of Science, Rehovot, Israel
C. Pandu Rangan
  Indian Institute of Technology, Madras, India
Bernhard Steffen
  TU Dortmund University, Dortmund, Germany
Demetri Terzopoulos
  University of California, Los Angeles, CA, USA
Doug Tygar
  University of California, Berkeley, CA, USA
Gerhard Weikum
  Max Planck Institute for Informatics, Saarbrücken, Germany

More information about this series at http://www.springer.com/series/7410

Rolf Haenni · Reto E. Koenig
Douglas Wikström (Eds.)

E-Voting
and Identity

5th International Conference, VoteID 2015
Bern, Switzerland, September 2–4, 2015
Proceedings

 Springer

Editors
Rolf Haenni
Bern University of Applied Sciences
Biel
Switzerland

Reto E. Koenig
Bern University of Applied Sciences
Biel
Switzerland

Douglas Wikström
Royal Institute of Technology
Stockholm
Sweden

ISSN 0302-9743   ISSN 1611-3349   (electronic)
Lecture Notes in Computer Science
ISBN 978-3-319-22269-1   ISBN 978-3-319-22270-7   (eBook)
DOI 10.1007/978-3-319-22270-7

Library of Congress Control Number: 2015944731

LNCS Sublibrary: SL4 – Security and Cryptology

Springer Cham Heidelberg New York Dordrecht London
© Springer International Publishing Switzerland 2015
This work is subject to copyright. All rights are reserved by the Publisher, whether the whole or part of the material is concerned, specifically the rights of translation, reprinting, reuse of illustrations, recitation, broadcasting, reproduction on microfilms or in any other physical way, and transmission or information storage and retrieval, electronic adaptation, computer software, or by similar or dissimilar methodology now known or hereafter developed.
The use of general descriptive names, registered names, trademarks, service marks, etc. in this publication does not imply, even in the absence of a specific statement, that such names are exempt from the relevant protective laws and regulations and therefore free for general use.
The publisher, the authors and the editors are safe to assume that the advice and information in this book are believed to be true and accurate at the date of publication. Neither the publisher nor the authors or the editors give a warranty, express or implied, with respect to the material contained herein or for any errors or omissions that may have been made.

Printed on acid-free paper

Springer International Publishing AG Switzerland is part of Springer Science+Business Media
(www.springer.com)

Preface

This volume contains the papers presented at VoteID 2015, the fifth edition of the International Conference on E-Voting and Identity held during September 2–4, 2015, in Bern, Switzerland. Previous VoteID conferences were held in Guildford, UK (2013), Tallinn, Estonia (2011), Luxembourg (2009), and Bochum, Germany (2007). This year's VoteID conference was hosted by the Bern University of Applied Sciences. There were 17 submissions by authors from 11 different countries. Each submission was reviewed by at least three, and on average 4.3, Program Committee members in a double-blind procedure. The committee decided to accept ten papers. The conference program also included one keynote and three invited talks. The paper submission, reviewing, and proceedings preparation process was supported by the EasyChair conference management tool.

Bringing one of the world's leading e-voting conferences to Switzerland was a long-desired objective of the conference organizers. In Switzerland's long tradtion of federalism and direct democracy, frequent referendums are held on national, cantonal, and communal levels. Citizens can vote about changes to the constitution or about accepting new laws up to four times a year. This guarantees not only a maximum amount of self-determination to the citizens, but is also an important stabilizing factor for the political system of the country. In addition to the frequent referendums, regular elections take place on all federal levels, usually every four years. Traditionally, voting used to take place either at the ballot box in local election offices or at the cantonal assembly (called *Landsge- meinde*) in a public space by raising hands. Both traditional voting channels still exist today, but their importance has descreased with the general introduction of postal voting on a national level in 1994. Today, postal voting is the most common form of voting in Switzerland and is widely accepted.

Given the high frequency of referendums and elections, providing the most efficient voting channels to Swiss voters is an obvious objective of Swiss election administrations on all levels. It is therefore not surprising that Switzerland has been a pioneering country not only in postal voting, but also in introducing remote voting over the Internet. The first pilots in the cantons of Geneva and Zurich started almost 15 years ago, and another pilot in the canton of Neuchâtel followed a few years later. All three systems are still in use today and are used by multiple cantons. Just recently, they all received a major update in the underlying security concept by introducing individual verifiability based on confirmation codes. Further updates toward universal verifiability are planned for the near future. The results of scientific research have therefore found fertile soil in Switzerland's fundamental democratic processes.

To establish a link between this year's conference location and the general conference topic, we invited Barbara Perriard, Head of the Political Rights Section of the Federal Chancellery, to give a keynote talk on "Vote électronique: The Long Path Towards the Digitalization of Political Rights." She presented the past and the future of the Swiss e-voting projects and outlined the strategy of the federal administration and the cantons. We also invited Dr. Uwe Serdült from the Centre for Democracy Studies Aarau (ZDA) to give a talk on "The Use and Users of Swiss Internet Voting." He presented Switzerland's experience with e-voting from a political science perspective. On the more technical side of the topic, we had two invited talks by Prof. Alex Halderman from the University of Michigan on "Security Analysis of Estonia's Internet Voting System" and by Prof. Steve Schneider from the University of Surrey on "Verifiable Voting in Victoria: The vVote Project."

We would like to thank everyone who helped in bringing this conference together: the VoteID Steering Committee for their trust in putting this year's edition into our hands; the authors for their submissions; the Program Committee and the external reviewers for their conscientious and timely efforts in reviewing and discussing the submissions; the keynote speaker for her insights into the process of introducing electronic voting in Switzerland; the invited speakers for delivering high-quality presentations on current research issues; the administration of the Swiss Federal Palace for offering a free guided tour to all participants; and Scytl for their generous sponsorship that allowed us to extend the list of invited speakers and to support students in attending the conference. Finally, we thank our home institution, the Bern University of Applied Sciences, for its support.

June 2015

Rolf Haenni
Reto E. Koenig
Douglas Wikström

Organization

Program Committee

Michael Alvarez	California Institute of Technology, USA
Roberto Araujo	Universidade Federal do Pará, Brazil
David Bernhard	University of Bristol, UK
David Bismark	Votato
Jeremy Clark	Concordia University, Canada
Chris Culnane	University of Surrey, UK
Eric Dubuis	Bern University of Applied Sciences, Switzerland
Aleks Essex	University of Waterloo, Canada
J. Paul Gibson	Telecom & Management SudParis, France
Kristian Gjøsteen	Norwegian University of Science and Technology, Norway
Rajeev Gore	The Australian National University, Australia
Jens Groth	University College London, UK
Rolf Haenni	Bern University of Applied Sciences, Switzerland
Hugo Jonker	University of Luxembourg, Luxembourg
Reto E. Koenig	Bern University of Applied Sciences, Switzerland
Robert Krimmer	Tallinn University of Technology, Estonia
Ralf Kuesters	University of Trier, Germany
Tal Moran	IDC Herzliya
Stephan Neumann	TU Darmstadt, Germany
Olivier Pereira	Université Catholique de Louvain, Belgium
Peter Y.A. Ryan	University of Luxembourg, Luxembourg
Steve Schneider	University of Surrey, UK
Berry Schoenmakers	Eindhoven University of Technology, The Netherlands
Carsten Schuermann	IT University of Copenhagen, Denmark
Philip Stark	University of California, Berkeley, USA
Vanessa Teague	The University of Melbourne, Australia
Melanie Volkamer	TU Darmstadt, Germany
Poorvi Vora	The George Washington University, USA
Roland Wen	The University of New South Wales, Australia
Douglas Wikström	KTH Royal Institute of Technology, Sweden
Filip Zagorski	Wroclaw University of Technology, Poland
Dimitrios Zissis	University of the Aegean, Greece

Local Organizers

Eric Dubuis	Bern University of Applied Sciences, Switzerland
Stephan Fischli	Bern University of Applied Sciences, Switzerland
Rolf Haenni	Bern University of Applied Sciences, Switzerland
Severin Hauser	Bern University of Applied Sciences, Switzerland
Reto E. Koenig	Bern University of Applied Sciences, Switzerland
Philipp Locher	Bern University of Applied Sciences, Switzerland

Additional Reviewers

Chaidos, Pyrros
Müller, Johannes
Ronquillo, Lorena
Vogt, Andreas

Contents

Real-World Election Systems

2015 Neuchâtel's Cast-as-Intended Verification Mechanism

David Galindo, Sandra Guasch[(✉)], and Jordi Puiggalí

Scytl Secure Electronic Voting, Barcelona, Spain
sandra.guasch@scytl.com

Abstract. Cast-as-intended verification seeks to prove to a voter that their vote was cast according to their intent. In case ballot casting is made remotely through a voting client, one of the most important dangers a designer faces are malicious voting clients (e.g. infected by a malware), which may change the voter's selections. A previous approach for achieving cast-as-intended verification in this setting uses the so-called Return Codes. These allow a voter to check whether their voting options were correctly received by the ballot server, while keeping these choices private. An essential ingredient of this approach is a mechanism that allows a voter to discard a vote that does not represent their intent. This is usually solved using multiple voting, namely, if the return codes received by the voter do not match their choices, they cast a new vote. However, what happens if voters are not allowed to cast more than one ballot (aka single vote casting)? In this paper we propose a simple ballot casting protocol, using return codes, for allowing a voter to verify votes in a single vote casting election. We do so without significantly impacting the number of operations in the client side. This voting protocol has been implemented in a binding election in the Swiss canton of Neuchâtel in March 2015, and will be the canton's new voting platform.

Keywords: Electronic voting protocols · Binding election · Cast-as-intended verifiability · Malicious voting client · Return codes

1 Introduction

Switzerland has a long history on direct participation of its citizens in decision making processes. Besides traditional elections where voters choose their representatives in the Federal Assembly, citizens can participate in several other voting events. Citizens can propose popular voting initiatives on their own (after having obtained enough popular support by collecting signatures), and then parties and governments themselves (at the communal, cantonal or federal level) can organize referendums in order to ask the citizens for their opinion on a new law or a modification of the Constitution, among others. At the end, Swiss citizens have the chance to participate in 3–4 voting processes a year in average.

Remote electronic voting was first introduced in Switzerland in three cantons: Geneva, Zurich and Neuchâtel [14]. The first binding trials were held in 2004.

© Springer International Publishing Switzerland 2015
R. Haenni et al. (Eds.): VoteID 2015, LNCS 9269, pp. 3–18, 2015.
DOI: 10.1007/978-3-319-22270-7_1

Nowadays 14 cantons offer the electronic voting channel to their electors, which until recently has been restricted to be used by up to 10 % of the eligible voters. In 2011 the Federal Council of Switzerland started a task force for studying the security issues of electronic voting. As a result, the Federal Council published, in 2013, a report with the requirements for extending the use of the electronic voting systems to a larger part of the electorate. This framework [11], which became binding in January 2014, provides requirements of functionality, security, verifiability and testing/certification which allow the electronic voting systems to be extended to 30 %, 50 % or up to 100 % of the electorate. More specifically, while current electronic voting systems may be allowed to be used for up to 30 % of the electorate provided that they fulfil a certain set of functional and security requirements, systems to be used for up to 100 % of the electorate are required to additionally provide verifiability features. Although the modality of electronic voting (DRE, remote, ...) is not specified in the report, it refers to electronic voting systems where the vote is cast electronically. In this paper, we will talk specifically of remote electronic voting systems.

Verifiability in remote electronic voting is traditionally divided in three types, which are related to the phase of the voting process which is verified [5]. The first step to audit is the vote preparation at the voting client application run in the voter's device. This application is usually in charge of encrypting the selections made by the voter prior to casting them to a remote server so that their secrecy is ensured. *Cast-as-intended* verification methods provide the voters with means to audit that the vote prepared and encrypted by the voting client application contains what they selected, and that no changes have been performed. *Recorded-as-cast* verification methods provide voters with mechanisms to ensure that, once cast, their votes have been correctly received and stored at the remote voting server. Finally, *counted-as-recorded* verification allows voters, auditors and third party observers to check that the result of the tally corresponds to the votes which were received and stored at the remote voting server during the voting phase.

According to the report by the Federal Council, systems to be used for up to the 50 % of electors are required to provide methods for cast-as-intended verification, and systems for up to 100 % of the electorate are required to additionally provide methods for recorded-as-cast and counted-as-recorded verification, while also enforcing the separation of duties on operations impacting the privacy, integrity and verifiability of the system.

Our Contribution. In this paper we present a protocol which provides cast-as-intended verification, according to the requirements of the Federal Council for systems to be used by up to 50 % of the electorate. The protocol has the particularity of only allowing voters to cast one vote through the electronic channel, and therefore gives provisions for ensuring that such vote is considered to be cast only in case that it represents the voter intention, by means of a confirmation phase executed by the voter. The protocol is an evolution of the so-called *Norwegian voting protocol* [15,16,23] that was used in the Norwegian elections in 2011 and 2013. Importantly, it substantially improves the Norwegian scheme by not needing to rely on the strong assumption that two independent server-side entities do not collude to preserve voter privacy. Furthermore, the scheme also represents a great performance improvement of the voting client application compared with the original Puiggali-Guasch scheme [6], from which the Norwegian scheme was initially derived.

This protocol has been implemented and used for a binding election in the canton of Neuchâtel, in the federal referendum conducted on March 8th 2015. From 111,080 eligible voters, 23,927 were registered at the citizen electronic portal Guichet Unique [20] (from which the electronic voting application could be accessed) and 5,132 chose to cast their vote electronically using this protocol, which represents 21,45 % of the voters who had the chance to use the electronic voting channel. General participation in the referendum, all voting channels considered, was 41,24 %.

The paper is structured as follows: the related work and the main contributions are detailed in Sect. 2. The syntax and a formal description of the solution are provided in Sect. 3. The building blocks and the instantiation of the protocol implemented for the election in Neuchâtel are presented in Sects. 4 and 5. Then, some details on the usability and verifiability aspects are provided in Sect. 6. Finally, an informal analysis on the security aspects of the protocol is provided in Sect. 7 and the conclusions are shown in Sect. 8.

2 Related Work

There have been several proposals of cast-as-intended verification schemes during the last decade. In [9], Benaloh presents the *Immediate decryption* scheme, where the voter's device encrypts a vote and the voter is allowed to challenge the encryption generated. In case they choose to challenge it, the device reveals the randomness which was used to perform the encryption of the voting options. Using this randomness, the voter can check that the encrypted vote was constructed correctly. After the audit, the voting options are encrypted again with fresh randomness prior to casting the vote, so that the voter cannot use the randomness provided for audit as a proof to a third party of how they voted. However, this approach presents several drawbacks, such as usability (this randomness is a rather large string, cumbersome to be typed by a voter), and the fact that it does not allow for simple verification (i.e. verification must be done using a secondary computing device, under the assumption that at least one of the two devices is not compromised). This approach is used by the Helios voting system [2–4] and in the Wombat system [24]. A similar approach is used in VoteBox [25], by disclosing audited votes in the poll station local network in order to allow them to be verified.

A different approach consists on using the so-called return codes, which are targeted against malicious voting clients while enjoying some degree of usability [6,15,18,19,23]. In these proposals the voter selects their voting options and the voting client sends an encrypted vote to the remote voting servers, where return codes are calculated from the encrypted vote and sent back to the voter for verification. Voters possess a *verification card* where return codes (pre-computed in a configuration phase) are shown against matching voting options, and verification can be made by rather simple visual inspection. The current proposals assume that the voter can cast multiple votes. If the return codes do not match the selected voting options, then voters can cast another vote that invalidates the previous one (typically, this would happen if the voting client is malicious and encrypts voting options independently of the voter). However, some countries do not allow voters to cast multiple votes (such as France or Switzerland [11,22]), so it is important to provide a proposal for these cases. Still, multiple voting is also used as a countermeasure for vote selling and voter coercion in such schemes, so they have to be taken into account when single voting is used[1].

One possible solution to support single vote casting is to add a *confirmation phase* to validate the vote after checking the return codes. In the first phase, the vote is encrypted and sent to the voting server, which calculates the return codes, stores the vote and communicates the return codes to the voter. In the second phase, the voter, after inspection of the return codes, sends a *confirmation code* to the voting server, that stores it together with the ballot as a proof that the vote has been confirmed by the voter. Only votes with a valid voter confirmation code will be taken into account during the tally phase.

The return codes are computed from the probabilistic encryption of voting options, but at the same time they have to be deterministic: during the voting phase, the values computed by the server-side from an encrypted vote have to match those computed during the verification card generation phase (which happens at election configuration time) for the same set of voting options. Therefore, the randomness from the voting options encryption has to be removed for computing the return codes, which poses a serious risk on the vote secrecy. This was solved in the Norwegian voting system [15,16,23] by splitting the generation of the return codes in two independent entities: a ballot box server and a code generation server, which were assumed not to collude. To prevent these components from colluding and compromising the election privacy [15,16], both components were located in independent locations and managed by different companies. However, this approach is not always feasible to implement (the economic and organizational cost of setting up two different and independent environments are high).

In contrast, in the Puiggali-Guasch [6] scheme one of the previous independent entities is embedded in the voting client application. In their proposal there is no need of two separate components at the server-side of the voting platform, although then vote casting becomes computationally more expensive for the voting client (2,5 times more exponentiations than in the Norwegian protocol are required approximately). This is important considering the fact that the cryptographic operations done at the voting application level are often performed using web technologies such as Java Applets or Javascript, so the performance is slowed down when compared to a C/assembly implementation that uses lower

---

[1] For example, the risk of voter coercion or vote selling in Switzerland is assumed to be affordable given the fact that many voters already use the postal channel.

level instructions. Naturally, ballot construction and casting needs to be executed in an acceptable time-frame to prevent voter disenfranchisement.

In this paper, we present a modification of the protocol [23] which, while very similar to [6] in the sense that it *moves* the operations of one of the server-side entities to the voting client application, reduces dramatically the number of operations to be performed at the voting client application (as it will be shown in Sect. 5, the cost of encryption and of proofs computation does not depend on the number of options anymore). Moreover, we add a confirmation phase in order to support single vote casting, so that it fulfils the requirements of the Swiss Federal Council [11].

3 Single Voting with Return Codes

We start by presenting a syntax for a voting scheme with return codes, which will be later used to describe the protocol[2]. We build on existing definitions of single-pass voting schemes, such as [10], and enrich them by adding a second interaction of the voter with the system, in order to confirm a cast vote.

3.1 Syntax

The scheme has the following participants: *Election Authorities*, who are in charge of setting up the election, computing the tally and publishing the results; *Voters*, who participate in the election by choosing their preferred options; *Registrars*, who are responsible for providing to the voters all the information they need to vote and, in particular, the return codes that provide the cast-as-intended integrity property; the *Voting Server*, which receives, processes and stores the ballots cast by eligible voters in the Ballot Box, and may as well publish some information; the *Voting Device*, which is in charge of casting a ballot given the voting options selected by the voter; the *Code Generator*, which is in charge of generating return codes from the ballots cast by the voting device. Finally, *Auditors*, who are responsible for verifying the integrity of the procedures run in the counting phase.

We assume that non-cryptographic election specifications such as the sets of administrators and voter identities are fixed in advance. Furthermore we assume a counting function $\rho : (V \cup \{\bot\})^n \to R$ is given, where Vs is the set of voting options, $\bot$ denotes abstention, n is the number of voters and R is the set of results. Voters may use credentials in order to be able to cast their ballots. However, how the voters obtain and use such credentials is out of the scope of this presentation.

There exists a public bulletin board PBB to which every algorithm in the voting scheme has read-only access to. As is common in the literature, some authorized parties have writing append-only access to it.

---

[2] As usual, the terms "scheme" and "protocol" can be read interchangeably without much loss of precision.

The voting scheme is characterized by the following protocols/algorithms:

- Setup(1^λ) is an interactive protocol run by the election authorities. On input a security parameter 1^λ, it generates and outputs an election public key pk_e and an election private key sk_e. In addition, it generates a global code generation public/private key pair (pk_c, sk_c), a signing public/private key pair (pk_s, sk_s), and the set of values which will represent the voting options: $V = \{v_1, \ldots, v_k\}$. The public keys pk_e, pk_c and pk_s, and the set of voting options V, are implicit inputs to the remaining algorithms.
- Register(id, sk_c, sk_s) is an interactive protocol run by the registrars. It takes as input a voter identity id, the global code generation private key sk_c and the signing private key sk_s. It outputs a voter's code generation public/private key pair $(pk_{\mathrm{id}}, sk_{\mathrm{id}})$, a set of voter return codes linked to voting options $\{v_i, \mathtt{RC}_i^{\mathrm{id}}\}_{i=1}^k$, a voter confirmation value $\mathtt{CV}^{\mathrm{id}}$, a voter finalization value $\mathtt{FC}^{\mathrm{id}}$ and a validity proof for such finalization code, $\Pi_{\mathtt{FC}^{\mathrm{id}}}$. Additionally, the registrars publish a set of reference values $\{\mathtt{RF}_i^{\mathrm{id}}\}_{i=1}^k$ that are linked to the codes $\{\mathtt{RC}_i^{\mathrm{id}}\}_{i=1}^k$. We sometimes refer to the set $\left\{\{v_i, \mathtt{RC}_i^{\mathrm{id}}\}_{i=1}^k, \mathtt{CV}^{\mathrm{id}}, \mathtt{FC}^{\mathrm{id}}\right\}$ as the *Verification Card*.
- Vote(id, sk_{id}, $\{v_{j_1}, \ldots, v_{j_t}\}$) is a probabilistic algorithm run at the voting device. It receives as input a set of values $\{v_{j_1}, \ldots, v_{j_t}\}$, the voter identifier id $\in$ ID and the voter's code generation private key sk_{id}; outputs a ballot b.
- ProcessBallot(BB, b, id, pk_{id}) is run by the voting server. It receives as input a ballot box BB, a ballot b, an identity id and a voter's code generation public key pk_{id}. It outputs 1 in case of success, 0 otherwise.
- RCGen(b, id, sk_c) is an algorithm run by the code generator. On input a ballot b, the voter identifier id and the global code generation private key sk_c, it outputs an (unordered) set of return codes $\{\overline{\mathtt{RC}^{\mathrm{id}}}\}$ if the operation is successful, or $\perp$ in case of error/rejection. Typically this algorithm will look-up at PBB to check the list of legitimate reference values $\left\{\{\mathtt{RF}_i^{\mathrm{id}}\}_{i=1}^k\right\}_{\mathrm{id}\in\mathrm{ID}}$.
- RCVerif($\{v_{j_1}, \ldots, v_{j_t}\}$, $\{\overline{\mathtt{RC}^{\mathrm{id}}}\}$, $\{v_i, \mathtt{RC}_i^{\mathrm{id}}\}_{i=1}^k$) is an algorithm run by the voter. On input a set of voting options $\{v_{j_1}, \ldots, v_{j_t}\}$, a set of return codes $\{\overline{\mathtt{RC}^{\mathrm{id}}}\}$ and a voting card $\{v_i, \mathtt{RC}_i^{\mathrm{id}}\}_{i=1}^k$, it outputs 1 if $\{\mathtt{RC}_{j_i}^{\mathrm{id}}\}_{i=1}^t = \{\overline{\mathtt{RC}^{\mathrm{id}}}\}$ as sets, 0 otherwise.
- Confirm($\mathtt{CV}^{\mathrm{id}}$, id, sk_{id}) is a simple algorithm run by the voting device. On input a voter confirmation value $\mathtt{CV}^{\mathrm{id}}$, the voter identity id, and the voter code generation private key sk_{id}, it outputs a confirmation message $\mathtt{CM}^{\mathrm{id}}$.
- FCGen($\mathtt{CM}^{\mathrm{id}}$, id, sk_c, $\Pi_{\mathtt{FC}^{\mathrm{id}}}$) is an algorithm run by the code generator. It receives as input a confirmation message $\mathtt{CM}^{\mathrm{id}}$, a voter identity id, the global code generation private key sk_c and the proof $\Pi_{\mathtt{FC}^{\mathrm{id}}}$. It outputs a finalization code $\overline{\mathtt{FC}^{\mathrm{id}}}$ if the operation is successful, or $\perp$ in case of error/rejection.
- Tally(BB, sk_e, $\{\Pi_{\mathtt{FC}^{\mathrm{id}}}\}_{\mathrm{id}\in\mathrm{ID}}$) is an interactive protocol run by the election authorities. It takes as input the ballot box BB, the election private key sk_e and the set of validity proofs $\{\Pi_{\mathtt{FC}^{\mathrm{id}}}\}_{\mathrm{id}\in\mathrm{ID}}$. It outputs a result $r \in R$ and a proof π of the tally correctness, or $\perp$.
- Verify(PBB, r, π) is an interactive protocol run by the auditors/election observers. It takes as input the bulletin board PBB, the tally result r and

the proof π of correct tally. The output is 1 if their verification succeeds, 0 otherwise.

3.2 Workflow

Configuration Phase: Election authorities define the set ID of voter identities participating in the election and run the Setup algorithm. They publish the election public key pk_e, the global code generation public key pk_c, the set of voter identities ID, the signing public key pk_s and the set of voting options V in the bulletin board. They provide the global code generation private key sk_c to both the registrars and the code generator. Finally the signing private key sk_s is provided to the registrars.

Registration Phase: Voters register to participate in the election. To register, a voter first provides their identity $id \in$ ID to the registrars, who run the Register algorithm. The outputs (pk_{id}, sk_{id}), $\{v_i, \mathrm{RC}_i^{id}\}_{i=1}^k$, CV^{id}, and FC^{id} are provided to the voter, while the voter's code generation public key pk_{id}, the proof $\Pi_{\mathrm{FC}^{id}}$ and the reference values $\{\mathrm{RF}_i^{id}\}_{i=1}^k$ are published in the bulletin board PBB.

Voting phase: This phase consists of several steps:

1. The voter authenticates through the voting device to the voting server. If the authentication is successful, the values id, pk_{id} are stored in the voting device. The voter chooses a set of voting options $\{v_{j_1}, \ldots, v_{j_t}\} \in V$ and enters them into the voting device as her choices for the election, together with the private key $sk_{id}{}^3$. The voting device then runs the Vote protocol and produces a ballot b. The ballot b and the voter identity id are sent to the voting server.
2. Upon reception of (b, id), the voting server calls the ProcessBallot algorithm. In case the result of the execution is 1, the ballot box BB is updated with the ballot b and the voter identity id, with the state *ballot received*. Otherwise, the voting device is notified of the error.
3. The code generator is notified of the new update in BB and executes the RCGen algorithm with the newly arrived ballot. In case the operation is successful, a set of return codes $\{\overline{\mathrm{RC}^{id}}\}$ is generated and sent to the voting server, which updates the status of the ballot in the BB to *return code generated*, and forwards the return codes to the voting device. In case the operation is not successful the voting device is notified accordingly.
4. The voting device shows the voter the set of generated return codes $\{\overline{\mathrm{RC}^{id}}\}$. The voter is then asked to confirm the ballot cast by providing the confirmation value CV^{id} to the voting device, which they will do **only** in case the RCVerif algorithm accepts. The voting device then runs Confirm and outputs a confirmation message CM^{id}, which is sent to the voting server together with the voter identity id.

---

^{3} How this key is provided to the voting device in the Neuchâtel protocol is explained in Sect. 6.1.

5. The voting server forwards the confirmation message $\mathsf{CM^{id}}$ to the code generator, which executes the $\underline{\mathsf{FCGen}}$ algorithm. If the operation is successful, the resulting finalization code $\overline{\mathsf{FC^{id}}}$ is sent back to the voting sever, which stores it together with the ballot, updates the ballot status to *confirmed* and forwards $\overline{\mathsf{FC^{id}}}$ to the voting device. In case the operation is not successful, the voter is notified accordingly.

6. Finally, the voter checks whether the displayed finalization code $\overline{\mathsf{FC^{id}}}$ matches the value $\mathsf{FC^{id}}$ received during registration. In case of a successful verification, the received finalization code serves the voter as a confirmation of the correct submission and confirmation of their vote. Otherwise, they complain to the election administrators, and might need to cast their vote using a different channel (i.e. at a polling station).

Counting Phase: The election authorities run the interactive protocol Tally on BB, obtaining and publishing in the bulletin board the result r and the proof π, or set $r =\perp$ in case of error. The auditors run the Verify protocol. In case their output is 1, the result r is announced to be fair. Otherwise, an investigation is opened to detect the reason of failure.

3.3   Trust Assumptions

The following conditions are assumed in order to provide cast-as-intended verification and voter privacy with the proposed protocol:

For **cast-as-intended verifiability**, it is assumed that the following entities, as pairs, are not simultaneously malicious: the voting device and (1) the code generator, (2) the registrar, or (3) the voting server; (4) the code generator and the registrar.

For **privacy**, the following conditions are necessary: (1) the voting device is not compromised; (2) the election authorities are honest; (3) the verification card contents are only known to the voter.

4   Building Blocks

ENCRYPTION SCHEME. Our protocol uses the ElGamal asymmetric encryption scheme [13], which consists of three algorithms: key generation, encryption and decryption (KGen, Enc, Dec). The key generation algorithm KGen takes on input a subgroup $\mathbb{G}$ which has a generator g of order q of elements in $\mathbb{Z}_p^*$, where p is a safe prime such that $p = 2q + 1$ and q is a prime number. It outputs an ElGamal public/secret key pair (pk, sk), where $pk \in \mathbb{G}$ such that $pk = g^{sk} \bmod p$ and $sk \in \mathbb{Z}_q$. On input $m \in \mathbb{G}$ and the public key pk, the Enc algorithm chooses a random $r \in \mathbb{Z}_q$ and computes $(c_1, c_2) = (g^r, pk^r \cdot m)$. The Dec algorithm receives (c_1, c_2) and the private key sk and outputs $m = c_2/c_1^{sk}$.

VOTING OPTIONS. The voting options $V = \{v_1, \ldots, v_k\}$ are chosen as small bit-length primes belonging to the group $\mathbb{G}$. A vote is encoded as the product of voting options chosen by the voter (prior to encryption), and the individual voting options are recovered via factorisation after decryption. Therefore, it has to be ensured that the product of t of such primes, where t is the number of selections a voter can make, is not larger than p.

PSEUDO-RANDOM FUNCTION FAMILY. A function family is a map $F : K \times D \to R$, where K is the set of keys, D is the domain and R is the range. A pseudo-random function family (PRF) is a family of efficiently computable functions, with the following property: a random instance of the family is computationally indistinguishable from a random function, as long as the key remains secret. We use the HMAC algorithm as a PRF [7], parametrized by the key K.

SIGNATURE SCHEME. A signature scheme is defined by three probabilistic algorithms SignKeyGen, Sign, SignVerify, that stand for key generation, signature generation and signature verification. Our protocol uses the RSA signature algorithm with the hash variant (or *RSA Full Domain Hash signature scheme (RSA-FDH)* [8]), therefore the key generation algorithm SignKeyGen outputs a pair of keys (pks, sks), for which $pks = \{pk_{\mathrm{rsa}}, N_{\mathrm{rsa}}\}$, $N_{\mathrm{rsa}} = p \cdot q$ where p and q are two distinct primes, and $sks = sk_{\mathrm{rsa}}$. The signature algorithm Sign takes as input a message m, which is not restricted to a specific space, and the private key sks, and outputs $\sigma = H(m)^{sk_{\mathrm{rsa}}} \bmod N_{\mathrm{rsa}}$, where H denotes a hash function. The signature verification algorithm SignVerify takes as input the public key pks, the message m and the signature σ, and checks that $H(m) = \sigma^{pk_{\mathrm{rsa}}} \bmod N_{\mathrm{rsa}}$. It outputs 1 if successful, 0 otherwise.

NON-INTERACTIVE ZERO-KNOWLEDGE PROOFS OF KNOWLEDGE. We use

$$\mathsf{EqDL}_G(g_1, \ldots, g_n, h_1, \ldots, h_n),$$

a generalization of the NIZK proof system [12], to prove in zero-knowledge that $\log_{g_1} h_1 = \log_{g_2} h_2 = \ldots = \log_{g_n} h_n$ for $g_1, \ldots, g_n, h_1, \ldots, h_n \in \mathbb{G}$ (with proof builder ProveEq and proof verifier VerifyEq); and the NIZK proof system [26] $\mathsf{PrDL}_G(g, h)$ to prove in zero-knowledge the knowledge of $\log_g h$ for $g, h \in \mathbb{G}$ (with proof builder ProveDL and proof verifier VerifyDL). G is a hash function mapping strings to $\mathbb{Z}_q$.

5 A Protocol for Cast-as-Intended Verification with Single Voting

The protocol implemented for the elections in Neuchâtel consists of the following algorithms:

– Setup(1^λ): the algorithm chooses a group $\mathbb{G}$ and runs KGen to generate an encryption key pair (pk, sk). As discussed before, the voting options $V = \{v_1, \ldots, v_k\}$ are chosen as small bit-length primes belonging to the group $\mathbb{G}$. The algorithm then generates a random K to choose a pseudorandom function $f_K \in F$, and chooses hash functions H, G.
  The election public key is $pk_e = (pk, \mathbb{G}, H, G)$, and the election private key is sk_e, where $sk_e = sk$ if there is only one trustee; alternatively sk_e consists

of the shares of sk if there are several trustees (for instance, by using [21]). Finally, the global code generation key pair is set to $pk_c = \perp$, $sk_c = K$, and SignKeyGen is run and the result is set to be the signing key pair $(pk_s, sk_s)^4$.

- Register(id, sk_c, sk_s): the algorithm runs KGen with input $\mathbb{G}$ to generate a keypair (pk, sk) which is set to be the voter public/private code generation[5] key pair $(pk_{\mathrm{id}}, sk_{\mathrm{id}}) \in \mathbb{G} \times \mathbb{Z}_q$. Then it generates the voter confirmation value $\mathrm{CV}^{\mathrm{id}}$ by selecting a random element from $\mathbb{G}$. For each voting option $v_i \in V$ it computes the corresponding return code $\mathrm{RC}_i^{\mathrm{id}} = f_{sk_c}(v_i^{sk_{\mathrm{id}}})$, and computes the finalization value $\mathrm{FC}^{\mathrm{id}} = f_{sk_c}((\mathrm{CV}^{\mathrm{id}})^{sk_{\mathrm{id}}})$. The validity proof for the finalization code $\Pi_{\mathrm{FC}^{\mathrm{id}}}$ is computed by running Sign($\mathrm{FC}^{\mathrm{id}}, sk_s$). Finally, the set of reference values $\{\mathrm{RF}_i^{\mathrm{id}}\}_{i=1}^k$ is generated by computing $\mathrm{RF}_i^{\mathrm{id}} = H(\mathrm{RC}_i^{\mathrm{id}})$ for each return code.

- Vote($\mathrm{id}, sk_{\mathrm{id}}, \{v_{j_1}, \ldots, v_{j_t}\}$): the algorithm receives the voting options selected by the voter as input, sets $v = \prod_{l=1}^t v_{j_l}$ and encrypts them, obtaining $(c_1, c_2) = \mathrm{Enc}(pk, v)$. The algorithm then makes a partial computation of the return codes corresponding to such voting options using the voter private key sk_{id}: $(v_{j_1}^{sk_{\mathrm{id}}}, \ldots, v_{j_t}^{sk_{\mathrm{id}}})^6$. Finally, it also computes $(c_1^{sk_{\mathrm{id}}}, c_2^{sk_{\mathrm{id}}})$. The following NIZK proofs are computed to prove the correct computation of these values:

  - A proof $\pi_{enc} \leftarrow \mathrm{ProveDL}(g, c_1)$, which proves knowledge of the randomness used for computing the encryption of v.

Two proofs to demonstrate that the voting options in the ciphertext (c_1, c_2) and the voting options used to for the partial computation of return codes are the same:

  - A proof $\pi_{exp} \leftarrow \mathrm{ProveEq}(g, c_1, c_2, pk_{\mathrm{id}}, c_1^{sk_{\mathrm{id}}}, c_2^{sk_{\mathrm{id}}})$ which proves that $(c_1^{sk_{\mathrm{id}}}, c_2^{sk_{\mathrm{id}}})$ are computed by raising the ciphertext (c_1, c_2) to the voter's code generation private key sk_{id} corresponding to the public key pk_{id}.

  - A proof $\pi_{prod} \leftarrow \mathrm{ProveEq}\left(g, pk, c_1^{sk_{\mathrm{id}}}, c_2^{sk_{\mathrm{id}}} \cdot (v_{j_1}^{sk_{\mathrm{id}}}, \ldots, v_{j_t}^{sk_{\mathrm{id}}})^{-1}\right)$ which proves that the ciphertext $(c_1^{sk_{\mathrm{id}}}, c_2^{sk_{\mathrm{id}}})$ is the encryption of the product $(v_{j_1}^{sk_{\mathrm{id}}} \cdots v_{j_t}^{sk_{\mathrm{id}}})$ under the election public key pk_e.

The result of the above computations is a ballot b consisting of

$$b = \left(\mathrm{id}, (c_1, c_2), (v_{j_1}^{sk_{\mathrm{id}}}, \ldots, v_{j_t}^{sk_{\mathrm{id}}}), (c_1^{sk_{\mathrm{id}}}, c_2^{sk_{\mathrm{id}}}), pk_{\mathrm{id}}, \underset{enc}{\pi}, \underset{exp}{\pi}, \underset{prod}{\pi}\right).$$

---

4 Note that sk_c is not considered to be divided in shares in this protocol. This is due to the fact that the secrets for computing the return codes (sk_c and sk_{id}) belong to two different entities that are assumed not to collude for providing vote secrecy. However, distributing sk_c might be considered to weaken the trust assumptions.

5 Notice that this is formally an encryption key pair, but it is being used here differently.

6 As explained in Sect. 2, return codes have to be computed between two entities which are assumed not to collude, in order to ensure vote secrecy. In this implementation, the voting device computes a partial computation in the Vote algorithm, while the voting server computes the final values in the ProcessBallot algorithm.

- ProcessBallot(BB, b): in the first place, the algorithm checks if there already exists a ballot for the voter identity id in the ballot box BB; if this is the case, it outputs 0. Otherwise, it continues by validating the NIZK proofs π_{enc}, π_{exp}, π_{prod}. In case all the validations are successful, 1 is returned.

- RCGen(b, id, sk_c): the algorithm computes the set of return codes contained in ballot b as follows:
  - Computes the final return code value $\overline{RC_{j_l}^{id}} = f_{sk_c}(v_{j_l}^{sk_{id}})$ for each of the partially computed return codes $(v_{j_1}^{sk_{id}}, \ldots, v_{j_t}^{sk_{id}})$ from b.
  - Checks that $\left\{\overline{RC_{j_1}^{id}}, \ldots, \overline{RC_{j_t}^{id}}\right\}$ is a subset of $\{RF_i^{id}\}_{i=1}^k$. In a positive case, the set of return codes $\{\overline{RC^{id}}\} = \left\{\overline{RC_{j_1}^{id}}, \ldots, \overline{RC_{j_t}^{id}}\right\}$ is output. In a negative case, $\perp$ is returned.

- Confirm(CV^{id}, id, sk_{id}): the algorithm computes $CM^{id} = (CV^{id})^{sk_{id}}$.

- FCGen(CM^{id}, id, sk_c, $\Pi_{FC^{id}}$): runs SignVerify(pk_s, $\overline{FC^{id}}$, $\Pi_{FC^{id}}$), where $\overline{FC^{id}} = f_K(CM^{id})$. $\overline{FC^{id}}$ is returned if the signature verification is successful, $\perp$ otherwise.

- Tally(BB, sk_e, $\{\Pi_{FC^{id}}\}_{id \in ID}$): for all the ballots in the ballot box which have a finalization code $\overline{FC^{id}}$ stored together with the ballot, this algorithm runs SignVerify(pk_s, $\overline{FC^{id}}$, $\Pi_{FC^{id}}$) to select the ones which have been confirmed by the voters. The resulting set is shuffled, and then for each ballot it runs Dec($\{c_1, c_2\}$, sk_e) and obtains the cleartext v (in case sk_e was divided in shares, a secret reconstruction algorithm [21] is used to recover the private key previous to decryption). The cleartext v is factorized to recover from $v = v_1^{\beta_1} \cdots v_k^{\beta_k}$ the factors v_i such that $\beta_i = 1$. The small primes representing the voting options v_i are then used to compute the final result r.

6 Usability and Vote Correctness Layers

The protocol described in the previous sections may pose significant usability problems to the voters. In order to cast a vote, the voter is asked to type in the voting device a series of secret values from their voting card, such as the confirmation value CM^{id} and the private key sk_{id}. In order to confirm their vote, the voter is asked to compare the return codes RC^{id} shown by the voting device with those in their verification card. The same applies to the finalization code $\overline{FC^{id}}$.

The problem is that, according to current cryptographic key length recommendations [1], the aforementioned values have a length of 256 or 2048 bits, depending on whether they are the output of a symmetric or an asymmetric key cryptographic operation. To be more concrete, in case a Base32 encoding is used to represent such values, this implies 52 and 410 characters, respectively. It is clearly not realistic to ask a voter to perform such task.

Therefore, an additional layer for improving usability is required on top of the protocol from Sect. 5. This layer allows to reduce the length of the values in the verification card, and to provide the voter's code generation key to the voting device in a way that is transparent to the voter. This usability layer was used in the referendum conducted in Neuchâtel.

6.1   Private Key Provision

Details about the authentication layer have been deliberately omitted in previous sections, for the sake of clarity. In Neuchâtel there are two layers of authentication: the first one is handled by the citizen portal *Guichet Unique* [20], and the second one is managed by the electronic voting system. This second layer consists on a username/PIN-based authentication. The PIN is generated during registration and printed onto the voter's verification card, while the username is provided by the first layer of authentication, i.e. the *Guichet Unique*. The authentication layer managed by the electronic voting system is used not only to qualify a user as an authorized voter in the election, but also to transparently provide her with some cryptographic secrets, such as the voter's code generation key pair $(pk_{\texttt{id}}, sk_{\texttt{id}})$.

6.2   Short Return Codes

The usability layer is in charge of generating short values $\{\texttt{sRC}^{\texttt{id}}\}_{i=1}^{k}, \texttt{sFC}^{\texttt{id}}$, that are printed in the verification card. One key ingredient of this layer is the length of such values, which actually represents a neat trade-off between usability and security: the longer they are, the harder it is to guess them by a corrupted voting device, but the harder is to use them by the voter. Specifically, in Neuchâtel they are of 4 and 7 numeric digits respectively[7].

Additionally, the registrar secretly generates a table which relates each code $\texttt{sRC}_i^{\texttt{id}}$ or $\texttt{sFC}^{\texttt{id}}$ to the corresponding long codes $\texttt{RC}_i^{\texttt{id}}$ or $\texttt{FC}^{\texttt{id}}$. We call this table the *mapping table*, and *mapping* to each one of the correspondences. During the voting phase, the code generator uses this table to obtain the corresponding short codes. The mapping table is designed to be an injective function from codes $\{\texttt{RC}^{\texttt{id}}\}_{i=1}^{k}, \texttt{FC}^{\texttt{id}}$ to short codes $\{\texttt{sRC}^{\texttt{id}}\}_{i=1}^{k}, \texttt{sFC}^{\texttt{id}}$.

Our implementation of the mapping table contains one entry for each (long) return code $\texttt{RC}_i^{\texttt{id}}$ of the form: $[H(\texttt{RC}_i^{\texttt{id}}), E_{\texttt{RC}_i^{\texttt{id}}}(\texttt{sRC}_i^{\texttt{id}})]$, where H denotes a hash function, and $E_k(m)$ denotes the encryption of the message m with a symmetric encryption algorithm[8] and a secret key k.

An additional entry is computed in the same way with the (long) finalization code $\texttt{FC}^{\texttt{id}}$ and the short finalization code $\texttt{sFC}^{\texttt{id}}$.

6.3   Vote Correctness

Additionally, we use the mapping table to ensure that a ballot that is accepted by the voting server, contains valid choices as per the election. For example, in case a ballot contains some $v_j' \notin V$, the (long) return code computed by the code

---

[7] Since the voting device has only one chance to show the values to the voter, a brute force attack succeeds with probability at most 10^{-4t} in changing the value of t voting choices without detection.

[8] The SHA-256 hash and the AES-128 symmetric encryption algorithms are used in the implementation made in Neuchâtel.

generator as $f_{sk_c}(v_j'^{sk_{id}})$ will not find an entry on the mapping table described above (and the same happens for the reference values $\{RF_i^{id}\}_{i=1}^k$ in the underlying protocol). Moreover, there is other information that can be checked: imagine the scenario where a voter can select one party list, and then can give some weight to individual candidates. Metadata can be added to the return code mechanism, so that it is verified that a vote contains voting options which fulfill this rule without breaking the voter privacy.

In the case of the Neuchâtel voting protocol, type identifiers such as $'party'$ or $'candidate'$ are added in the ballot cast by the voter, and then used to compute the return codes at the server. The ballot cast by the voter, then, has the following contents:

$$b = \left(id, (c_1, c_2), (v_{j_1}^{sk_{id}}\text{-}'party', \dots, v_{j_t}^{sk_{id}}\text{-}'candidate'), (c_1^{sk_{id}}, c_2^{sk_{id}}), pk_{id}, \dots \right)$$

In a first step the type identifiers are checked (in the example, that there is only one type identifier for party list and that the rest are for candidates). In the second step, these type identifiers are added to the computation of the return codes:

$$\overline{RC_{j_l}^{id}} = f_{sk_c}(v_{j_l}^{sk_{id}} v_{j_l}^{sk_{id}}, 'party' \text{ or } 'candidate'),$$

where ',' denotes a concatenation. The same is done in the configuration phase, when generating the *mapping table*. Therefore, an invalid combination of partial return code $(v_{j_l}^{sk_{id}})$ and of type identifier will result on an entry of the table only with negligible probability, given the properties of cryptographic hash functions.

7   (Informal) Security Analysis

The protocol is focused on preventing a corrupt voting client from changing the voter intention without being detected, while maintaining the privacy of such voter in front of a malicious voting server/code generator. In this section we informally discuss how these security properties are fulfilled given the trust assumptions presented in Sect. 3.3.

7.1   Cast-as-Intended Verifiability

The voting device can try to modify the voter's intention without detection in two ways: (i) by showing to the voter return codes which do not correspond to the maliciously modified contents of the vote (but that correspond with those of the voter's choices); (ii) by confirming a vote without the participation of the voter.

For the first attack, the voting device could try to send a ballot where the encrypted options do not correspond to the partial computation of return codes. However, in that case the proofs π_{exp}, π_{prod} would not be successfully verified by the voting server. The collaboration of the code generator is needed to generate the return codes. However, the only way the code generator receives a ballot cast by the voting device is that the voting server verifies the proofs first. Therefore, the code generator and the voting device cannot collaborate in case of a honest voting server and the only strategy the voting device can follow is to guess the return codes the voter expects. A brute force attack cannot be done in this case, since the voter will detect consecutive attempts of displaying wrong return codes.

A possibility for the second attack is that the voting device generates a fake cofirmation message, so that the code generator computes a fake finalization value. Even in case the code generator does not verify the proof of validity of this finalization value (because it colludes with the voting device), the election authorities or the auditors would detect that it is fake at the counting or audit phases, so that the vote would not be counted. The alternative is that the voting device guesses a valid confirmation message. In order to limit the possibility of a brute force attack, the voting server allows a limited number of retries.

7.2   Privacy

Privacy in electronic voting is understood as the property of maintaining the intention of a voter unknown. Besides recovering the voter selections or the encryption randomness from the voting device (which we assume that cannot happen because for privacy the voting device is assumed to be honest), there are two ways to attack the voter privacy in this scheme.

The first one is to target the voting options encryption. This can be done by brute forcing the encryption, by decrypting the votes without shuffling them (so that they could be connected to the voter's identities), or by recovering the shuffling permutation. However, according to the assumptions previously detailed and using a strong encryption algorithm, none of these attacks are feasible.

The second attack is to target the return code generation mechanism. The ballot cast by the voter includes some partial computations of the return codes, which consist on the voter selections raised to some exponent known by the voting device. As far as it does not reveal such secret exponent, neither the voting server nor the code generator (even in coalition) can compute back the voter's original voting options (see [15] for the analysis). Given that the relation between return codes and voting options is only known to the voter, neither the voting server nor the code generator (or any third party who could have access to them) can use the generated return codes to infer which are the choices selected by the voter.

Finally, a voter cannot copy a vote of another voter and cast it as it was theirs, so that they receive return codes matching those in their voting card. In order to do that they need to compute the exponentiation the original selections to an exponent they know (while not knowing the selections themselves). Otherwise, they would get return codes that they would not be able to understand (because they would belong to another verification card).

8   Conclusions

In this paper, we have presented a technique for cast-as-intended verification in the case of single voting. This mechanism improves on the performance and infrastructure requirements of previous proposals using return codes. Besides a syntax (that could be useful to design other return code-based voting protocols) and a formal description of the scheme, we have provided various details on the implementation of this mechanism for the new Internet voting platform of the Swiss canton of Neuchâtel, where it has already been used for a binding federal election in March 2015. These details include techniques applied to improve the usability of the system, and to check that the contents of an encrypted vote are correct before being added to the ballot box, without breaking vote privacy. Finally, an informal security analysis has been provided. As a future work we foresee the formalization of the security properties of the scheme and a rigorous study of their fulfillment, as well as further improvements with respect to usability and computational cost.

Acknowledgements. We are thankful to the comments and suggestions made by the anonymous reviewers.

References

1. Crytographic key length recommendation (2015). http://www.keylength.com
2. Adida, B.: Helios: web-based open-audit voting. In: van Oorschot, P.C. (ed.) USENIX Security Symposium, pp. 335–348. USENIX Association, Berkeley (2008)
3. Adida, B., de Marneffe, O., Pereira, O.: Helios voting system. http://heliosvoting. org
4. Adida, B., de Marneffe, O., Pereira, O., Quisquater, J.J.: Electing a university president using open-audit voting: analysis of real-world use of Helios. In: Proceedings of the 2009 Conference on Electronic Voting Technology/Workshop on Trustworthy Elections (2009)
5. Adida, B., Neff, C.A.: Ballot casting assurance. In: Wallach, D.S., Rivest, R.L. (eds.) 2006 USENIX/ACCURATE Electronic Voting Technology Workshop, EVT 2006, Vancouver, BC, Canada, 1 August 2006. USENIX Association (2006)
6. Allepuz, J.P., Castelló, S.G.: Internet voting system with cast as intended verification. In: Kiayias, A., Lipmaa, H. (eds.) VoteID 2011. LNCS, vol. 7187, pp. 36–52. Springer, Heidelberg (2012)
7. Bellare, M.: New proofs for NMAC and HMAC: security without collision-resistance. Cryptology ePrint Archive, Report 2006/043 (2006)
8. Bellare, M., Rogaway, P.: Random oracles are practical: a paradigm for designing efficient protocols. In: Proceedings of the 1st ACM Conference on Computer and Communications Security. CCS 1993, pp. 62–73. . ACM, New York (1993)
9. Benaloh, J.: Simple verifiable elections. In: Proceedings of the USENIX/Accurate Electronic Voting Technology Workshop 2006. EVT 2006, p. 5. USENIX Association, Berkeley (2006)
10. Bernhard, D., Pereira, O., Warinschi, B.: On necessary and sufficient conditions for private ballot submission. Cryptology ePrint Archive, Report 2012/236 (2012)

11. Chancellery, S.F.: Explications relatives à l'ordonnance de la chancellerie fédérale sur le vote électronique (OVotE) (2013). http://www.bk.admin.ch/themen/pore/evoting/07979

12. Chaum, D., Pedersen, T.P.: Wallet databases with observers. In: Brickell, E.F. (ed.) CRYPTO 1992. LNCS, vol. 740, pp. 89–105. Springer, Heidelberg (1993)

13. El Gamal, T.: A public key cryptosystem and a signature scheme based on discrete logarithms. In: Blakely, G.R., Chaum, D. (eds.) CRYPTO 1984. LNCS, vol. 196, pp. 10–18. Springer, Heidelberg (1985)

14. Gerlach, J., Gasser, U.: Three case studies from Switzerland: E-voting (2009)

15. Gjøsteen, K.: Analysis of an internet voting protocol. Cryptology ePrint Archive, Report 2010/380 (2010)

16. Gjosteen, K.: The Norwegian internet voting protocol. Cryptology ePrint Archive, Report 2013/473 (2013)

17. Kripp, M.J., Volkamer, M., Grimm, R. (eds.): 5th International Conference on Electronic Voting 2012, (EVOTE 2012), Co-organized by the Council of Europe, Gesellschaft für Informatik and E-Voting.CC, 11–14 July 2012, Castle Hofen, Bregenz, Austria, LNI, vol. 205. GI (2012)

18. Lipmaa, H.: Two simple code-verification voting protocols. Cryptology ePrint Archive, Report 2011/317 (2011)

19. Malkhi, D., Margo, O.: E-voting without 'Cryptography'. In: Blaze, Matt (ed.) FC 2002. LNCS, vol. 2357. Springer, Heidelberg (2003)

20. Neuchatel: Guichet unique citizen portal. https://www.guichetunique.ch/

21. Pedersen, T.P.: Non-interactive and information-theoretic secure verifiable secret sharing. In: Feigenbaum, J. (ed.) CRYPTO 1991. LNCS, vol. 576, pp. 129–140. Springer, Heidelberg (1992)

22. Pinault, T., Courtade, P.: E-voting at expatriates' MPs elections in France. In: Kripp et al. [17], pp. 189–195

23. Puigalli, J., Guasch, S.: Cast-as-intended verification in Norway. In: Kripp et al. [17], pp. 49–63

24. Rosen, A., Ta-shma, A., Riva, B., Ben-Nun, J.: Wombat voting. http://www.wombat-voting.com/

25. Sandler, D., Derr, K., Wallach, D.S.: Votebox: a tamper-evident, verifiable electronic voting system. In: van Oorschot, P.C. (ed.) USENIX Security Symposium, pp. 349–364. USENIX Association, Berkeley (2008)

26. Schnorr, C.: Efficient signature generation by smart cards. J. Cryptology 4(3), 161–174 (1991)

Log Analysis of Estonian Internet Voting 2013–2014

Sven Heiberg[1], Arnis Parsovs[2,3], and Jan Willemson[4]([✉])

[1] Smartmatic-Cybernetica Centre of Excellence for Internet Voting,
Ülikooli 2, Tartu, Estonia
[2] Software Technology and Applications Competence Centre,
Ülikooli 2, Tartu, Estonia
[3] Institute of Computer Science, Tartu University, J. Liivi 2, Tartu, Estonia
[4] Cybernetica, Ülikooli 2, Tartu, Estonia
jan.willemson@gmail.com

Abstract. This paper presents analysis of Internet voting system logs of
2013 local municipal and 2014 European Parliament elections in Estonia.
We study both sociodemographic characteristics of voters and technical
aspects of voting. Special attention is paid to voting and verification
sessions that can be considered irregular (e.g. inability to cast a valid
vote or failed verifications). We observe several interesting phenomena,
e.g. that older people are generally faster Internet voters and that women
use the vote verification option significantly less than men.

1 Introduction

The 2011 parliamentary elections were a significant landmark in Estonian i-
voting. The share of votes cast over the Internet reached the as high as 24.3 % [7].
Such a share makes Internet voting an appealing target for various attackers, and
indeed, several different attacks observed in 2011 [9]. The most interesting
one was proposed by a student who developed a proof-of-concept vote-rigging
malware that exploited the lack of a feedback channel in 2011 elections.

As a result of these events, Estonian National Electoral Committee (NEC)
took the initiative to improve the security of Internet voting in various ways.
The i-voting protocol was extended by adding a new scheme providing cast-as-
intended verification for Estonian i-voting [11]. A separate effort was established
to perform in-depth analysis of logs produced by i-voting servers in order to
study voter behaviour and to detect attacks against i-voting system and system
malfunction.

This paper presents the results of these analysis efforts for 2013 and 2014
Estonian elections. Internet voting in 2013 local municipal elections (KOV2013)
took place from 2013-10-10 09:00 to 2013-10-16 18:00 [5], and Internet voting in
2014 European Parliament elections (EP2014) took place from 2014-05-15 09:00
to 2014-05-21 18:00 [8].

To facilitate this kind of analysis, NEC has taken a decision to provide
pseudonymised log records for research purposes. During pseudonymisation, the

© Springer International Publishing Switzerland 2015
R. Haenni et al. (Eds.): VoteID 2015, LNCS 9269, pp. 19–34, 2015.
DOI: 10.1007/978-3-319-22270-7_2

voters' identities and client certificates have been replaced by pseudonyms (leaving the option of studying repeating voting patterns). Sociodemographic data (gender, age) and technical session data (e.g. time stamps, OS identifiers) have been preserved in the logs in their original form.

There have been several reports on electronic voting log monitoring, but they have mostly been concerned with voting machines. Antonyan *et al.* analyse AccuVote optical scanning terminal logs [2]. Peisert *et al.* discuss the need for a detailed forensic audit trail to enable auditors to analyze the actions of e-voting systems [14]. Michel *et al.* present a grammar-based log analysis framework automating the analysis of event logs recorded by the electronic voting tabulators [12]. To the best of our knowledge, the current paper presents the first analysis of remote voting system logs.

The paper has the following structure. Section 2 describes the logging framework together with the criteria used to determine successful voting sessions. Sections 3 and 4 present various sociodemographic and technical metrics observed while studying the logs. Sections 5 and 6 analyse failed voting and verification sessions, respectively. Finally, Sect. 7 discusses the most interesting findings and makes some conclusions.

2   Log Monitoring for Estonian Internet Voting Scheme

2.1   Estonian Internet Voting Scheme

The basic Internet voting scheme used in Estonia follows the double-envelope postal voting system where the inner envelope is replaced by encryption and the outer envelope by digital signature (see [9] for a more detailed description). For cryptographic operations, each voter can use either smart card-based eID tools (ID card, Digi-ID) or cellphone SIM card-based Mobile-ID. The voter is supplied with the official i-voting client application (IVCA) and she can use it to download the candidate list and cast her vote to the server. Since 2013 elections it is also possible to verify one's vote using a mobile device [11]. In case the Internet voter feels coerced, she can resubmit her vote via Internet or in the polling station during the advance voting period.

The three protocols implemented by the i-voting system – voting with smart card, voting with Mobile-ID and verification – are defined by finite-state machines. The transitions between the states generate log messages. For example Fig. 1 displays the protocol for candidate list retrieval with a smart card-based eID tool. After TLS authentication to Vote Forwarding Server (VFS) has succeeded, a unique session identifier *sid* is generated. The *sid* is used throughout the voting session to identify log messages belonging to this protocol run. Before proceeding to eligibility checks and candidate list retrieval, the IP-address, HTTP User-Agent, personal code and client certificate of the voter are logged. The protocol proceeds by determining eligibility of the voter, checking the re-voting status at Vote Storage Server (VSS) and returning the candidate list to IVCA. Each of those steps is logged accordingly. The candidate

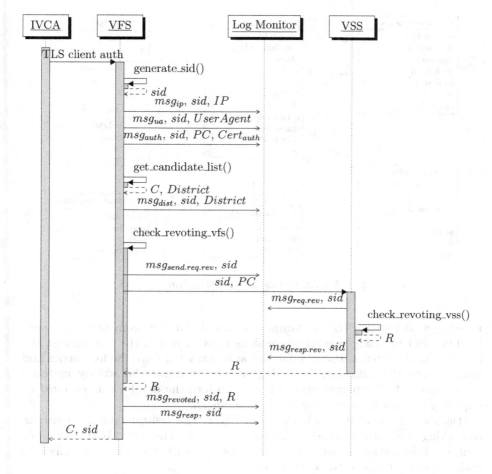

Fig. 1. Logs generated on candidate list retrieval

list retrieval is later followed by the vote casting where the same *sid* is submitted by the IVCA.

During the i-voting period, a large amount of log entries is produced (e.g. in 2013, 4 086 512 messages). Since it is not feasible for election officials to manually review every log entry, a solution was required to process the produced audit trail and generate a meaningful summary report that could be used to assess the current state of the i-voting system and perform informed decisions upon it. For example, unusually high system load could signal a possible bug in server software or an ongoing denial-of-service attack. Sudden increase in the number of unfinished voting sessions could be caused by a bug in i-voting software or an attack being performed on Internet voters, etc.

A log monitor has been introduced to the architecture. The monitor is connected to VFS and VSS receiving copies of log messages in quasi real-time using

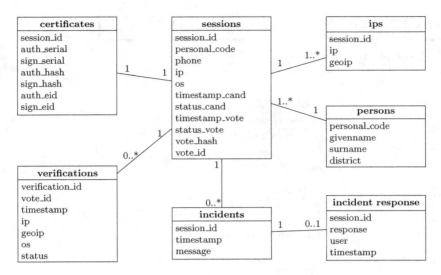

Fig. 2. Database table structure

`rsyslog` utility with UDP as transport protocol. The log monitor parses every log line, and by using regular expressions tries to match the line against the list of defined patterns. Useful information is extracted from the log entries and inserted into the database. Every log entry that cannot be strictly matched against the list of expected entries is written into the database as an incident requiring manual inspection by an election official.

Database table structure is shown in Fig. 2. The central table is `sessions` containing the data describing the voting session. The `verifications` table contains information about vote verification requests which can be linked to voting sessions through the `vote_id` field.

The `incidents` table stores incidents that have been logged by the log processor. The incidents are linked to `incident_response` table, which stores incident resolutions created by election officials.

2.2   Specification-Based Log Analysis

The relative simplicity of voting and verification protocols makes it feasible to apply the specification-based approach to monitoring where manually developed specifications are used to characterize legitimate program behaviours. Sessions that describe valid protocol runs and end with a successful result or acknowledged error state are generally not interesting for detailed analysis. These sessions are white-listed, they may become the subject of analysis in case some external condition characterizes them as a part of some bigger pattern – e.g. somebody re-voting a number of times over a certain threshold.

Associated with each session is a set of data which should be consistent within the session and/or across the sessions. In case certain conditions are not met the session is labelled for further analysis. The main criteria to call a voting session normal are given below.

1. *The encrypted vote is signed with the same eID tool that was used for authentication.* The i-voting protocol allows, e.g., for the voter to authenticate using ID card and submit a vote signed by Mobile-ID eID tool. However, that would be an anomaly since the official IVCA does not implement such a feature and there is no clear reason why the voter would use two eID tools in one voting session.

2. *The IP address and the OS of the voter do not change through the voting session.* Voter's IP address or OS change in the middle of the voting session might indicate voting session hijacking. Although we do not see the benefit or the flaw that would allow to hijack the i-voting session, we believe that detection of such an anomaly is advisable.
   Note that an IP address change could happen also for a completely legitimate reason, such as voter switching Internet connections in the process of i-voting.

3. *The vote cryptogram is unique.* To encrypt the vote, RSA-OAEP encryption scheme with random padding is used. Therefore, there should be no duplicate votes received by the i-voting servers. Several encrypted votes sharing the same cryptogram could indicate either randomness failure in IVCA (as was the case in 2013 parliamentary elections in Norway [3]), vote manipulation malware that uses hard-coded version of encrypted vote, or a ballot copying attack [4].

4. *Verification is requested only for those vote identifiers that have been issued.* Verification request containing a vote identifier which has not been issued by the i-voting server could indicate a vote identifier brute-force attack or a bug in the i-voting system or verification software. This event may also trigger legitimately if the voter is for some reason using a QR code from a previous election.

In addition to labelling sessions as normal or anomalous we also aggregate descriptive metrics about ongoing election. The gathered data contains sociodemographic metrics such as age and gender, technical data such as OS, eID tool, IP-addresses, etc. Some metrics are described below.

1. *Amount of voters sharing an IP address.* Several voters using the same IP address could indicate that a collective voting is being performed or the votes are cast by a single person who is using eID tools of other persons. However, several voters can be legitimately using a single IP if they are voting from a large organization where shared connection is used to access the Internet.

2. *The overall percentage of revoters.* In order to prevent vote selling and coercion, voters can change their i-vote by casting another i-vote. Through previous elections in 2005–2011 the revoter proportion has been between 1.15 % and 3.9 % [7]. A sudden increase in revoter proportion should be considered an anomaly indicating a large scale coercion or malware installed on the voting devices that revotes using voter's eID tool connected to the device, thus escaping detection by vote verification scheme [11, Section 5.E].

Increase in revoter ratio could also have a legitimate reason, e.g. a significant political scandal occurring during the voting period.

3. *Number of IP addresses for verifying a single vote.* By design, the vote verification protocol allows anyone knowing the vote reference to download the encrypted vote from the server. Under normal circumstances, we should see the vote verified from only a few devices (mostly just one). Verification requests coming from different devices may be an indication of the QR code containing the vote reference being misused.

4. *Amount of verifiers sharing an IP address.* Large number of votes verified from a single IP address may indicate a large-scale vote-buying attempt. On the other hand, verification from the same IP address can also happen if one mobile device or Internet connection is shared by several verifiers legitimately or a dynamic IP address is reassigned to different mobile devices.

3   Sociodemographic Metrics in 2013–2014

In this Section we will summarize some of the more interesting findings we observed from the vote session logs w.r.t. sociodemographic metrics (age and gender). In 2013, 170 804 voting sessions were made. In total, 133 808 voters cast at least one successful i-vote and 4542 (3.39 %) of them attempted to verify their vote. In 2014, 114 799 voting sessions were made. In total, 103 151 voters cast at least one successful i-vote and 4250 (4.12 %) of them attempted to verify their vote.

3.1   Age Distribution

The youngest person who (unsuccessfully) attempted i-voting in 2013 was 3 years old (in 2014, 7), and the oldest i-voter was 102 (in 2014, 103). The youngest vote verifier was 18 (in 2014 also 18) and the oldest was 97 (in 2014, 93).

The activity by age of voters (expressed as a percentage of all the eligible voters) and verifiers (expressed as a percentage of all the voters) are shown in Figs. 3 and 4 for 2013, and in Figs. 5 and 6 for 2014. We see that the most active voters are people of age 30–40.

An interesting phenomenon was observed when studying the relationship between the voter's age and voting session length (which is defined as the time between downloading the candidate list and submitting the vote). It turns out that contrary to what one might expect, older people are faster i-voters. The phenomenon is illustrated in Fig. 7 for 2013 and in Fig. 8 for 2014. We note that this phenomenon does not disappear when splitting the data by gender or eID tool used. The cause of this phenomenon remains unclear, possible reasons include older people having made up their minds already when starting to vote and younger people being more affected by multitasking.

Figures 9 and 10 show the histogram of general voting session lengths observed in 2013 and 2014 respectively.

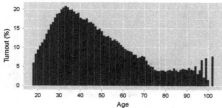

Fig. 3. KOV2013: Voter activity by age

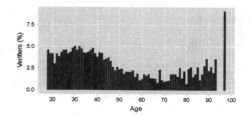

Fig. 4. KOV2013: Verifier activity by age

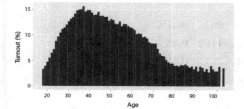

Fig. 5. EP2014: Voter activity by age

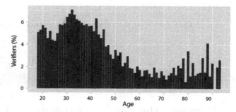

Fig. 6. EP2014: Verifier activity by age

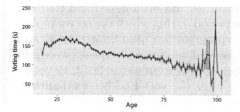

Fig. 7. KOV2013: Age vs voting time

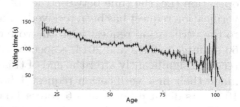

Fig. 8. EP2014: Age vs voting time

Table 1 gives 0.5 %, 1 %, 99 % and 99.5 % quantiles on the length of the voting session. It allows us to estimate that a normal length for a voting session could be considered between 20 s and 20 min (in 2014, 20 s and 13 min). Note that for 91.28 % (in 2014, 96.11 %) voting sessions the session length was less than 6 min.

3.2 Verification

It has been observed several times that women cast more i-votes than men. This observation was also confirmed in 2013 and 2014 elections when 52,2 % and 51.53 % of successful Internet voters were women, respectively.

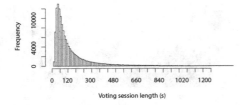

Fig. 9. KOV2013: Distribution of the voting session lengths

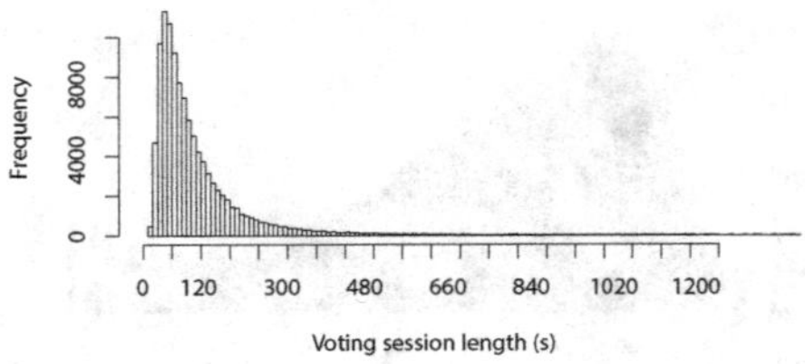

Fig. 10. EP2014: Distribution of the voting session lengths

Table 1. Quantiles of voting session lengths in seconds

Quantile	0.5 %	1 %	99 %	99.5 %
KOV2013	20	22	1182	1685.4
EP2014	21	23	751	1080

However, the gender distribution of verification is completely different, as only 31.6 % and 26.35 % of vote verifiers were women in 2013 and 2014, respectively.

It is also interesting to look at the length distribution of the verification operation (i.e. the time between the vote identifier has been issued and the vote verification request has been received). The period during which the server replies to the verification request with the vote cryptogram has been limited to 30 and 60 minutes in 2013 and 2014, respectively. Several verification requests were still received significantly after the end of this period. For example, in 2013, 19 voters made their first verification request 1 hour after the vote had been submitted, 10 voters did it 6 hours and 6 voters 1 day after the vote submission.

Frequencies of verification lengths (taking into account only the first verification request made by the voter) are shown in Figs. 11 and 12 for 2013 and 2014, respectively.

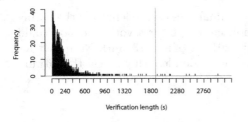

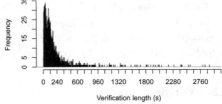

Fig. 11. KOV2013: Distribution of verification lengths

Fig. 12. EP2014: Distribution of verification lengths

4   Technical Metrics in 2013–2014

4.1   OS and eID Distribution

The official IVCA is available for three operating system families. Table 2 shows the popularity of Windows, Mac OS X and GNU Linux for voting.

As mentioned in Sect. 2.1, an i-vote can be cast using three eID tools. Popularity of these tools is shown in Table 3. Note that in Tables 2 and 3 we only take the final votes into account, thus excluding the votes annulled by revoting.

Table 2. OS distribution

OS	Windows	Mac OS X	GNU Linux
KOV2013	93.87 %	5.35 %	0.78 %
EP2014	93.4 %	5.46 %	1.14 %

Table 3. eID distribution

eID	ID card	Mobile-ID	Digi-ID
KOV2013	90.27 %	8.49 %	1.23 %
EP2014	87.69 %	10.86 %	1.45 %

4.2   IP Address Shared by Several Voters

In 2013, 133808 (in 2014, 103151) voters used 68503 (in 2014, 52191) unique IP addresses to cast their successful votes.

There were 28 (in 2014, 22) IP addresses which were each shared by more than 100 voters with the top IP address shared by 1127 (in 2014, 970) voters. We reviewed the top shared voting IP addresses and did not notice any strange patterns – voting was evenly distributed over the voting period, different OS versions were used and several voting sessions overlapped. This is consistent with the expected behaviour of people voting from one large organisation having just one external IP address.

We observed a large number of IP addresses shared by two and more voters where the voting sessions were not evenly distributed over the voting period, e.g. voters' casting their votes shortly after each other. Table 4 shows the number of voter groups observed, where voters voting in 5 min interval between each other and using the same OS are considered to belong to one group.[1] The table contains data only about those IP addresses which do no have overlapping voting sessions and those with the first and last voting activity falling into a 24 hour window.

4.3   Revoting

In 2013, 1.93 % (in 2014, 1.69 %) voters (altogether 2586; in 2014, 1743) cast more than one vote. From these revoters majority revoted only once. It appears that 30 % (in 2014, 28 %) of the revoters revote in the first 10 min, and 41 % (in 2014, 38 %) of revoters revote in the first hour after casting the vote.

---

[1] This definition of a group is limited to phenomena observable from system logs. A proper group voting study would require a more detailed social science approach.

Table 4. Voter groups in 2013 and 2014

Group size	KOV2013	EP2014
2	8476	6033
3	697	523
4	108	60
5	15	9
6	3	1

Figures 13 and 14 show distribution of votes and revotes over the voting period. We see that revoting activity pattern over the voting period follows the voting activity pattern.

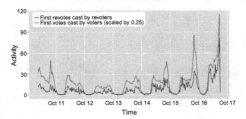

Fig. 13. KOV2013: Distribution of votes and revotes

Fig. 14. EP2014: Distribution of votes and revotes

We can estimate that in the worst case in KOV2013 2586 (in 2014, 1743) voters could have been coerced or fallen as a victims for revoting malware described in Sect. 2.2.

However, since in the previous elections revoter proportion was similar (see Sect. 2.2) and some amount of revoters is normal, it is unlikely that most of the revotes would have been caused by an attack.

5   Unsuccessful Voting Sessions

From those persons who attempted to i-vote in 2013, 96.6 % (in 2014, 98.5 %) succeeded to cast at least one successful vote (possibly by retrying). Still in 2013, 19.88 % of the voting sessions (in 2014, 8.39 %) did not result in a successfully cast vote. In this section we present the causes for unsuccessful voting sessions.

5.1   Sessions Failing with an Error Condition

It is natural for some voting sessions to fail – e.g. it is possible that a person is not in the list of eligible voters by mistake and finds it out only during the failed attempt to vote. The breakdown of error conditions, the number of unique voters affected in these voting sessions and the number of voters who did not manage to successfully i-vote (column "Voters (u)") are given in Table 5.

Looking at the row "Ineligible voters", we can see that in 2013 some voters who were originally declared ineligible eventually still managed to submit a vote. This is because a person's eligibility status can change during the voting period.

Table 5. Failed voting sessions in KOV2013 and EP2014

Reason of failure	KOV2013			EP2014		
	Sessions	Voters	Voters (u)	Sessions	Voters	Voters (u)
Maintenance of voting servers	11	11	1	–	–	–
Under-aged voter	28	25	25	16	16	15
Ineligible voter	1063	774	766	315	199	199
Voting not started	3	2	0	5	3	0
Voting already ended	1	1	1	38	35	28
Pre-2011 Mobile-ID user	1490	876	332	549	407	160
Bad Mobile-ID number	2051	–	–	491	–	–
Mobile-ID failure (auth)	2004	1394	122	1200	776	54
Mobile-ID failure (sign)	1043	926	29	609	562	33
Revoked ID card	1933	872	755	270	146	128
Revoked Mobile-ID	41	–	–	23	–	–
Incident	93	60	6	1173	325	88

5.2 Failure to Cast a Vote

Some voting sessions did not fail because of an error, but were from the i-voting system perspective simply abandoned – the candidate list was success-fully downloaded, but the vote submission request did not follow. Table 6 shows the number of affected voters and the number of voters who did not manage to cast any i-vote.

From these 2889 (in 2014, 869) voters, 176 (in 2014, 20) voters had at least one voting session with failed status. From the remaining 2713 (in 2014, 849) voters, 2000 (in 2014, 700) voters had made only a single voting session which did not continue after candidate list retrieval, 370 (in 2014, 79) voters had two such sessions, 52 (in 2014, 9) voters had more than six such sessions.

Some of these unfinished voting sessions in KOV2013 can be explained by a bug [1] in libcurl library used by the IVCA which caused a connection timeout when sending vote submission request over a slow network connection.

We can only speculate why these voters did not get past the candidate list retrieval in EP2014. Possible reasons include forgetting the PIN required to sign a vote with an eID tool, not finding a suitable candidate in the downloaded candidate list, or simply not realising that the i-voting session has to be completed by signing the vote.

5.3 Incidents

In addition to previously defined error conditions and abandoned voting sessions, there were 93 (in 2014, 1178) voting sessions raising an incident alert caused by unexpected log entries.

KOV2013. We observed 37 ID card voting sessions failing with the incident message which stated that the signing certificate digest did not match the digest specified in the vote. In total 12 voters were affected. Almost all of the voters were using GNU Linux OS except one voter who was using Windows OS. The incident was traced to the bug in OpenSC smart card library which was shipped with some GNU Linux distributions [13]. The bug failed to remove zero padding from the certificate when reading it from the smart card.

On 2013-10-15 from 15:12:26 to 15:13:08 there were 36 failed voting sessions logged with an incident message which informed about unavailability of VSS. The reason for VSS downtime was vote backup routine which required to stop Apache process running on VSS. Starting from the next elections (EP2014) LVM snapshots were used which allow to backup the votes without stopping the Apache process.

We observed 17 incidents caused by malformed votes – some votes were rejected as invalid. Altogether 13 voters were affected, all of them later managed to successfully cast an i-vote. Some of these incidents were traced back to the bug in IVCA. The IVCA continued with vote submission even if the certificate could not be read from the smart card or the digital signature generation in the smart card failed. In case of one voter it was found that the failure was caused by a defective Mobile-ID SIM card. Without the corresponding invalid votes, some of those incidents could not be thoroughly investigated.

We observed 3 Mobile-ID voting sessions which raised an incident alert about invalid phone number received. The problem was traced back to IVCA which failed to correctly enforce valid phone number input from the voter.

EP2014. We observed 1131 voting sessions failing with an error message stating that the certificate used to sign the vote is not yet valid. The error was traced back to a bug in server-side software updated in EP2014, which did not take into account timezone information when checking the certificate validity date. The error affected voters who had renewed their eID tool on the day of i-voting. The voters who approached NEC support centre were instructed to retry after a

Table 6. Abandoned voting sessions in KOV2013 and EP2014

	KOV2013			EP2014		
	Sessions	Voters	Voters (u)	Sessions	Voters	Voters (u)
Sessions without cast votes	24103	15563	2889	4921	3889	869

few hours. From the 310 voters affected, 229 managed to successfully cast their i-vote later in the i-voting period.

We observed five ID card voting sessions where the person submitting the vote was not the same who obtained the candidate list. The behaviour can be explained by the new "Retry" button feature introduced in IVCA which allows to obtain the candidate list using one ID card, but sign and submit the vote with another by swapping the cards between these operations. These votes were accepted and counted without creating a problem. While it is not the case in European Parliament Elections, it may happen that the voter obtaining the candidate list and the voter casting the vote have different candidate lists, which will result in an invalid vote in the vote counting phase. Therefore, server-side software was modified to reject the vote if the candidate list was not obtained by the same person who cast the vote.

It is not clear why these five voters decided to swap their ID card with other person's ID card before signing the vote. The persons involved in these sessions were paired as 79 years old male and 72 years old female, 50 years old male and 71 years old female, 74 years old male and 68 years old female, 56 years old male and 58 years old female, and 52 years old male and 33 years old female. From the voters who obtained the candidate list, two submitted their own vote a few minutes later, but three voters did not cast their vote at all.

We observed one ID card voting session using Windows IVCA failing with the incident alert stating that the vote signature could not be verified. Three minutes later the voter successfully revoted using the same ID card authentication certificate, but a different digital signature certificate. The hash of the digital signature certificate used in the failed voting session could not be found in any other voting session. We suspect that the voter swapped the currently valid ID card before signing the vote with an older ID card which had been officially reported lost.

The rest of the incidents were caused by the bug in a smart card library or person retrying the failed Mobile-ID session.

6   Unsuccessful Verification Sessions

6.1   Failure to Verify

In 2013, NEC received no complaints about unsuccessful vote verifications. However, we see that for 33 (in 2014, 26) voters their first verification attempt was not successful, resulting in an error message shown to the voter. Those voters tried to verify after the verification time-window had passed or after a new vote was submitted by them. In 2013, one verifier failed because VSS was unreachable due to backup procedures.

In 2014, we observed 196 vote verification requests having a malformed vote ID. Some of malformed vote ID requests were caused by a bug in iOS-based vote verification application which truncated the vote identifiers that contained a 0-byte. Four voters called to NEC support centre complaining about iOS verification application being unable to find their vote on VSS. The bug was fixed during elections and updated iOS application was pushed in iOS app store [11, Sect. 6].

However, other malformed verification requests could not be attributed to 0-byte bug. The malformed vote verification requests were traced back to iOS vote verification application, which failed to validate contents of the captured QR code before forming the vote verification request sent to VFS. This bug in iOS-based vote verification application has been fixed.

6.2 Verification Requests that Could Not Be Linked to Votes

We observed vote verification requests for three (in 2014, five) unique vote identifiers that were not issued by i-voting system. Some of those vote identifiers were queried multiple times by several unique IP addresses. One of the identifiers seen in EP2014 was also seen in KOV2013. We were able to track one of those identifiers to a QR code from information materials about Internet voting.

7   Discussion and Conclusions

7.1   Summary of the Findings

Log monitoring has proven to be a useful tool for the election officials for troubleshooting voters' problems and understanding the state of ongoing i-voting. In KOV2013 and EP2014 several malfunctions in IVCA, i-voting system, verification apps and external systems were discovered and fixed. From the i-voting perspective, those bugs were causing minor inconveniences to voters, in most cases it was possible to re-vote successfully.

In those elections we did not observe any event which could qualify as an attack against i-voting system. Furthermore, taking into account all observations, we can conclude that during KOV2013 and EP2014 no large-scale attack has been executed against i-voters.

There were several interesting phenomena observed in the logs that were unknown before. We were able to determine that older people are generally faster i-voters and vote verifiers are predominantly men, even though among the general population of i-voters the share of women is slightly higher.

7.2   Limitations of the Approach

The main limitation of our analysis is the ability to find the causes for some anomalies observed in the data.

In some of these cases the causes might be found if the voter could be contacted for an explanation. However, there is no simple way to contact the voter[2] and there is no legal basis for it, unless there is convincing evidence that illegal

---

[2] Although, if the voter used Mobile-ID to cast the vote, the phone number registered to the voter is available to NEC.

activity might have been performed. The only event when the voter was contacted, was the case of voter who cast more than 500 votes in RK2011 [10], and even then the inquiry did not provide a plausible explanation for the anomalous behaviour observed.

Some incidents could not be investigated because of technical reasons, such as unavailability of the vote involved in an incident. Logging and availability of such data for investigation is deliberately limited by NEC due to the vote privacy concerns.

Obviously, the approach used in this work can detect only the attacks executed by external attackers who attack voters' voting devices or eID tools, since none of the anomalous patterns applied can be used to detect large-scale vote manipulation attacks carefully executed by i-voting servers. Therefore, server-side attacks must be detected using different means.

After the i-voting server-side source code was published on GitHub [6], the described log monitoring solution is unlikely to observe incidents caused by reconnaissance exploitation attempts against i-voting servers, since now the attacker does not have to develop his attacks on a live election system. The exploit can be developed using a cloned i-voting system fully operated by the attacker.

Note that Internet voting still has a significant human component and hence not all the errors can be expected to manifest themselves only on digital media. For example, the mobile application for vote verification only displays the candidate number found in the cryptogram, but the decision about its match with the voter's intention is taken inside her head. Thus, some parts of the analysis of events depends on the voters' willingness to report them.

Also note that most of the reasons for suspicion do not necessarily indicate a malicious attack and can occur for perfectly acceptable reasons. However, they can be a starting point for more in-depth analysis to draw more complex conclusions (e.g. in case several of the items trigger a flag).

7.3   Future Work

Most of the anomalous patterns – e.g. IP address changing in the middle of the voting session, voter revoting several times – are not easily distinguishable from the legitimate behaviour. In some of those cases sessions become interesting only if a certain threshold is reached. Setting threshold values is a delicate trade-off between missing an attack and getting too many false positives. The statistical model of the expected behaviour built from KOV2013 and EP2014 data can be used to implement better anomaly detection for further elections. However, human behaviour is ever-changing, so these kinds of log monitoring efforts must be continued to adjust the normality profiles in the future accordingly.

Acknowledgements. This research was supported by the Estonian Research Council under Institutional Research Grant IUT27-1, Estonian Doctoral School in Information and Communication Technology (IKTDK) and the European Regional Development Fund through the Centre of Excellence in Computer Science (EXCS) and grant project number 3.2.1201.13-0018 "Verifiable Internet Voting – Event Analysis and Social Impact".

References

1. Timeout for Expect: 100-continue as an option, Oct 2013, Curl-library mailing list archives. http://curl.haxx.se/mail/lib-2013-10/0142.html
2. Antonyan, T., Davtyan, S., Kentros, S., Kiayias, A., Michel, L., Nicolaou, N., Russell, A., Shvartsman, A.: Automating voting terminal event log analysis. In: Electronic Voting Technology Workshop/Workshop on Trustworthy Elections (EVT/WOTE09) (2009)
3. Bull, C., Nore, H.: Problems encountered. Seminar on Internet voting, Sep 2013. https://www.regjeringen.no/contentassets/c41c2959b8d946bf8007b546552ff9dc/5_problems_encountered.pdf
4. Cortier, V., Smyth, B.: Attacking and fixing Helios: an analysis of ballot secrecy. J. Comput. Secur. **21**(1), 89–148 (2013)
5. Estonian National Electoral Committee: Municipal Elections 2013 Results (2013). http://kov2013.vvk.ee/
6. Estonian National Electoral Committee: Source code of the server side components of Estonian internet-voting system, Jul 2013. https://github.com/vvk-ehk/evalimine
7. Estonian National Electoral Committee: Statistics about Internet Voting in Estonia (2013). http://vvk.ee/voting-methods-in-estonia/engindex/statistics
8. Estonian National Electoral Committee: European Parliament Elections 2014 Results (2014). http://ep2014.vvk.ee/detailed-en.html
9. Heiberg, S., Laud, P., Willemson, J.: The application of I-voting for estonian parliamentary elections of 2011. In: Kiayias, A., Lipmaa, H. (eds.) VoteID 2011. LNCS, vol. 7187, pp. 208–223. Springer, Heidelberg (2012)
10. Heiberg, S., Willemson, J.: Modeling threats of a voting method. In: Zissis, D., Lekkas, D. (eds.) Design, Development, and Use of Secure Electronic Voting Systems, pp. 128–148. IGI Global, Hershey (2014)
11. Heiberg, S., Willemson, J.: Verifiable internet voting in Estonia. In: Krimmer, R., Volkamer, M. (eds.) 6th International Conference on Electronic Voting 2014, (EVOTE 2014), 28–31 October 2014, Bregenz, Austria, pp. 23–29. TUT Press, Tallinn (2014)
12. Michel, L.D., Shvartsman, A.A., Volgushev, N.: A systematic approach to analyzing voting terminal event logs. USENIX J. Election Technol. Syst. (JETS) 2(2), April 2014. https://www.usenix.org/system/files/jets/issues/0202/overview/jets_0202-michel.pdf
13. OpenSC project: Regression in e35febe: compute cert length, Dec 2012. https://github.com/OpenSC/OpenSC/pull/114
14. Peisert, S., Bishop, M., Yasinsac, A.: Vote selling, voter anonymity, and forensic logging of electronic voting machines. In: 42nd Hawaii International Conference on System Sciences, 2009. HICSS 2009, pp. 1–10. IEEE (2009)

The New South Wales iVote System: Security Failures and Verification Flaws in a Live Online Election

J. Alex Halderman[1] and Vanessa Teague[2]($\boxtimes$)

[1] University of Michigan, Ann Arbor, USA
jhalderm@eecs.umich.edu
[2] University of Melbourne, Melbourne, Australia
vjteague@unimelb.edu.au

Abstract. In the world's largest-ever deployment of online voting, the iVote Internet voting system was trusted for the return of 280,000 ballots in the 2015 state election in New South Wales, Australia. During the election, we performed an independent security analysis of parts of the live iVote system and uncovered severe vulnerabilities that could be leveraged to manipulate votes, violate ballot privacy, and subvert the verification mechanism. These vulnerabilities do not seem to have been detected by the election authorities before we disclosed them, despite a pre-election security review and despite the system having run in a live state election for five days. One vulnerability, the result of including analytics software from an insecure external server, exposed some votes to complete compromise of privacy and integrity. At least one parliamentary seat was decided by a margin much smaller than the number of votes taken while the system was vulnerable. We also found protocol flaws, including vote verification that was itself susceptible to manipulation. This incident underscores the difficulty of conducting secure elections online and carries lessons for voters, election officials, and the e-voting research community.

1 Introduction

Internet voting has rarely been used in significant elections for public office, due to numerous, well established security risks [15], such as compromise of election servers, of voters' client devices, of the network in between, and of the voter authentication process. To better understand how these risks can play out in real elections, we studied what may be the largest deployment of Internet voting to-date, the March 2015 state election in New South Wales, Australia.

In this election, voters had the option to use an online voting system called iVote, which was developed by e-voting vendor Scytl for the New South Wales Electoral Commission (NSWEC). Prior to the election, NSWEC performed multiple security studies (e.g. [23,24]), and officials publicly claimed that the vote was "...completely secret. It's fully encrypted and safeguarded, it can't be tampered with" [1]. Over 280,000 votes were reportedly returned through iVote

© Springer International Publishing Switzerland 2015
R. Haenni et al. (Eds.): VoteID 2015, LNCS 9269, pp. 35–53, 2015.
DOI: 10.1007/978-3-319-22270-7_3

(about 5 % of the election total), exceeding the 70,090 Norwegian votes submitted online in 2013 [27] and the 176,491 online votes in the 2015 Estonian election [13].

While the election was going on, we performed an independent, uninvited security analysis of public portions of the iVote system. We discovered critical security flaws that would allow a network-based attacker to perform downgrade-to-export attacks [5,12], defeat TLS, and inject malicious code into browsers during voting. We showed that an attacker could exploit these flaws to violate ballot privacy and steal votes. We also identified several methods by which an attacker could defeat the verification mechanisms built into the iVote design.

After we reported these problems to authorities, NSWEC patched iVote to correct the network security flaws, but by this time the election had been running for five days and 66,000 votes had been cast on the vulnerable system. After the vulnerabilities were removed, we made our findings public in a technical blog post on *Freedom to Tinker* [29] and an essay in *The Conversation.*

The election count is now complete [21], with the final seat in the proportionally represented Legislative Council having come down to a margin of 3177 votes, a tiny fraction of the number of votes cast over iVote before it was patched. To our knowledge, this is the first time enough votes to affect a parliamentary seat in a state election have been returned over an Internet voting system while it was demonstrably vulnerable to attacks that would allow external vote manipulation. While we do not know whether anyone exploited the opportunity for electoral fraud, we know the opportunity was there.

This paper details our security findings and draws broader lessons from the iVote vulnerability. It reinforces findings of security problems in other Internet voting systems, such as Washington, D.C.'s [31] and Estonia's [28], and it demonstrates once again that no amount of pre-election review can guarantee that such a system is secure. These problems also highlight the brittleness of the web platform and TLS protocol—a fragility which may be incompatible with the intensive security requirements and time pressure of political elections.

iVote's vulnerabilities should encourage skepticism of other Internet voting systems claimed to be verifiable. Years of research on electronic methods of election verification are only just beginning to produce end-to-end verifiable voting systems appropriate for use in low-stakes, low-coercion elections [4], or in government elections using a postal mail step [32], or in the much easier case of supervised polling places [7,10,11]. The iVote verification protocol ignores basic insights and techniques from that research, opting instead for a telephone-based vote reading service that substantially reduces voter privacy while providing only very limited assurances of integrity. Furthermore, an election verification protocol, like any other security protocol, should not be relied upon without an extensive period of public review; in the case of the iVote protocols, there was none.

Securing Internet voting requires overcoming some of the most difficult problems in computer security, and, with existing technology, even the smallest mistakes can undermine the integrity of the election result. The experience in

New South Wales is a real-world example demonstrating online voting security problems that many security researchers, including us, have warned about for many years. We recommend that election officials refrain from conducting high-stakes elections online until there are fundamental security advances.

2   iVote Background

The iVote system was a complex interaction of many components, some managed by the NSWEC and some by other administrators. Registration and voting could each be done by three different methods: by telephone, over the Internet, or from a NSWEC computer in a polling place. There were four steps in using iVote:

1. The voter registered, received an 8-digit iVote ID, and chose a 6-digit PIN.
2. The voter logged in to the voting server (or the telephone voting system) with her iVote ID and PIN, cast a vote, and received a 12-digit receipt number. The vote was encrypted on the client, sent to the voting server, and forwarded to a separate verification service.
3. Optionally, the voter telephoned the verification service, an interactive voice response (IVR) system. She entered her iVote ID, PIN, and receipt number and heard her vote read back. This service stopped at the close of polls.
4. Optionally, the voter visited an online receipt service to query whether any votes with her receipt number were included in the final count. No login was needed. This service remained active after the close of polls.

More details are described in the Security Implementation Statement [24] and other reports published by NSWEC [22]. These include prose descriptions of the methods of encrypting and processing the vote. The protocol evolved over several drafts, but all of them differ in some important respects from what the system actually did during the election (see Sect. 5.1). No source code was made available for any of the server-side processes, including the main voting web server, verification server, registration server, and receipt server.

In the 2015 state election, each voter could cast one vote for the Legislative Assembly and one for the Legislative Council. Although iVote was officially reserved for the disabled and other eligible absentee voters, voters could qualify by self-certifying that they would be out of the state during election day. iVote opened to the public on the morning of March 16 and closed at 6 P.M. on March 28, the same time as other polls closed in the state election. Officials reported that about 280,000 votes (5 % of all counted ballots) were cast over iVote.

3   Vulnerabilities in iVote

Shortly after iVote voting opened, we began an independent security review of the publicly accessible components of the system. Although election officials did not publish the source code, client-side portions of this code were necessarily delivered to voters' browsers. Since we were not eligible voters, we did not

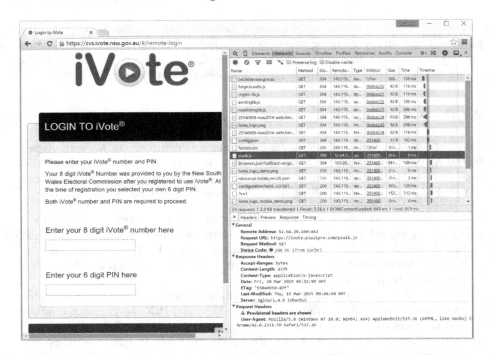

Fig. 1. Like most web applications, iVote was made up of dozens of resources that were loaded in the background by the browser. Using the Chrome Developer Tools, we could see that most of the iVote resources came from the "core voting system" server, `cvs.ivote.nsw.gov.au`, but one component, JavaScript for the Piwik analytics tool, was loaded from an external server, `ivote.piwikpro.com`.

proceed past the login screen of the voting web application, http://cvs.ivote. nsw.gov.au, but we did inspect the HTML, CSS, and JavaScript code that made up the application. In addition, NSWEC made a practice version of the iVote system available to the public at https://practise.ivote.nsw.gov.au. The practice site allowed anyone to log in using provided credentials and vote a mock ballot. We confirmed that the practice system used substantially the same client-side code as the real election server and used it to perform further hands-on tests.

iVote delivers the web application using HTTPS. This is intended to prevent an adversary from modifying or replacing the code in transit to the user's web browser. We tested the security of the main iVote HTTPS server using the Qualys SSL Labs SSL Test, which indicated that the server configuration complied with current best practices and was secure against known vulnerabilities. However, a closer analysis of the structure of the iVote application showed that when the voter loads the iVote site, the site imports and executes JavaScript for a third-party analysis tool called Piwik. As shown in Fig. 1, this code is loaded from a URL at the third-party server https://ivote.piwikpro.com. When we tested the SSL configuration of this site, we found that it was extremely poor—scoring an

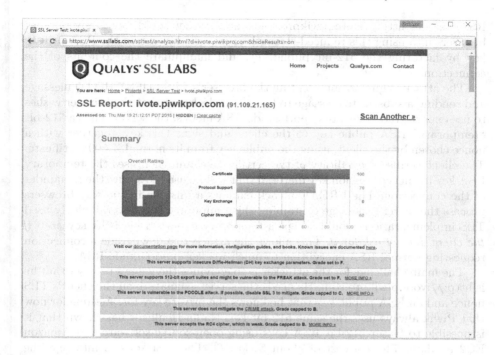

Fig. 2. The `ivote.piwikpro.com` server scored an F on the Qualys SSL Labs tests. Among other reported problems, the server used insecure Diffie-Hellman parameters, allowed 512-bit export cipher suites that are subject to the FREAK attack, and was vulnerable to the POODLE attack. We showed that these problems would allow a man-in-the-middle attacker to inject vote-stealing code into the iVote application.

'F' grade in the SSL Labs test, as shown in Fig. 2. Among a variety of other security problems, the server supported 512-bit "export-grade" ciphersuites for both RSA and ephemeral Diffie-Hellman key exchange. As we will show, this weak configuration allowed multiple ways for an attacker to bypass the security provided by HTTPS and inject malicious code into the user's iVote session without triggering any browser security warnings.

3.1   Vulnerability to the FREAK Attack

The FREAK attack [8,12], short for Factoring RSA Export Keys, is a TLS vulnerability that was publicly disclosed on March 3, 2015, less than two weeks before the iVote voting opened. The Piwik server's configuration problems made it vulnerable to FREAK, and a network-based man-in-the-middle attacker could exploit the attack against the Piwik server in order to compromise iVote.

As the name implies, FREAK exploits the weakness of 512-bit "export-grade" RSA keys that are supported by the TLS protocol as a legacy feature of 1990s era U.S. cryptographic export restrictions. If a server supported export-grade

RSA—as did http://ivote.piwikpro.com—an attacker could fool many popular browsers into using this reduced-strength cryptography, obtain the RSA private key by factoring the 512-bit public key, and manipulate the contents of the connection.

The attack begins by intercepting the browser's TLS CLIENT_HELLO message and sending a substitute message to the server declaring that the browser wishes to use export-grade RSA. In export-grade RSA modes, the server sends a 512-bit "temporary" RSA public key to the client and signs this key, together with a nonce chosen by the client, using the public key from its normal X.509 certificate. The client verifies the validity of the certificate chain, then uses the temporary RSA key to encrypt session key material that will be used to secure the remainder of the connection. The FREAK attack exploits a mistake in the way browsers process the server's message containing this temporary key. Several widely used TLS implementations would accept a temporary export-grade RSA key *even if the client did not ask for it*. This allows the attacker to downgrade a connection requesting normal RSA encryption to much weaker export-grade RSA.

The main challenge for the attacker is to convince the voter's browser that he is http://ivote.piwikpro.com. He needs the server's signature on the client's TLS nonce and an RSA public key that he knows the private key for. Assume for now that Piwik always uses the same 512-bit key. Nadia Heninger has shown that it is possible to factor 512-bit RSA keys using open-source software and Amazon EC2 in about 7 h at a cost of about \$100 [16]. The attacker can intercept the user's connection, note the client's nonce, and make a request to the real Piwik server with the same nonce—in effect, using it as a signature oracle. He can send the resulting signature on the RSA key as part of the connection to the voter's browser, which will see the key as valid and use it to encrypt its session key material. Since the attacker has factored the key, he can decrypt this key material and impersonate the Piwik server for the rest of the connection.

One complication is that Piwikpro, unlike many TLS servers, periodically rotated its temporary key. We saw the key change approximately every hour—too frequently to apply the factoring methods available to us. However, we found that we could force the Piwik server to use the same temporary RSA key for much longer by maintaining a long-lived TLS connection and repeatedly invoking client-initiated renegotiation. Each renegotiation can use a different client nonce, so we could use the Piwik server as a signature oracle to attack as many clients as we wanted and use the same key for as long as this connection stayed open.

In tests, we were able to sustain the connection for 17–21 h, and, with Heninger's assistance, we factored the temporary RSA key from one such session. An attacker could start such a connection, spend the first 7 h factoring the key, and then attack an unlimited number of voters' TLS connections for the remainder of the connection lifetime. By making multiple such connections in a staggered fashion, the attacker could have continuously attacked iVote users for the duration of the connection at a cost of about \$100 per 12 h period.

Many popular browsers were vulnerable to FREAK, including Internet Explorer, Safari, and Chrome for Mac OS and Android [12]. Although patches were released for most browsers around March 10, iVote voting opened on March 16, and many users likely had not applied the relevant patches.

3.2 Vulnerability to the Logjam Attack

The ivote.piwikpro.com server was also vulnerable to an even more power-ful downgrade-to-export attack that affected *all* popular browsers: the Logjam attack [5], which was publicly disclosed on May 20, 2015. We knew about this flaw during the election because one of us was part of the team that developed the attack, but we could not talk about it publicly because responsible disclosure to the browser-makers was still ongoing. In other words, we had a zero-day TLS vulnerability that would have allowed us to attack any voter's iVote session.

Logjam is reminiscent of the FREAK attack, but it affects ephemeral Diffie-Hellman (DHE) ciphersuites rather than RSA ciphersuites, and it is made pos-sible by a flaw in the TLS protocol rather than a client-side implementation error. If a server supports export-grade Diffie-Hellman with parameters that an attacker can break, a man-in-the-middle can force browsers to use it, obtain the session keys, and intercept or arbitrarily change the contents of the connec-tion [5].

In Diffie-Hellman, two public parameters, a prime p and a group generator g, are used to compute a public key y from a secret key x as $y = g^x \bmod p$. An attacker can breach the security by computing the discrete logarithm of y to recover x. Although computing one discrete log is harder than factoring one RSA key of equivalent parameter size, a large part of the discrete log computation can be reused for all connections that use the same p [5]. The Piwik server supported export Diffie-Hellman using a fixed 512-bit p:

a705d4b834119d78e434e47be531ae602209c4810fa3baca2b781d49f847bc27
7681d93375522e41aae5de77d86d124852951be54145c9417f603ea96e5024b7

The team that developed the Logjam attack used open-source software to per-form the precomputation step for three other common 512-bit values of p, each of which took about a week of wall-clock time using idle cycles on a cluster [5]. Following precomputation, they could break individual key exchanges based on those values in about 90 s using a single 24-core machine. The same kind of attack would be possible against Piwik's p, and would allow us to effectively attack all iVote sessions from any browser by paying a fixed up-front cost for the precomputation. In that case, since the browser connects to Piwik in the background, the 90 s delay to compute the session key would not be noticeable by the voter.

3.3 Proof-of-Concept, Exploitability, and Responsible Disclosure

We developed a proof-of-concept demonstration to show how an attacker could leverage the FREAK or Logjam vulnerability to compromise an iVote voting session. Following the scheme in Fig. 3, this attack replaced the code loaded

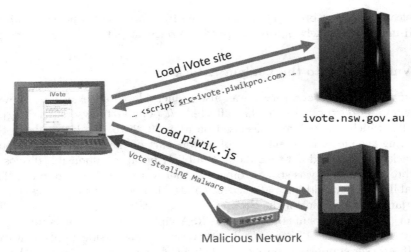

Fig. 3. Although the NSW web server used a secure HTTPS configuration to deliver the iVote application, the app subsequently loaded additional JavaScript from an insecure external server, `ivote.piwikpro.com`. An attacker who intercepted connections between the voter's browser and the PiwikPro server could tamper with this JavaScript to inject arbitrary malicious code into the iVote application.

from http://ivote.piwikpro.com with malicious JavaScript. Since this code was executed in the context of the user's iVote session, it could arbitrarily change the operation of the iVote web application. iVote used AngularJS to run a series of worker JavaScript threads which implemented cryptographic operations. Crucial election data, including the contents of the vote, were passed between these workers as messages. Our code intercepted these messages to change the intended vote to a different vote before it was sent to the iVote server. Our code also exposed the vote that the voter intended to cast and sent it, along with the voter's authentication credentials, to a command-and-control server operated by the attacker. Screenshots from our demonstration are in Fig. 4.

To exploit these attack against iVote, the attacker would need to intercept and manipulate connections from the voter's browser destined for the Piwik server. (Such man-in-the-middle attacks are, of course, one of the main threats that HTTPS is intended to guard against.) Criminal attackers have many well documented ways to achieve this. It could be done, for example, using client-side malware (including functions of widespread pre-existing botnets [2,9]), by compromising insecure WiFi access points, by poisoning ISP DNS caches to redirect the traffic to an attacker-controlled IP address [17], by attacking vulnerable routers or links along the path to the server, or by redirecting packets by hijacking BGP prefixes [6]. These attacks are especially practical in an election scenario, because the attacker can be highly opportunistic—he does not

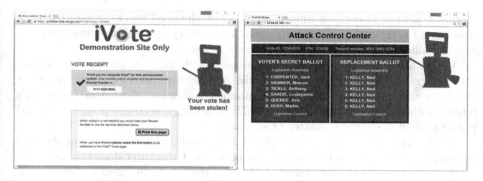

Fig. 4. As a proof of concept, we showed that we could exploit the FREAK attack against iVote to inject malicious code that would surreptitiously manipulate the voter's choices (*left*) and report them to a command-and-control server (*right*). Our mock attacker's symbol invokes Ned Kelly, an iconic Australian outlaw.

care which NSW voters he compromises, so he can target any insecure hosts or infrastructure in the entire state, or anywhere in the world with large numbers of iVote voters. In addition to large scale criminal fraud, many individuals and employers have legitimate administrator privileges on home or workplace networks that others might use for voting, and could abuse these privileges to target votes.

Since we (of course) would not attempt to steal actual votes, we tested our demonstration attack only on our own votes, cast only on the iVote practice system, which was identical in all relevant respects to the real voting system. After confirming that the attack was possible, we notified the Australian CERT of the vulnerabilities around 2 P.M. on Friday, March 20. CERT took responsibility for notifying the NSW Electoral Commission, which fixed the problem around midday on Saturday, March 21, by modifying the iVote server configuration to disable Piwik. By then, about 66,000 votes had already been cast. We cannot know with certainty whether any real iVote votes were attacked; however, the final Legislative Council margin of 3177 votes represented less than 5 % of the votes cast over iVote while the server was vulnerable.

4   Circumventing Verification

Vote manipulation attacks should be detectable with some probability by the verification mechanism. However, the verification mechanism itself suffers from a number of straightforward circumventions and at least one important protocol flaw.

4.1   Simple Verification Avoidance

The telephone-based verification scheme is easily sidestepped for last-minute votes because it shuts down at the close of polls. So an attacker could confidently modify votes that were cast immediately before the deadline, knowing that they could not be verified. A malicious client (or server) could slow down near the end of polling to exacerbate this problem.

Voters are told how to verify by the same website they use to vote, so the attacker could use the man-in-the-middle methods we describe above to direct the voter to a fake verification phone number that would read back the voter's intended choices. Thanks to modern VoIP technology, setting up an automated phone system is simply a matter of software.

Even more simply, the attacker could delay submitting the vote and showing the receipt number for a few seconds, in hopes that the voter does not intend to verify and simply leaves the website. (Perhaps the site could show a progress bar in place of the number.) If the voter navigates away, there will be no chance to verify, and the attacker can confidently submit a fraudulent vote. Otherwise, the attacker can give up, submit the genuine vote, and display the receipt number.

4.2   Using the "clash" Attack to Reduce Verification Failures

The following attack coordinates multiple compromised iVote sessions to manipulate a large number of votes with limited detection. The attack is a variant of the "clash" attack [18]. We believe it would work, but of course we could not test it during the election without interfering with real votes.

When verification fails to produce the expected vote, the voter is supposed to complain to the authorities. Inevitably, some voters will falsely complain, either mistakenly or maliciously, that their correctly entered vote has been dropped or misrecorded. The iVote verification design does not provide any evidence to support or disprove voter complaints, making it difficult to distinguish an attack from the baseline level of complaints due to voter error. This observation is important in the following attack, which reduces the number of complaints, but probably does not eliminate them altogether. Although this attack would sometimes be detected, the percentage of verification complaints would substantially underrepresent the fraction of manipulated votes, perhaps leading to an incorrect result appearing to have been verified. The attack requires the ability to:

- misdirect some voters' registrations,
- assign these voters a PIN at registration, instead of letting them choose, and
- compromise some iVote clients, using the attack from Sect. 3 or simple misdirection.

First observe that, while the registration server itself was protected by HTTPS, the main iVote gateway from which voters reached it ran plain HTTP[1]. This gave a man-in-the-middle attacker the opportunity to misdirect registration attempts to a site of the attacker's choosing, for instance by using the SSL_strip attack [19]. The attacker could substitute a look-alike registration site which assigned a PIN rather than accepting one, under the assumption that a typical voter would not realize this was not the normal behavior.

---

[1] Or rather, it did for the first week of voting, until we pointed this out to NSWEC.

Now note that Australian elections use multi-candidate preferential voting, so two voters who support party A may subsequently list quite different lower preferences. However, some common patterns recur very often, for example the vote consisting of a single (first) preference on each ballot. Many voters also follow official party "How to Vote" cards. Although we are not aware of data for NSW, studies in the neighboring state of Victoria show that overall about 40 % of voters follow their how-to-vote card exactly [30].

The main idea of this attack is to intercept a voter's registration and give him the iVote ID and PIN of a like-minded person who has already voted, preferably one who has cast a simple vote likely to be repeated. If the target voter's choices exactly match those of the first voter, then all of the verification will look exactly right to both voters. The attacker can safely reuse the target voter's registration credentials to get a new iVote ID and PIN and cast an arbitrary vote. If the target voter's choices are different from the first voter, he will detect a problem if he uses the verification service, but not if he contacts the receipt service only.

This attack removes a party-A vote and substitutes a vote of the attacker's choice. While it may sometimes be detected, if prediction of voter behavior is good then it raises far fewer complaints than that quantity of attacked votes ought to. For example, if prediction is perfect then it raises no alarm; if prediction is near-perfect then it manipulates many more votes than the number of verification complaints indicates. Note that it is not hard to predict how someone will vote when you have their registration credentials and hence their electoral roll record.

We find it notable that issues mentioned in the academic literature on verifiable voting—including the absence of dispute resolution (or accountability) and the prospect of a particular kind of attack—here turn out to be relevant in the context of a real-world online election.

5   Other Issues

We discuss additional problems related to privacy, integrity and usability.

5.1   Integrity, Auditing, and Verification

The iVote verification and audit systems are incompletely described in public documents, and no source code is publicly available, so it is not possible for external independent observers like us to rule out the existence of other substantial risks to integrity, beyond those we have already described. However, we can make several high-level observations about limitations of the design.

For instance, the design cannot achieve the same level of assurance for integrity as an ordinary post-election scrutineering process, since a related compromise of the Core Voting System and the Verification Service could undetectably alter votes. For instance, the Verification Service could simply lie to the voter about what vote was recorded on their behalf. Then the Core Voting System and Verification System could show consistent misrepresented votes to the Auditor.

The process for auditing is incompletely described, so it is not clear whether a related compromise of the Core Voting System and the Auditor would also suffice to alter votes undetectably. A simple potential attack would be for the auditor to turn a blind eye to inconsistencies between the Core Voting System's data and the Verification Server's. Would this be caught? The Security Implementation Statement [24] refers to some independent parties being allowed to observe some parts of the audit process and receive some software, but it does not say exactly what data they may check.

Votes that were present on the verification server (and possibly verified) could subsequently be removed if the voter re-registered or voted via another channel. It is not clear from the published system description how or whether the auditor (or anyone else) could verify that only the correct votes were removed.

A compromised web server or Voice Server (*i.e.* the IVR system for phone voting) could perform the attack from Sect. 4.1 on last-minute votes just as easily as a compromised web client. This would be a low-risk attack, since the malicious server would know that the verification server would be turned off before the voter could perform verification and detect this.[2]

There are important inconsistencies between the code and the documentation describing how votes are encrypted. Early iVote documents [22], including The iVote System Overview, describe them as being encrypted with the Receipt Number; the Security Implementation Statement [24] describes them as being encrypted using the ElGamal public key encryption system with the public keys of the Election and Verification Servers. Our inspection of the JavaScript used by iVote clients indicates that neither description is completely accurate: votes are encrypted using a "digital envelope" which consists of a randomly-generated symmetric key, encrypted once each with the Election and Verification Servers' ElGamal public keys, plus the vote choices encrypted with AES using the symmetric key. This has implications for both the privacy and the integrity of the system. Furthermore, the deviation of the actual code from the published specifications, particularly for such a central aspect of the voting protocol, raises broader questions about the accuracy of the published descriptions of iVote.

5.2   Privacy

Having voters telephone a third-party server to have their votes read back to them is unprecedented, either in Australia or (to our knowledge) elsewhere in the world. It introduces many different opportunities for privacy breaches and coercion after voting that do not exist in traditional paper-based voting.

---

[2] In the case of the web server, this would require forging a signature attached to the vote by the client. This signing step is evident in the JavaScript, but we could not find any documentation on how the signing key was derived or how the signature was verified. Hence we do not know whether a compromised web server could have simply created a new signature on any vote it received, or whether it would have needed to modify the JavaScript served to the client in order to get a valid signature on an altered vote.

For instance, a criminal could offer money in return for iVote verification credentials that produced the desired vote from the verification server, or a coercer could threaten punishment if such credentials are not provided. As noted by McKay [20], such an attacker could use the Receipt Server to check that the voter had not revoted to change their selections. Such attacks could originate anywhere in the world, and vote buying could even be automated—imagine a Tor hidden service that offered Bitcoin payments for proper votes.

Although the iVote design appears to give up on using technology to protect against vote buying and coercion, the system employs elaborate privacy measures to try to separate the voter's identity from their ballot internally. Encryption alone does not guarantee vote privacy, as the vote must eventually be counted somehow. Some electronic voting systems, including the Norwegian Internet voting system [14], use verifiable mixing in order to hide the link between the decrypted vote and the encrypted form submitted by the voter.[3] The "cryptographic envelope" form of encryption used in iVote does not seem conducive to these privacy-preserving tabulation methods. It is therefore crucial for privacy that the voter's identity cannot be reconnected with her symmetrically-encrypted vote, which seems to remain in the same recognizable form throughout the process.

iVote tries to achieve this by storing various items of unique or private data in various different parts of the system, and the Security Implementation Statement [24] makes reference to associations between these being destroyed. However, compared to traditional postal ballots, for which the physical separation of the voter's identity from the ballot can occur irrevocably, the destruction of electronic links is much more difficult to achieve. This is especially true if components of the system are compromised or malfunctioning in ways that allow data to be observed, recorded, or transferred elsewhere.

Unfortunately, there are several critical places in the system where compromised components or malicious insiders could potentially associate voter identities with ballot contents. For example:

1. In the polling-site version of iVote, voters register and then vote via the same machine. This creates a single point of attack, as their identity and their vote are both present.
2. All the phone communications, including voting and verifying by IVR system, are potentially susceptible to eavesdropping if the encryption used by the phone company is weak or absent. This is particularly serious since both voting and verification involve transmitting the ballot contents over this channel, and since many voters use identifiable telephone numbers.
3. A compromise of the registration server, which knows the link between an individual's iVote ID and name, could be combined with only one other compromise (of the Verification Server, Voice Server, or possibly the Auditor) to link the name to the decrypted vote.

---

[3] Some also use homomorphic tallying, but that would not work for Australian (preferential) voting.

4. The verification server has simultaneous access to the voter's ballot contents and iVote ID. If the voter accesses the service in a way that reveals their identity (for example, with a phone that has caller ID), then the verification server has all the information necessary to link the voter to their vote.

5.3   Usability and Operations

iVote suffered other problems during the election period. The system was suspended for six hours because two minor parties had been left off the "above the line" section of the ballot.

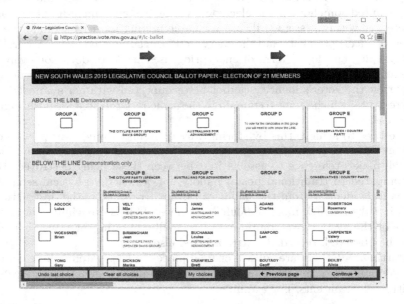

Fig. 5. iVote suffered from problems beyond security. Two parties were mistakenly left off the "above the line" section of the ballot for the first 19,000 votes, and the ballot interface (which required scrolling both horizontally and vertically to access all 394 candidates) was criticized for usability problems.

Other commentators drew attention to serious usability problems with the ballot interface, which was very similar to the practice ballot design shown in Fig. 5. Navigating the ballot required scrolling horizontally and vertically to access all 24 party groups and 394 candidates. Scroll bars failed to appear on some browsers, and the red arrows at the top of the screen had no effect. The "Continue" button with the right-pointing arrow ended the voting session and took the voter to a review, rather than scrolling right as might be expected. This would seem to suggest that the system's core voting functionality was not adequately tested prior to deployment.

6   Lessons

Security: The Difficulty of Correcting Known Problems in Time, and Unknown Problems at all

iVote's vulnerability to the FREAK and Logjam attacks illustrates once again why Internet voting is hard to do securely. The system had been in development for years, but FREAK was made public about two weeks before the election. New vulnerabilities are discovered regularly in software and protocols that an Internet voting system depends on for its security, including web browsers and TLS. When this happens near election day, there may not be time to ensure that election servers and voters' clients are properly retested and patched.

Moreover, mechanisms for trying to ensure that correct software is running in the voting system conflict with the necessity for rapid patching. A last minute change to fix one serious problem could introduce new vulnerabilities—as happened in Washington, D.C. [31]—or could conceal a deliberate attempt at fraud.

The ability to test for and patch such problems assumes they are publicly known, but attackers may also have access to unpublished "zero-day" vulnerabilities for which, by definition, no patches yet exist. This was the case for us with Logjam, which would have allowed us to compromise iVote connections to all popular browsers during the election. It is sheer luck that NSWEC's method of removing the vulnerability to FREAK also protected iVote from Logjam, as the attack was not disclosed publicly until two months later. The only responsible assumption is that there are more major HTTPS vulnerabilities waiting to be discovered and perhaps already known to sophisticated attackers.

Fragility: Standard Web Development Practices are Inadequate for Critical Applications such as Elections

Many pieces of software contribute to a typical web application experience, including off-the-shelf server software and library code and, commonly, packages such as analytics tools that are loaded from third-party services. While reliance on such components might be appropriate for a blog or even an e-commerce site, they are often not engineered to the level of security that is required for critical, high-risk applications. (Indeed, analytics software has been shown to leak critical private information in certain online banking systems [25]). Given the economic and foreign policy stakes involved in the outcome of a large election, such contests need to be treated as national security matters, which require a wholly different technical approach than typical IT systems.

Moreover, the decision to import code from a third party into the election system creates the possibility for that party to attempt to undermine the system. Even if the PiwikPro server had not been vulnerable to man-in-the-middle attacks, anyone with administrative access to that server (whether legitimate or otherwise) would have been able to mount the same attack. Insider threats represent some of the most insidious security risks, and reliance on external code greatly expands the set of insiders who are able to affect the security of the election, adding possibly unknown employees of third-party service providers.

Verifiability: When Does an Advertised Verification Mechanism Truly Provide Verifiable Evidence of a Correct Election Outcome?

Although some schemes do provide genuine electronic election verification remotely, including Helios [3], Remotegrity [32], and Pretty Good Democracy [26], achieving this in a privacy-preserving way requires real verification work from the voter. Such techniques hold promise for the future, and have been used successfully in elections with relatively educated voters and low stakes [4]. However, extending them to state-level elections remains impractical for now. Issues such as voter authentication and usability are especially problematic. New South Wales is particularly challenging, since it has no public key infrastructure and requires voters to number multiple preferences on a ballot with 394 candidates.

Considering these limitations of state-of-the-art verification schemes, it is not surprising that the iVote verification mechanism was vulnerable to circumvention. It was not based on any peer-reviewed end-to-end verifiable scheme, and there was no detailed public review to allow such problems to be pointed out prior to the election. When an Internet voting system is claimed to be verifiable, this claim should be supported with a clear argument based on a complete description of the system. Otherwise the verification protocol itself could be incomplete, erroneous, or open to manipulation.

7   Conclusion

We discovered serious flaws in the iVote online voting system that would have allowed a malicious attacker to expose voters' secret ballots, substitute replacement votes, and sidestep the verification mechanism. Despite years of planning, development, and pre-election security assessment, the system was susceptible to both publicly known and zero-day vulnerabilities that were at our disposal during the state election. These findings demonstrate yet again why conducting Internet voting with existing security technologies poses grave real-world risks.

NSWEC's decision to keep the system's source code and detailed design secret prevented independent analysts like us from being able to bring these specific problems to the officials' attention before the election. Even now, we cannot know whether there are other critical flaws in the iVote software and protocols that would be evident if the relevant details were made public.

We recommend that NSWEC and others avoid large-scale Internet voting deployments until there are fundamental advances in computer security that can appropriately mitigate the risks. If Internet voting tests must proceed, future tests should firmly restrict eligibility to voters unable to vote via a more secure channel; incorporate genuine, peer-reviewed verification mechanisms; ensure that the design and implementation are made openly available for rigorous independent scrutiny; and include a clear public statement of the risks to voter privacy and electoral integrity.

Elections should produce not only an outcome but also sufficient evidence supporting that outcome. This is the reason for Australia's tradition of transparent electoral processes, as well as for more recent research on auditable and verifiable elections. In the case of the 2015 New South Wales state election, there is neither evidence that the vulnerabilities we discovered were exploited nor adequate proof that they were not. A demonstrable vulnerability exposing a large number of votes to potential manipulation constitutes a serious failure of the electoral process.

Acknowledgments. The authors thank David Adrian, Ed Felten, Rajeev Goré, Nadia Heninger, Harri Hursti, and Liz Minchin for assistance during this project. For their support and encouragement after we made our results public, we would also like to thank the tremendous community of election integrity scholars and advocates, including but not limited to: Duncan Buell, David Dill, Joseph Hall, Candice Hoke, David Jefferson, Noel Runyan, Ronald Rivest, Barbara Simons and Pamela Smith. This material is based in part upon work supported by the U.S. National Science Foundation under grants CNS-1345254 and CNS-1409505, and by the Morris Wellman Faculty Development Assistant Professorship.

References

1. ABC News. Computer voting may feature in March NSW election, February 2015. http://www.abc.net.au/news/2015-02-04/computer-voting-may-feature-in-march-nsw-election/6068290
2. Abendan, O.: How DNS changer Trojans direct users to threats. In: Trend Micro Threat Encyclopedia (2012)
3. Adida, B.: Helios: web-based open-audit voting. In: 17th USENIX Security Symposium, August 2008. https://vote.heliosvoting.org
4. Adida, B., De Marneffe, O., Pereira, O., Quisquater, J.-J.: Electing a university president using open-audit voting: analysis of real-world use of Helios. In: Electronic Voting Technology Workshop (EVT) (2009)
5. Adrian, D., Bhargavan, K., Durumeric, Z., Gaudry, P., Green, M., Halderman, J.A., Heninger, N., Springall, D., Thomé, E., Valenta, L., VanderSloot, B., Wustrow, E., Zanella-Béguelin, S., Zimmermann, P.: Imperfect forward secrecy: how Diffie-Hellman fails in practice, May 2015. https://weakdh.org/
6. Ballani, H., Francis, P., Zhang, X.: A study of prefix hijacking and interception in the Internet. In: Proceedings of ACM SIGCOMM, August 2007
7. Bell, S., Benaloh, J., Byrne, M.D., DeBeauvoir, D., Eakin, B., Fisher, G., Kortum, P., McBurnett, N., Montoya, J., Parker, M., et al.: Star-vote: a secure, transparent, auditable, and reliable voting system. USENIX J. Election Technol. Syst. **1**(1), 18–37 (2013)
8. Beurdouche, B., Bhargavan, K., Delignat-Lavaud, A., Fournet, C., Kohlweiss, M., Pironti, A., Strub, P.-Y., Zinzindohoue, J.K.: A messy state of the union: taming the composite state machines of TLS. In: 36th IEEE Symposium on Security and Privacy (2015)
9. Bilodeau, O., Dupuy, T.: Dissecting Linux/Moose: the analysis of a Linux router-based worm hungry for social networks, May 2015. http://www.welivesecurity.com/wp-content/uploads/2015/05/Dissecting-LinuxMoose.pdf

10. Carback, R., Chaum, D., Clark, J., Conway, J., Essex, A., Herrnson, P.S., May-berry, T., Popoveniuc, S., Rivest, R.L., Shen, E. et al.: Scantegrity II municipal election at Takoma Park: the first E2E binding governmental election with ballot privacy. In: Proceedings of the 19th USENIX Security Symposium (2010)

11. Culnane, C., Ryan, P.Y.A., Schneider, S., Teague, V.: vVote: A verifiable voting system. ACM Transactions on Information and System Security. To appear. Technical report at http://arxiv.org/abs/1404.6822

12. Durumeric, Z., Adrian, D., Mirian, A., Bailey, M., Halderman, J.A.: Tracking the FREAK attack. https://freakattack.com/

13. Estonian Internet Voting Committee. Statistics about Internet voting in Estonia, May 2014. http://www.vvk.ee/voting-methods-in-estonia/engindex/statistics

14. Gjøsteen, K.: The Norwegian Internet voting protocol. In: Kiayias, A., Lipmaa, H. (eds.) VoteID 2011. LNCS, vol. 7187, pp. 1–18. Springer, Heidelberg (2012)

15. Hastings, N., Peralta, R., Popoveniuc, S., Regenscheid, A.: Security considerations for remote electronic UOCAVA voting. National Institute of Standards and Technology, NISTIR 7770, February 2011. http://www.nist.gov/itl/vote/upload/NISTIR-7700-feb2011.pdf

16. Heninger, N.: Factoring as a service. Crypto 2013 rump session. https://www.cis.upenn.edu/nadiah/projects/faas/

17. Kaminsky, D.: It's the end of the cache as we know it. In: Toorcon (2008)

18. Kusters, R., Truderung, T., Vogt, A.: Clash attacks on the verifiability of e-voting systems. In: 33rd IEEE Symposium on Security and Privacy, pp. 395–409 (2012)

19. Marlinspike, M.: New tricks for defeating SSL in practice. Black Hat (2009). http://www.thoughtcrime.org/software/sslstrip/

20. McKay, R.: Flaws in iVote's re-vote process which attempts to defeat coercers. http://www.bigpulse.com/governmentelections#changevoteflaw. BigPulse

21. NSW Electoral Commission. legislative council–final distribution of preferences (2015). http://vtr.elections.nsw.gov.au/lc-home.htm#lc/state/dop/dop_index

22. NSW Electoral Commission. Index of iVote reports. http://www.elections.nsw.gov.au/about_us/plans_and_reports/ivote_reports

23. NSW Electoral Commission. iVote threat analysis and risk assessment, January 2014. http://www.elections.nsw.gov.au/_data/assets/pdf_file/0008/175760/NSW_Election_iVote_Threat_Analysis_and_Risk_Assessment_v3.0.pdf

24. NSW Electoral Commission. iVote system security implementation statement, March 2015. http://www.elections.nsw.gov.au/_data/assets/pdf_file/0007/193219/iVote-Security_Implementation_Statement-Mar2015.pdf

25. Räisänen, O.: The bank deal. http://oona.windytan.com/pankki.html

26. Ryan, P.Y.A., Teague, V.: Pretty good democracy. In: Christianson, B., Malcolm, J.A., Matyáš, V., Roe, M. (eds.) Security Protocols 2009. LNCS, vol. 7028, pp. 111–130. Springer, Heidelberg (2013)

27. Segaard, B., Christensen, D.A., Folkestad, B., Saglie, J.: Internettvalg: hva gjør og mener velgerne? (2014). https://www.regjeringen.no/globalassets/upload/kmd/komm/rapporter/isf_internettvalg.pdf

28. Springall, D., Finkenauer, T., Durumeric, Z., Kitcat, J., Hursti, H., MacAlpine, M., Halderman, J.A.: Security analysis of the Estonian internet voting system. In: ACM Conference on Computer and Communications Security (CCS), November 2014

29. Teague, V., Halderman, J.A.: Security flaw in New South Wales puts thousands of online votes at risk. Freedom to Tinker blog post, 22 March 2015. https://freedom-to-tinker.com/blog/teaguehalderman/ivote-vulnerability/

30. Victorian Electoral Commission. Report to Parliament on the 2010 Victorian State election; Section 11: Statistical overview of the election (2011). http://www.vec. vic.gov.au/files/ER-2010-Section11.pdf
31. Wolchok, S., Wustrow, E., Isabel, D., Halderman, J.A.: Attacking the Washington, D.C. Internet voting system. In: 16th International Conference on Financial Cryptography and Data Security (FC), February 2012
32. Zagórski, F., Carback, R.T., Chaum, D., Clark, J., Essex, A., Vora, P.L.: Remotegrity: design and use of an end-to-end verifiable remote voting system. In: Jacobson, M., Locasto, M., Mohassel, P., Safavi-Naini, R. (eds.) ACNS 2013. LNCS, vol. 7954, pp. 441–457. Springer, Heidelberg (2013)

Advanced Voting Protocols

Extending Helios Towards Private Eligibility Verifiability

Oksana Kulyk[1]([⊠]), Vanessa Teague[2], and Melanie Volkamer[1,3]

[1] Technische Universität Darmstadt/CASED, Darmstadt, Germany
Oksana.kulyk@secuso.org
[2] University of Melbourne, Melbourne, Australia
vjteague@unimelb.edu.au
[3] Karlstad University, Karlstad, Sweden
Melanie.volkamer@secuso.org

Abstract. We show how to extend the Helios voting system to provide eligibility verifiability without revealing who voted which we call private eligibility verifiability. The main idea is that real votes are hidden in a crowd of null votes that are cast by others but are indistinguishable from those of the eligible voter. This extended Helios scheme also improves Helios towards receipt-freeness.

1 Introduction

Electronic voting protocols must allow the public to verify the accuracy of the election outcome. Much of the research focus has been devoted to *universal end-to-end verifiability*, which includes *cast-as-intended*, *stored-as-cast* and *tallied-as-stored* verifiability. In particular, the Helios voting system [1] was designed to ensure these requirements. Another crucial property is *eligibility verifiability*, meaning that anyone can verify that only the votes of eligible voters have been accepted and included into the tally, thus preventing ballot stuffing by the voting system. The original version of Helios requires trust in the voting system for accepting votes from eligible voters only, thus lacking the option to verify eligibility by the general public.

In Helios and related systems, votes are cast encrypted and are anonymized before decryption and tallying. One simple way to ensure eligibility verifiability would be to make use of an existing public-key infrastructure (PKI), letting voters sign their encrypted vote and publishing all signed encrypted votes on the Bulletin Board. In that case, everyone could verify that each vote had been signed by an eligible voter. However, this approach inevitably reveals who voted in the election and who abstained.

It is worth noting that different democracies take slightly different attitudes to vote privacy in practice. In Australia and many other countries, voting is compulsory and hence a matter of (somewhat) public record. However, in other countries including Germany and Switzerland, the fact of whether or not a person has voted is regarded as private; in the United States political organisations

© Springer International Publishing Switzerland 2015
R. Haenni et al. (Eds.): VoteID 2015, LNCS 9269, pp. 57–73, 2015.
DOI: 10.1007/978-3-319-22270-7_4

quite openly target likely voters on an individual basis. Hence it is sometimes important to hide who voted—we call this *participation privacy*.

This work shows how to extend Helios to ensure both universal eligibility verifiability and participation privacy for voters, *i.e.* private eligibility verifiability. The proposal could also be used to improve other schemes like the Estonian voting scheme [23], or could be implemented as an independent system.

The main idea is to pad out the Helios votes with null votes cast by others. Anyone may add null votes to any voter's row; and voters can update their votes. We have decided to identify specific participants called "posting proxies" who do most of the padding with null votes (according to some, presumably randomised, algorithm).

These null votes need to have some important properties: They should not have any effect on the election outcome. The null votes must also be indistinguishable from the voter's contributions, and numerous and unpredictable enough to provide proper cover for voters. We achieve it by introducing witness-indistinguishable disjunctive proofs that ensure that each cast vote is either a null vote (represented by an encryption of 1), or a vote cast by an eligible voter. We rely on an anonymous channel that is used by posting proxies as well as by voters, in order to hide the origin of the cast votes. Our scheme uses an existing PKI rather than relying on a dedicated credential-based mechanism like JCJ/Civitas or caveat coercitor [18]. All voters must use their signing key to vote. The list of assumptions for the overall scheme as well as for the individual security requirements are listed and discussed in Sect. 5. Our construction also prevent voters from proving which valid vote they have cast. Thus, it improves Helios even fruther as it offers some level of receipt-freeness as protection against vote selling. The remaining security properties, such as preserving the integrity and secrecy of the vote, should hold for honest voters under the same assumptions as in the original Helios system. Note, we use the same cast-as-intended verification methods as Helios.

We would not claim that our protocol satisfies all the requirements necessary for government elections. It remains susceptible to coercion for abstaining and randomizing the vote. Also the strong assumptions about the public key infrastructure, and the smart card's good behaviour mean that it is not truly end-to-end verifiable. The necessity of participation of other contributors in each person's row may also be too strong for sufficient privacy for some elections.

The paper is structured as follows. In Sect. 2 we describe the related work relevant for our proposal. In Sect. 3 we give the background information with the building blocks used in our scheme. In Sect. 4 we describe the scheme itself, followed by its security analysis, including the ensured security requirements and the assumptions needed for this, in Sect. 5. Section 6 gives an efficiency analysis of the scheme, and Sect. 7 provides the conclusion.

2   Related Work

Haenni and Spycher [22] provide a scheme with eligibility verifiability and participation privacy (which they call anonymity). The scheme, however, does not provide receipt-freeness. Eligibility verifiability for Helios was considered in [40]. This work takes a complementary approach to ours, because it assumes that there is no public key infrastructure and relies instead on tokens generated specifically for the election. The protocol provides eligibility verifiability and prevention of ballot stuffing under reasonable assumptions, but does not attempt either to hide who voted or to provide receipt freeness.

The goal of ensuring both eligibility verifiability and the participation privacy of the voters is addressed, among other security requirements, by the schemes aiming to provide the property of coercion resistance. The issue of coercion resistance in remote voting was addressed in the work of Juels, Catalano and Jacobson (JCJ) in [25], presenting a scheme that provides coercion resistance – the definition of which includes receipt freeness as well as protection against forced abstention, randomization and simulation attacks – against strong attacker. This scheme, however, is unsuited for practical use, due to the fact, that its performance is $\mathcal{O}(N^2)$ with N as the number of eligible voters. Therefore, a number of works have presented the improvements to the JCJ system, that preserve the coercion-resistance properties while achieving linear complexity – among others, approaches based upon group signatures [2], panic passwords [10], concurrent ballot authorization [15], anonymity sets [34] or using the voter roll [38]. Furthermore, several improvements focused on improving other shortcomings in JCJ scheme, such as addressing the issue of board flooding [26], or improving usability with using tamper-resistant smartcards [29]. These improvements, however, still require complex forms of credential management, thus lacking in usability from the voter's perspective. A number of other schemes has been suggested that provide some level of coercion resistance [27,32], which, however, also require complex actions from the voter. The Caveat Coercitor scheme [18] aims at detecting whether coercion took place during the election, but not at preventing it.

3   Background

In this section we provide the background information we base our scheme upon.

3.1   Helios

The Helios voting system incorporates a simple yet powerful collection of methods for end-to-end verifiable voting. Each person's encrypted vote is tabulated, along with some authentication information, on a public bulletin board. Well-behaved voting clients are supposed to delete the randomness they use when generating the ciphertext—if they do so, the person cannot subsequently prove how they voted. If they fail to do so, that randomness can be used to open the ciphertext and prove its contents to a coercer. It is obvious from the bulletin board which voters have participated and which have abstained.

The client is trusted for privacy. If more than a threshold of talliers collude they too can violate privacy. No entities are trusted for integrity though of course verification procedures for the voting process and the bulletin board must be followed. Helios uses the "Benaloh challenge" [5] to allow voters to verify that their vote is cast as they intended.

3.2 Cryptographic Building Blocks

We describe the cryptographic primitives and protocols that underlie our scheme.

ElGamal Encryption: Let $(g, h) \in \mathbb{G}_q^2$ be a public ElGamal key, where $\mathbb{G}_q \subset \mathbb{Z}_p$ is a multiplicative group of order q, with both p, q large primes, $p = 2q + 1$. An ElGamal encryption of $v \in \mathbb{G}_q$ using the public key (g, h) is defined as a tuple $Enc_{(g,h)}(v) = (a, b) := (g^r, v \cdot h^r)$ for some randomness $r \in \mathbb{Z}_q$. In case it is necessary to ensure for a ciphertext (a, b) encrypts a vote in $\mathbb{G}_q$, one checks whether $a^q = b^q = 1 \mod p$.

Proof of an Encryption of 1: In order to prove that a given ciphertext (a, b) encrypts 1, one has to present a zero-knowledge proof:

$$ZKP\{\exists r : a = g^r \mod p \land b = h^r \mod p\}$$

The proof, presented in [9], is given in Appendix A.1.

Note, that this as well as further proofs can be made non-interactive according to Fiat-Shamir heuristic [16], by providing the challenge c as a hash function of the "commitment" values sent in the first step of the proof, as well as to other relevant parameters, as suggested in [7].

Proof of Knowledge of DSA Signing Key: Let $(g_s, h_s = g^s) \in \mathbb{G}_q$ be the DSA public key. Proving the possession of valid secret key s could be done with Schnorr's proof of knowledge of discrete logarithm [35], restated in Appendix A.2. The proof is easily extended to a proof of knowledge of an ElGamal plaintext.

Proof of Knowledge of RSA Signatures: Let (N, e) with e prime be a public RSA signature key, d secret signature key. For a message m and some encoding function $h(m)$ that is used for signing[1], in order to prove the knowledge of a valid signature on m, one has to show:

$$ZKP\{\exists s : s^e \equiv h(m) \mod N\}$$

The proof, described in [20,21], is given in Appendix A.3.

---

[1] Usually a hash value of m and/or padding, according to common RSA signature standards.

Reencryption Mix Nets: Re-encryption mix nets shuffle a set of ciphertexts without needing to know the private key, and provide a proof of correct shuffling. Modern re-encryption mixnets run efficiently, and many are appropriate for ElGamal encryption, including [17, 19, 28, 41].

It is important to defend against Pfitzmann's attack on mixnet privacy [31], in which a malicious participant copies someone else's vote as a way of exposing it. Our scheme hence requires a proof of the validity and knowledge of the vote when it is posted, as in [6].

Plaintext Equality Tests: There are two approaches to prove the validity of encrypted vote (i.e. that the plaintext belongs to the set of allowed voting options) while preserving voter privacy. The first is to make the voter attach the proofs of validity during vote casting. This approach is inapplicable to our scheme because the product of several valid votes may be invalid. The second approach is to discard non-valid votes after vote casting and anonymization. A simple way would be to decrypt and publish all the votes. This approach destroys receipt freeness, however. For example, a coercer could demand a particular vote v and then, with 50 % probability, either let a voter keep their vote or demand that they add some large number x, and then see whether the $x + v$ appeared in the list of decrypted votes.

To prevent this, instead of decrypting, we use plaintext equality tests ($\mathcal{PET}$) [24]. For a pair of ElGamal ciphertexts $e, e' \in \mathbb{G}_q^2$, $e = Enc_{(g,h)}(v) = (a, b)$, $e' = Enc_{(g,h)}(v') = (a', b')$, these tests are performed in a distributed way by a group of trustees that own the shared corresponding decryption key. The trustees compute and jointly decrypt

$$((\frac{a}{a'})^z, (\frac{b}{b'})^z)$$

for a jointly generated random secret z.

The result is the value of $(\frac{v}{v'})^z$ which is 1 if $v = v'$, or a random value in $\mathbb{G}_q$ that reveals no information about v, v' or their relation to each other otherwise.

Other Cryptographic Tools: We use the disjunctive witness-hiding proofs of Cramer et al. [13]. The trustees share the decryption key using Shamir threshold secret sharing [36], jointly generated using Pedersen's scheme [30], as recommended for Helios by Cortier et al. [11].

4   Proposed Scheme

In this section we describe the proposed voting scheme. The key generation, decryption trustees, mix nodes, bulletin board, and basic voter behaviour are the same or similar as for Helios. The main difference to Helios is the tallying stage, because we now allow multiple votes against one voter's name. Each row (corresponding to one voter) will be homomorphically totalled, then all the totals will be mixed and interpreted by $\mathcal{PET}$.

If board flooding is considered a possible problem, we could incorporate the token-based mechanisms of [26], which restricts the total number of postings by any individual[2]. Even more simply, we could impose a restriction on the number of ciphertexts that could be posted by each person against each voter's row. Even a small number (such as one or two) might be entirely sufficient, as long as Assumption Sect. 5.2 remained true.

4.1   Preparations

The list of all eligible voters $V_1, ..., V_N$ is posted on the bulletin board, as the list of their public keys and voter IDs. We think of the bulletin board as having a row for each of those eligible voters—in other words, each posted ciphertext is explicitly allocated to one of the voter IDs. The available voting options are represented as $C = \{c_1, ..., c_L\}$, with $1 \notin C$ representing the null/abstaining vote. Using distributed threshold secret sharing [30], the trustees generate a pair of ElGamal keys (g, h) for encrypting the votes. Furthermore, the trustees publish the list of ciphertexts resulting from the deterministic encryption (i.e. using fixed and public randomness value) of voting options: $\widehat{E} = \{\hat{e}_1 = Enc_{(g,h)}(c_1), ..., \hat{e}_L = Enc_{(g,h)}(c_L)\}$.

4.2   Vote Casting

In order to post a vote $v \in C$ for the voter V_i, one sends an ElGamal ciphertext $e = Enc_{(g,h)}(v)$, and a disjunctive witness-hiding proof given in Algorithm 1.

Algorithm 1. Witness hiding proof of valid vote posting (Assuming that the DSA-based PKI is used.)

Public Input: The election ID, the ElGamal ciphertext e to be posted, the public key PK_V of the row to be posted on, the election ElGamal encryption parameters (p, q, g, h).

Poster's private input: Either the randomness used to produce e, or the private key corresponding to PK_V.

Proof: the poster proves
poster knows plaintext of e, using proof from Sect. 3.2
AND
{e encrypts 1, that is, is a null vote, using proof from Sect. 3.2
OR poster knows the private key corresponding to PK_V, using proof from Sect. 3.2}

The proof is made noninteractive using the Fiat-Shamir heuristic applied to the entire public input.

---

[2] As the complexity of the computations in the tallying stage depends on the amount of eligible voters rather than total cast votes, and the complexity of the computations in the voting stage is linear in the number of cast votes, we presume board flooding is less likely to significantly hinder the election than it is in [25].

An alternative method, applicable in case the RSA-based PKI is used, would be that instead of proving knowledge of the signing key, the prover proves knowledge of a digital signature on (election ID, e). Either way it is important to incorporate all of the public parameters of the proof into the Fiat-Shamir hash, to prevent reuse of the proof of knowledge.

As in the Helios system, the voter has the option to either audit the encrypted ballot via the Benaloh challenge, or to send the vote and the proof. Once the vote is sent, the voter can check the bulletin board in order to verify that it has been recorded. It follows that only the legitimate voter V_i can post non-null votes near her name, since she is the one possessing the secret signature key. If the voter wants to update her vote from v_A to v_B, she encrypts and casts the value of $v_A^{-1} v_B$.

All the cast votes are validated at the moment of posting: exact duplicated postings are removed[3], also discarded are the ciphertexts with invalid zero-knowledge proofs, or those that encrypt a value $v \in \mathbb{Z}_p \backslash \mathbb{G}_q$[4].

4.3   Tallying

At the end of vote casting stage, the bulletin board looks as shown on Table 1. It is assumed that for all $i = 1, ..., N$, it holds that $m_i > 0$. Furthermore, only the voter V_i knows how many of the votes $v_{i,1}, ... v_{i,m_i}$ are null votes, and how many are real ones.[5]

Table 1. Bulletin board prior to tallying stage

Voter ID	Cast votes
V_1	$e_{1,1}, \ldots e_{1,m_1}$
$\vdots$	$\vdots$
V_N	$e_{N,1}, \ldots e_{N,m_N}$

The final ciphertext for each V_i is computed by elementwise multiplication

$$e_i = \prod_{j=1}^{m_i} e_{i,j}$$

Since the null votes are all encryptions of 1, only the non-null votes influence the final vote included in tallying. If for some i, the voter V_i has abstained, the resulting ciphertext e_i is an encryption of a null vote.

---

[3] This prevents manipulating someone's vote by re-posting something they have genuinely contributed.

[4] This can be done by checking whether $b^q = 1$ for a ciphertext (a, b) with a valid proof of plaintext knowledge, and is needed to prevent information leakage about plaintext from $\mathcal{PET}s$ during tallying.

[5] This and other assumptions are further discussed in Sect. 5.

The resulting ciphertexts $e_1, ..., e_N$ are then processed through the mix net for the sake of removing the link between the voter and the decrypted vote, with the anonymized list $e'_1, ..., e'_N$ as output.

For each ciphertext $e'_i = Enc_{(g,h)}(v_i)$ that results from shuffling and each voting option c_j encrypted as $\hat{e}_j$, the trustees perform $\mathcal{PET}s$ for e'_i and $\hat{e}_j$. If the test is positive for some j, the trustees conclude that $v_i = c_j$; otherwise, they conclude that v_i is either a null vote, or an invalid vote, and thus should be discarded from tallying. The result can then be directly computed from the non-discarded votes.

5   Security Analysis

In this section we conduct the security analysis of our scheme, by listing the security requirements we want to ensure, and identifying the security assumptions that are needed for them. Further we discuss the ways to ensure the assumptions that we make.

5.1   Security Requirements

In general, we need to rely on the following assumptions regarding the cryprography used in the scheme:

- Cryptography Assumption: the cryptography used in witness-indistinguishable proofs and in the ElGamal encryption scheme is reliable:
  - the DDH assumption holds,
  - the random oracle model is instantiated by a hash function,
  - if RSA is used for PKI, the RSA assumption holds.

In the following we explain for each security requirement why it is ensured and under which further security assumptions:

Eligibility Verifiability: This requirement suggests, that everyone should be able to verify that only the votes from the eligible voters have been included in the tallying result.

This requirement is ensured due to the application of the proof in Algorithm 1 in Sect. 4.2 and its soundness (i.e. it that non voters can only cast null votes, which have no effect on the final tallying), if the following assumptions hold:

- Secret Key Leakage Assumption: The voter's secret key is not leaked to the adversary without voter's knowledge.
- Secret Key Re-Usage Assumption: The voting device cannot use the secret key to cast any additional votes without voter's knowledge.
- Authentic List of Keys Assumption: Only eligible voters have their public keys published in the voting register.

Individual Verifiability: Each voter should be able to verify, that her vote has been cast and stored by the voting system according to her intention.

This requirement is ensured due to the following mechanisms:
- the application of the Benaloh challenges for cast-as-intended verifiability;
- the possibility for voters to check that the encrypted votes that she submitted herself appear on the bulletin board for stored-as-cast verifiability;
- the functionality to re-send a vote if voters detect that a posting proxy withholds a vote (just like the single bulletin board in Helios); and
- the application of the proof in Algorithm 1 in Sect. 4.2 and its soundness

if the following assumptions hold:
- Secret Key Leakage Assumption: The voter's secret key is not leaked to the adversary without voter's knowledge.
- Secret Key Re-Usage Assumption: The voting device cannot use the secret key to cast any additional
- without voter's knowledge.

Universal Verifiability: Everyone should be able to verify, that the tallying result is computed from the valid votes stored by the voting system only.

This requirement is ensured due to the following mechanisms:
- all the ciphertexts posted on the bulletin board include a valid proof, thus being either encryptions of null votes or of votes from eligible voters,
- these ciphertexts are included in the product defining the final votes,
- the final votes are correctly processed through mix net, and
- each one of the plaintext equality tests outputs the correct result, either assigning a correct valid voting option to each vote, or determining that the vote is invalid

if the following assumption holds:
- Bulletin Board Assumption: The bulletin board is a reliable broadcast channel with memory.

Participation Privacy: The system should not disclose the fact, whether an individual voter has participated in the election, to the passive adversary, who only has access to the public output.

This requirement is ensured due to the the application of the proof in Algorithm 1 in Sect. 4.2 and its soundness if the following assumption hold:
- Hidden Origin Vote Assumption (Passive): There is at least one ciphertext which the adversary is unable to distinguish between a null vote and an effective vote from an eligible voter.

Note, the tallying process does not reveal information about individual votes, or even the presence of particular invalid votes.

Vote Secrecy: The adversary should not be able to learn for which candidate each individual voter has voted from the public output.

The secrecy of the vote relies on
- the vote anonymization performed in a proper way, and
- the individual ciphertexts not being decrypted prior to being anonymized.

if the following assumption holds:
- Trustee Assumption: Less than a threshold number of trustees disclose their private key shares to the adversary.

Receipt-Freeness: The voter should not be able to provide a receipt to the adversary, proving that she has voted for a particular candidate c.

The receipt-freeness relies on the fact, that even if the voter proves that she cast a ciphertext encrypting c^6, there are some additional ciphertexts in the voter's row, for which she would not be able to prove that it does not encrypt some value $c' \cdot c^{-1}$ thus replacing c with c'^7. This is ensured as long as the following assumption holds:
- Hidden Origin Vote Assumption (Active): There is at least one ciphertext in the voter's row, that the voter cannot prove whether she cast it.

An active coercer can force abstention or randomization, and a voter can prove that they have abstained by casting an invalid vote.

5.2 Discussion on the Assumptions

We summarize the assumptions identified in Sect. 5.1 in the list below:

1. Hidden Origin Vote Assumption (Passive): There is at least one ciphertext which the adversary is unable to distinguish between a null vote and an effective vote from an eligible voter.
2. Hidden Origin Vote Assumption (Active): There is at least one ciphertext in the voter's row, that the voter cannot prove whether she cast it.
3. Secret Key Re-Usage Assumption: The voting device cannot use the secret key to cast any additional votes without voter's knowledge.
4. Secret Key Leakage Assumption: The voter's secret key is not leaked to the adversary without voter's knowledge.
5. Trustee Assumption: Less than a threshold number of trustees disclose their private key shares to the adversary.
6. Bulletin Board Assumption: The bulletin board is a reliable broadcast channel with memory.
7. Cryptography Assumption: the cryptography used in witness-indistinguishable proofs and in the ElGamal encryption scheme is reliable:
   - the DDH assumption holds,
   - the random oracle model is instantiated by a hash function,
   - if RSA is used for PKI, the RSA assumption holds.
8. Authentic List of Keys Assumption: Only eligible voters have their public keys published in the voting register.

---

[6] She can do this for the ciphertext $(g^r, c \cdot h^r)$ by disclosing the randomness r to the adversary.

[7] Note, that v' can be the legitimate vote for another candidate (i.e. the one the voter actually intends to vote for), but also some random or even unknown to the voter value that results in an invalid vote.

We discuss possible ways the assumptions that our scheme requires could be implemented in the following paragraphs:

Hidden Origin Vote Assumption (Passive) and **Hidden Origin Vote Assumption (Active)** can be summarized in following: each voter, against every adversary, must have at least one opportunity to communicate with the bulletin board (perhaps via a third party) and which

- the adversary cannot detect whether the voter has communicated, and
- if the voter doesn't communicate to the BB, some other participant posts a null vote

In other words, it should not be possible for a voter to prove that they have cast all of the ciphertexts in their row that the adversary thinks they might possibly have cast.

It could be implemented by a few ways, for example:

- some posting proxy not colluding with the coercer, with whom the voter can communicate via an untappable channel,
- an anonymous channel to the bulletin board,
- a receipt-free attendance voting scheme (such as Prêt à Voter [33], Wombat [4], StarVote [3] or Scantegrity II [8]) that the voter can attend physically and not tell the coercer about.

This also implies, that at least one posting proxy faithfully adds null ciphertexts in a way that is sufficiently numerous and unpredictable for the adversary, in order to provide adequate cover for voters.

This is enough for participation privacy against a passive coercer. In order to achieve receipt freeness we need to assume that the cryptographic protocol does not allow an actively participating voter to cause Assumption 5.2 to fail by deviating from the protocol. This will be shown below.

The **Secret Key Re-Usage Assumption** is a particularly strong one for voting, though standard enough for electronic commerce and banking. The issue here is that in standard Helios each voter casts only one vote, and hence can see whether an extra one has been added on their behalf. In our scheme, the whole mechanism relies on the possibility of multiple additive vote casting. The assumption that the smartcard reader doesn't add extras implies a strong trust assumption on the hardware (with, for example, a display/PIN setup). This is also necessary for banking and other contracts, and is what a PIN-based smartcard reader is supposed to achieve. However, this is a stronger assumption than truly end-to-end verifiable protocols, such as basic Helios. We consider it an important aspect of future work to remove this assumption, which was identified as one source of vulnerability in the Estonian Internet voting protocol [37]. Similarly, **Secret Key Leakage Assumption** could also be facilitated by assuming the tamper-resistant and trusted smartcard that stores the key.

An alternative way of realising Secret Key Re-Usage Assumption without trusted hardware is to insist that all votes but one be cast in a physical polling place at which eligibility was carefully established. It would be important to do

Table 2. Efficiency of individual phases

Preparations	$3T + t - 2 + 2L$
Vote casting (cast)	5
Vote casting (verify)	$9N'$
Tallying	$(4T + 5t - 1)NL + (19N + 16)T$

this in a way that preserved the Hidden Origin Vote Assumption. Again anyone who was not concerned about coercion could simply cast their ordinary vote online, and check that exactly that vote appeared on the bulletin board. There would be no need to trust their hardware not to cast subsequent votes, because there would be no option to cast a second vote remotely.

The **Trustee Assumption** is common in voting protocols that employ distributed decryption, and might be facilitated by selecting e.g. representatives of groups with conflicting interests, such as of different parties as the trustees. The **Bulletin Board Assumption** can be facilitated either by establishing a central server, supervised by trusted third-party observers, or implemented in a distributed way (e.g. [14]). The **Cryptography Assumption** is common to the voting systems based on cryptographic mechanisms, and the **Authentic List of Keys Assumption** is based upon the public list of all eligible voters, the integrity of which is something that should be ensured in traditional elections as well.

6 Efficiency Analysis

Assuming T as the number of tallying trustees, that are responsible for both the mixing of the votes and performing the $\mathcal{PET}s$ with t as threshold parameter (usually suggested as $t = \lfloor T/2 \rfloor + 1$), $N' = \sum_{i=1}^{N} m_i$ as all the votes posted during vote casting (including null votes posted by posting proxies), L as number of candidates (for example, $L = 2$ for referendum), following estimations can be made regarding the performance of the scheme. We count the required number of modular exponentiations during each phase, summarizing the findings in Table 2. We assume, that the verifiable mix net scheme proposed in [41] is used during the tallying stage, requiring $8N + 5$ modular exponentiations for the proof of validity, and $9N + 11$ modular exponentiations for its verification. Furthermore, we assume that the DSA-based PKI is used in the election.

7 Conclusion

We have presented a novel method of achieving private eligibility verifiability and participation privacy by padding the real votes with null votes that are indistinguishable from the non-null ones. With this, the presence of null votes obscures who has actually voted.

Retaining the individual verifiability assumption of ordinary Helios depends on the strong assumption that the voter's signing key cannot be used to post a ciphertext without the voter's knowledge. (This issue does not arise in ordinary Helios because each voter can cast at most one vote).

The scheme further provides a level of receipt-freeness, preventing voters from proving that they have voted for a particular candidate. The protocol is still susceptible to forced abstention and randomization attacks.

It is important further work to quantify how many and how random padded votes we need. This depends of course on assumptions about collusion between the posting proxies. It is therefore important to consider developing an algorithm which an honest posting proxy should follow when deciding when to cast a null vote.

Usability and public understanding (both important to increase trust in an electronic voting system [39]) remain important open problems. In this system, a voter who doesn't want to participate in the receipt-freeness or participation privacy aspects may simply ignore them and cast a single vote (optionally using the Benaloh challenge for cast-as-intended verification). The possibility that they might have participated is still enough to offer them privacy.

However, possible issues of understandability or usability might arise: for example, the voters might get confused seeing several votes cast in their row, thus leading to distrust in the system; or the need to remember all the previously cast votes in order to be able to update them might become an issue. Many of the complexities of the protocol could be hidden behind a helpful user interface, for example one that remembered what votes had been cast before. Nevertheless the tradeoffs between security, verifiability, public understanding, and ease of use remain challenging, and require further exploration (for example, in forms of user studies).

Acknowledgment. This project (HA project no. 435/14-25) is funded in the framework of Hessen ModellProjekte, financed with funds of LOEWE – Landes-Offensive zur Entwicklung Wissenschaftlich-ökonomischer Exzellenz, Förderlinie 3: KMU-Verbundvorhaben (State Offensive for the Development of Scientific and Economic Excellence).

A   Cryptographic Building Blocks

A.1   Proof of an Encryption of 1

In order to prove that a given ciphertext (a, b) encrypts 1, one has to present a zero-knowledge proof:

$$ZKP\{\exists r : a = g^r \bmod p \land b = h^r \bmod p\}$$

The proof, presented in [9], is as follows:

1. Prover chooses a random $w \in_R \mathbb{Z}_q$, computes $\alpha = g^w \bmod p$, $\beta = h^w \bmod p$ and sends α, β to the Verifier.
2. Verifier sends the challenge $c \in_R \mathbb{Z}_q$ to the prover
3. Prover computes $u = w + cr \bmod q$ and sends u to Verifier
4. Verifier checks, that $g^u \equiv \alpha a^c \bmod p$ and $h^u \equiv \beta b^c \bmod p$ hold.

The proof has the soundness error of $1/q$.

A.2 Proof of Knowledge of Discrete Log

The following proof can be used to prove knowledge of a DSA or ElGamal signing key, or knowledge of an ElGamal ciphertext.

$$\texttt{Proof of knowledge}\{s : h = g^s\}$$

Public Parameters: ElGamal/DSA parameters (g, h, p, q)
   Prover knows: $s : h = g^s \bmod p$.

1. Prover selects a random value $w \in_R \mathbb{Z}_q$ and publishes $a = g^w$.
2. Verifier sends the challenge $c \in_R \mathbb{Z}_q$
3. Prover calculates and publishes $u = w + cs$
4. Verifier checks $g^u = ah^c$

The soundness error of the proof is $1/q$.

A.3 Proof of Knowledge of RSA Signature

$$\texttt{Proof of knowledge}\{s : s^e \equiv h(m) \bmod N\}$$

Public Parameters: Message m, encoding function $h(m)$, RSA public key (N, e) with e prime
   Prover knows: $s : s^e \equiv h(m) \bmod N$, $d : d = e^{-1} \bmod \phi(N)$.

1. Prover selects a random value $r \in_R \mathbb{Z}_N^*$ and calculates $x = r^e \bmod N$
2. Verifier sends the challenge $c \in_R \mathbb{Z}_e$
3. Prover calculates $z = rs^c \bmod N$ and sends z to Verifier
4. Verifier checks $z^e \equiv x \cdot h(m)^c \bmod N$.

The soundness error of the proof is $1/e$. Note, that often the small prime values of e are used as public key in RSA system: commonly, $e = 3$ or $e = 2^{16} + 1$. This leads to the proof being insufficiently sound. For this cases, a modification has been proposed in [12], where in order to prove the knowledge of e-th root s of $h(m)$, one proves the knowledge of e^t-th root s' of $h(m) \bmod N$, which can be calculated as $s' = h(m)^{d^t} \bmod N$. The modified proof has the soundness error of $1/e^t$.

References

1. Adida, B.: Helios: web-based open-audit voting. USENIX Security Symposium. vol. 17, pp. 335–348 (2008)
2. Araújo, R., Traoré, J.: A practical coercion resistant voting scheme revisited. In: Heather, J., Schneider, S., Teague, V. (eds.) Vote-ID 2013. LNCS, vol. 7985, pp. 193–209. Springer, Heidelberg (2013)
3. Bell, S., Benaloh, J., Byrne, M.D., DeBeauvoir, D., Eakin, B., Fisher, G., Kortum, P., McBurnett, N., Montoya, J., Parker, M., Pereira, O., Stark, P.B., Wallach, D.S., Winn, M.: STAR-vote: a secure, transparent, auditable, and reliable voting system. USENIX J. Election Technol. Syst. (JETS) 1(1), 18–37 (2013)
4. Ben-Nun, J., Fahri, N., Llewellyn, M., Riva, B., Rosen, A., Ta-Shma, A., Wikström, D.: A new implementation of a dual (paper and cryptographic) voting system. In: 5th International Conference on Electronic Voting (EVOTE) (2012). http://www.wombat-voting.com
5. Benaloh, J.: Simple verifiable elections. In: Proceedings of the USENIX/Accurate Electronic Voting Technology Workshop 2006 on Electronic Voting Technology Workshop, pp. 5–5. USENIX Association (2006)
6. Bernhard, D., Cortier, V., Pereira, O., Smyth, B., Warinschi, B.: Adapting helios for provable ballot privacy. In: Atluri, V., Diaz, C. (eds.) ESORICS 2011. LNCS, vol. 6879, pp. 335–354. Springer, Heidelberg (2011)
7. Bernhard, D., Pereira, O., Warinschi, B.: How not to prove yourself: pitfalls of the Fiat-shamir heuristic and applications to Helios. In: Wang, X., Sako, K. (eds.) ASIACRYPT 2012. LNCS, vol. 7658, pp. 626–643. Springer, Heidelberg (2012)
8. Carback, R., Chaum, D., Clark, J., Conway, J., Essex, A., Herrnson, P.S., Mayberry, T., Popoveniuc, S., Rivest, R.L., Shen, E., Sherman, A.T., Vora, P.L.: Scantegrity II municipal election at Takoma Park: the first E2E binding governmental election with ballot privacy. In: Proceedings of USENIX Security (2010)
9. Chaum, D., Pedersen, T.P.: Wallet databases with observers. In: Brickell, E.F. (ed.) CRYPTO 1992. LNCS, vol. 740, pp. 89–105. Springer, Heidelberg (1993)
10. Clark, J., Hengartner, U.: Selections: internet voting with over-the-shoulder coercion-resistance. In: Danezis, G. (ed.) FC 2011. LNCS, vol. 7035, pp. 47–61. Springer, Heidelberg (2012)
11. Cortier, V., Galindo, D., Glondu, S., Izabachène, M.: Distributed Elgamal à la Pedersen: application to Helios. In: Proceedings of the 12th ACM Workshop on Workshop on Privacy in the Electronic Society, pp. 131–142. ACM (2013)
12. Cramer, R., Damgård, I.B., MacKenzie, P.D.: Efficient zero-knowledge proofs of knowledge without intractability assumptions. In: Imai, H., Zheng, Y. (eds.) PKC 2000. LNCS, vol. 1751, pp. 354–373. Springer, Heidelberg (2000)
13. Cramer, R., Damgård, I.B., Schoenmakers, B.: Proof of partial knowledge and simplified design of witness hiding protocols. In: Desmedt, Y.G. (ed.) CRYPTO 1994. LNCS, vol. 839, pp. 174–187. Springer, Heidelberg (1994)
14. Culnane, C., Schneider, S.: A peered bulletin board for robust use in verifiable voting systems. In: 2014 IEEE 27th Computer Security Foundations Symposium (CSF), pp. 169–183. IEEE (2014)
15. Essex, A., Clark, J., Hengartner, U.: Cobra: toward concurrent ballot authorization for internet voting. In: Proceedings of the 2012 International Conference on Electronic Voting Technology/Workshop on Trustworthy Elections, EVT/WOTE, p. 3 (2012)

16. Fiat, A., Shamir, A.: How to prove yourself: practical solutions to identification and signature problems. In: Odlyzko, A.M. (ed.) CRYPTO 1986. LNCS, vol. 263, pp. 186–194. Springer, Heidelberg (1987)
17. Furukawa, J., Sako, K.: An efficient scheme for proving a shuffle. In: Kilian, J. (ed.) CRYPTO 2001. LNCS, vol. 2139, p. 368. Springer, Heidelberg (2001)
18. Grewal, G.S., Ryan, M.D., Bursuc, S., Ryan, P.Y.: Caveat coercitor: coercion-evidence in electronic voting. In: 2013 IEEE Symposium on Security and Privacy (SP), pp. 367–381. IEEE (2013)
19. Groth, J.: A verifiable secret shuffe of homomorphic encryptions. In: Desmedt, Y.G. (ed.) PKC 2003. LNCS, vol. 2567, pp. 145–160. Springer, Heidelberg (2002)
20. Guillou, L.C., Quisquater, J.-J.: A practical zero-knowledge protocol fitted to security microprocessor minimizing both transmission and memory. In: Günther, C.G. (ed.) EUROCRYPT 1988. LNCS, vol. 330, pp. 123–128. Springer, Heidelberg (1988)
21. Guillou, L.C., Quisquater, J.-J.: A "paradoxical" identity-based signature scheme resulting from zero-knowledge. In: Goldwasser, S. (ed.) CRYPTO 1988. LNCS, vol. 403, pp. 216–231. Springer, Heidelberg (1990)
22. Haenni, R., Spycher, O.: Secure internet voting on limited devices with anonymized dsa public keys. In: Proceedings of the 2011 Conference on Electronic Voting Technology/Workshop on Trustworthy Elections, pp. 8–8. EVT/WOTE 2011. USENIX Association (2011)
23. Heiberg, S., Laud, P., Willemson, J.: The application of i-voting for estonian parliamentary elections of 2011. In: Kiayias, A., Lipmaa, H. (eds.) VoteID 2011. LNCS, vol. 7187, pp. 208–223. Springer, Heidelberg (2012)
24. Jakobsson, M., Juels, A.: Mix and match: secure function evaluation via ciphertexts. In: Okamoto, T. (ed.) ASIACRYPT 2000. LNCS, vol. 1976, p. 162. Springer, Heidelberg (2000)
25. Juels, A., Catalano, D., Jakobsson, M.: Coercion-resistant electronic elections. In: Proceedings of the 2005 ACM workshop on Privacy in the electronic society, pp. 61–70. ACM (2005)
26. Koenig, R., Haenni, R., Fischli, S.: Preventing board flooding attacks in coercion-resistant electronic voting schemes. In: Camenisch, J., Fischer-Hübner, S., Murayama, Y., Portmann, A., Rieder, C. (eds.) SEC 2011. IFIP AICT, vol. 354, pp. 116–127. Springer, Heidelberg (2011)
27. Kutyłowski, M., Zagórski, F.: Verifiable internet voting solving secure platform problem. In: Miyaji, A., Kikuchi, H., Rannenberg, K. (eds.) IWSEC 2007. LNCS, vol. 4752, pp. 199–213. Springer, Heidelberg (2007)
28. Neff, C.A.: A verifiable secret shuffle and its application to e-voting. In: Proceedings of the 8th ACM conference on Computer and Communications Security, pp. 116–125. ACM (2001)
29. Neumann, S., Feier, C., Volkamer, M., Koenig, R.: Towards a practical jcj/civitas implementation. In: INF13 - Workshop: Elektronische Wahlen: Ich sehe was, das Du nicht siehst - öffentliche und geheime Wahl, pp. 804–818 (2013)
30. Pedersen, T.P.: Non-interactive and information-theoretic secure verifiable secret sharing. In: Feigenbaum, J. (ed.) CRYPTO 1991. LNCS, vol. 576, pp. 129–140. Springer, Heidelberg (1992)
31. Pfitzmann, B.: Breaking an efficient anonymous channel. In: De Santis, A. (ed.) EUROCRYPT 1994. LNCS, vol. 950, pp. 332–340. Springer, Heidelberg (1995)
32. Raykova, M., Wagner, D.: Verifable remote voting with large scale coercion resistance. Technical report CUCS-041-11, Columbia (2011)

33. Ryan, P.Y., Bismark, D., Heather, J., Schneider, S., Xia, Z.: Prêt à voter: a voter-verifiable voting system. IEEE Trans. Inf. Forensics Secur. 4(4), 662–673 (2009)
34. Schläpfer, M., Haenni, R., Koenig, R., Spycher, O.: Efficient vote authorization in coercion-resistant internet voting. In: Kiayias, A., Lipmaa, H. (eds.) VoteID 2011. LNCS, vol. 7187, pp. 71–88. Springer, Heidelberg (2012)
35. Schnorr, C.P.: Efficient signature generation by smart cards. J. Cryptol. 4(3), 161–174 (1991)
36. Shamir, A.: How to share a secret. Commun. ACM 22(11), 612–613 (1979)
37. Springall, D., Finkenauer, T., Durumeric, Z., Kitcat, J., Hursti, H., MacAlpine, M., Halderman, J.A.: Security analysis of the estonian internet voting system. In: Proceedings of the 2014 ACM SIGSAC Conference on Computer and Communications Security, pp. 703–715. ACM (2014)
38. Spycher, O., Koenig, R., Haenni, R., Schläpfer, M.: A new approach towards coercion-resistant remote e-voting in linear time. In: Danezis, G. (ed.) FC 2011. LNCS, vol. 7035, pp. 182–189. Springer, Heidelberg (2012)
39. Spycher, O., Volkamer, M., Koenig, R.: Transparency and technical measures to establish trust in Norwegian internet voting. In: Kiayias, A., Lipmaa, H. (eds.) VoteID 2011. LNCS, vol. 7187, pp. 19–35. Springer, Heidelberg (2012)
40. Srinivasan, S., Culnane, C., Heather, J., Schneider, S., Xia, Z.: Countering ballot stuffing and incorporating eligibility verifiability in Helios. In: Au, M.H., Carminati, B., Kuo, C.-C.J. (eds.) NSS 2014. LNCS, vol. 8792, pp. 335–348. Springer, Heidelberg (2014)
41. Terelius, B., Wikström, D.: Proofs of restricted shuffles. In: Bernstein, D.J., Lange, T. (eds.) AFRICACRYPT 2010. LNCS, vol. 6055, pp. 100–113. Springer, Heidelberg (2010)

Verifiable Internet Elections with Everlasting Privacy and Minimal Trust

Philipp Locher[1,2]($\boxtimes$) and Rolf Haenni[1]

[1] Bern University of Applied Sciences,
2501 Biel, Switzerland
{philipp.locher,rolf.haenni}@bfh.ch
[2] University of Fribourg,
1700 Fribourg, Switzerland
philipp.locher@unifr.ch

Abstract. This paper presents a new cryptographic Internet voting protocol based on a set membership proof and a proof of knowledge of the representation of a committed value. When casting a vote, the voter provides a zero-knowledge proof of knowledge of the representation of one of the registered voter credentials. In this way, votes are anonymized without the need of trusted authorities. The absence of such authorities reduces the trust assumptions to a minimum and makes our protocol remarkably simple. Since computational intractability assumptions are only necessary to prevent the creation of invalid votes during the voting period, but not to protect the secrecy of the vote, the protocol even offers a solution to the everlasting privacy problem.

1 Introduction

Two types of trust assumptions are commonly found in cryptographic voting protocols. First, it is usually assumed that a threshold number of non-colluding trusted authorities exists, for instance for mixing the list of encrypted votes or for decrypting them in a distributed manner. In an ideal setting, each trusted authority is completely independent from all the others, both in terms of the people engaged in providing the expected service and in terms of the available computer and software infrastructure. In practice, recruiting such a group of trusted authorities and equipping them with independent hard- and software is a very difficult problem.

The second type of assumptions in cryptographic voting protocols limits the adversary's computational capabilities, for example with respect to computing discrete logarithms or factoring large numbers. Such computational intractability assumptions are very common in many cryptographic applications, but they are very problematic in the context of electronic elections. It means that the secrecy of the votes of an election today may be at risk in the future, when more powerful computers and better methods of cryptanalysis are available. Choosing very conservative security parameters may postpone the privacy breach, but does not prevent it.

© Springer International Publishing Switzerland 2015
R. Haenni et al. (Eds.): VoteID 2015, LNCS 9269, pp. 74–91, 2015.
DOI: 10.1007/978-3-319-22270-7_5

1.1 Contribution

The contribution of this paper is a new cryptographic voting protocol for remote electronic elections, which guarantees the secrecy of the vote without relying on trusted authorities or on computational intractability assumptions. It offers therefore *everlasting privacy* in an information-theoretical sense. Trusted authorities are only needed for fairness, and computational intractability assumptions are only necessary to prevent the creation of invalid votes during the voting period.

From a technical point of view, our protocol differs strongly from mainstream approaches such as those based on homomorphic tallying, mix-nets, or blind signatures. The core of the protocol is a combination of a set membership proof [3] and a proof of known representation of a committed value [2]. When casting a vote, the voter provides a zero-knowledge proof of knowledge of the representation of one of the registered public voter credentials. Informally, the protocol consists of the following four consecutive steps (some details about preventing double voting or providing fairness are left out):

- **Registration:** Each voter creates a pair of private and public voter credentials and sends the public voter credentials over an authentic channel to the election administration.
- **Election Preparation:** The election administration publishes the list of public voter credentials—one for every registered voter—on the public bulletin board.
- **Vote Casting:** The voter creates an electronic ballot and sends it over an anonymous channel to the public bulletin board. The ballot consists of the vote, a commitment to the voter's public credential, and the above-mentioned composition of zero-knowledge proofs.
- **Public Tallying:** At the end of the election period, anyone can derive the final election result from the data published on the public bulletin board. The correctness of the result follows from verifying the zero-knowledge proofs included in the ballots.

The proofs included in every ballot are computationally sound and perfectly zero-knowledge. This implies with very high probability that every vote with a valid proof stems from an eligible voter, but nothing more than that. Every single voter remains completely anonymous within the set of registered voters, independently of the computational capabilities of a future adversary. In this way, our protocol achieves everlasting privacy without the help of trusted authorities. As a consequence, the protocol requires almost no central infrastructure and no complicated process coordination. Except during registration, interactions are limited to writing data to and reading data from the public bulletin board. The main computational efforts are spent by the voters themselves during vote casting and by anyone computing and verifying the final election result.

1.2 Related Work

The position that only the strongest notion of privacy is sufficient for electronic voting has first been proclaimed by Chaum [10]. He argued that ballot secrecy must be *unconditionally secure*, meaning that the partial tally of a group of voters can only be determined by a coalition of all other voters. In its strict sense, this definition includes an adversary with unlimited computational power. Two protocols by Kiayias and Yung [16] and Groth [15] achieve a weaker form of so-called *perfect ballot secrecy* under the Decisional Diffie-Hellman assumption. They are intended for use in the context of boardroom voting with a small number of participants. Both protocols are *self-tallying*, meaning that the election result can be computed without the aid of a trusted authority.

In a series of papers [18–20], Moran and Naor proposed several protocols with everlasting privacy (but not unconditional privacy according to Chaum's definition). They are intended for use in the traditional setting, in which ballots are cast in a private polling booth. In all three protocols, everlasting privacy is only achieved with the aid of a single or a group of trusted authorities, which could potentially cause voter privacy to be breached. Another protocol [21] for the traditional setting achieves everlasting privacy by combining concepts from Punchscan and Prêt àVoter.

In a more recent series of papers [6,11,12], everlasting privacy with the aid of trusted authorities has been brought into the context of remote elections. While the information published on the public bulletin board does not reveal anything about somebody's vote, the trusted server could potentially break the encrypted votes transmitted over the private channel between voter and server.

Another important line of related work are the protocols based on blind signatures [14]. They are also based on submitting votes over an anonymous channel, but they achieve everlasting privacy under much stronger trust assumptions. Their main problem is ballot-stuffing by malicious signing authorities, which cannot be detected. More generally speaking, protocols based on blind signatures do not support the verification of the electorate. Other disadvantages are the facts that voters need to interact with the authorities during vote casting and that the authorities learn who actually voted. To overcome some of the drawbacks of blind signatures, Canard and Traoré introduced a system based on list signatures [9].

1.3   Paper Overview

In the following section, we introduce the cryptographic building blocks of our protocol. In particular, we describe possible instances of a set membership proof and a proof of known representation of a committed value. In Sect. 3, we provide a detailed description of our protocol and a discussion of the underlying adversary model and the resulting system properties. In Sect. 4, we analyse the running times of the vote casting and tallying procedures and present the results from corresponding performance tests. Finally, we summarize the findings of this paper in Sect. 5.

2   Cryptographic Preliminaries

Let $\mathcal{G}_p$ be a multiplicative cyclic group of prime order p, for which the discrete logarithm assumption is believed to hold. Furthermore, let $\mathbb{G}_q \subset \mathbb{Z}_p^*$, be a large prime-order subgroup of the group of integers modulo p, where $\gamma = (p-1)/q$ denotes the corresponding co-factor. Finally, suppose that independent generators $g_0, g_1 \in \mathcal{G}_p$ and $h_0, \ldots, h_N \in \mathbb{G}_q$ are publicly known. Independence with respect to generators of a cyclic group means that their relative discrete logarithms are unknown.[1]

In our protocol, we use two instances of the perfectly hiding Pedersen commitment scheme, one over $\mathcal{G}_p$ and one over $\mathbb{G}_q$. We distinguish them by $com_p(u, r) = g_0^r g_1^u$ as a commitment to u with randomization r and $com_q(v, s) = h_0^s h_1^v$ as a commitment to v with randomization s, where $u, r \in \mathbb{Z}_p$ and $v, s \in \mathbb{Z}_q$. In the case of $\mathbb{G}_q$, we write $com_q(v_1, \ldots, v_N, s) = h_0^s h_1^{v_1} \cdots h_N^{v_N}$ for a commitment to N values $v_1, \ldots, v_N \in \mathbb{Z}_q$. Recall that Pedersen commitments are perfectly hiding, computationally binding, and additively homomorphic.

The main cryptographic tools in our protocol are non-interactive zero-knowledge proofs of knowledge. The voter uses them to demonstrate knowledge of some secret values involved in a mathematical statement, but without revealing any information about the secret values. One of the most fundamental type of zero-knowledge proofs of knowledge is a preimage proof for a one-way group homomorphism $\phi : X \to Y$, denoted by $NIZKP[(a) : b = \phi(a)]$, where $a \in X$ is the secret preimage of a public value $b = \phi(a) \in Y$. Examples of such preimage proofs result from the above additively homomorphic Pedersen commitment schemes, for example $NIZKP[(u, r) : c = com_p(u, r)]$ for proving knowledge of an opening $u, r \in \mathbb{Z}_p$ for a publicly known commitment $c \in \mathcal{G}_p$.

The most common construction of a non-interactive preimage proof is the Σ-protocol in combination with the Fiat-Shamir heuristic [13]. The transcript of such a non-interactive proof consists of one or multiple commitments and one or multiple responses to a challenge computed by a publicly known hash function. Some auxiliary information can be linked to the transcript by using it as an additional input to the hash function. In Sect. 3, we will write $\pi_i = NIZKP_x[\cdot]$ for the transcripts of the non-interactive proofs used in the voting protocol, where x represents some auxiliary information linked to the proof.

2.1 Set Membership Proof

Let $U = \{u_1 \ldots, u_M\}$ be a finite set of values $u_i \in \mathbb{Z}_p$ and $c = com_p(u, r)$ a commitment to an element $u \in U$. Both U and c are publicly known. With a *set membership proof*, denoted by $NIZKP[(u, r) : c = com_p(u, r) \wedge u \in U]$, the prover demonstrates knowledge of corresponding values $u \in U$ and $r \in \mathbb{Z}_p$, but without revealing any information about them. Such a proof can be constructed by a standard OR combination of individual preimage proofs for each $u \in U$, but this proof has a size linear to M and is therefore not efficient. The first set membership proof with a sub-linear size has been given by Camenisch et al. [7].

As suggested by Brands et al. [5], a general way of constructing a set membership proof is to compute the polynomial $P(X) = \prod_{i=1}^{M}(X - u_i)$ and

---

[1] To ensure that generators are independent, they need to be generated in some publicly reproducible way, for example by deriving them from a common reference string.

to demonstrate that $P(u) = 0$. This proof, denoted by $NIZKP[(u, r) : c = \mathrm{com}_p(u, r) \wedge P(u) = 0]$, is a particular case of a *polynomial evaluation proof* $NIZKP[(u, r, v, s) : c = \mathrm{com}_p(u, r) \wedge d = \mathrm{com}_p(v, s) \wedge P(u) = v]$ for $v = s = 0$. In a recent publication [3], Bayer and Groth proposed a polynomial evaluation proof with a logarithmic size, which is the current state-of-the-art. We use a non-interactive version of this proof in our voting protocol, instantiated to the special case of $v = s = 0$. A summary of the proof generation and verification is given in Fig. 1.

A complete proof transcript consists of $4\lfloor \log M \rfloor + 2$ elements of $\mathcal{G}_p$ and $3\lfloor \log M \rfloor + 3$ elements of $\mathbb{Z}_p$. The proof generation requires $8\lfloor \log M \rfloor + 4$ exponentiations in $\mathcal{G}_p$ and not more than $2M\lfloor \log M \rfloor$ multiplications in $\mathbb{Z}_p$. Similarly, $6\lfloor \log M \rfloor + 6$ exponentiations in $\mathcal{G}_p$ and $3M$ multiplications in $\mathbb{Z}_p$ are needed for the verification.[2] In terms of exponentiations only, the computational costs for generating and verifying a proof are both logarithmic with M, but for very large values M, the cost of the (quasi-)linear number of multiplications becomes dominant.

2.2 Proof of Known Representation of a Committed Value

In a cyclic group such as $\mathbb{G}_q$ with generators $h_1, \ldots, h_N$, a tuple $(v_1, \ldots, v_N)$ of values $v_i \in \mathbb{Z}_q$ is called *DL-representation* (or simply *representation*) of $u \in \mathbb{G}_q$ with respect to $(h_1, \ldots, h_N)$, if $u = h_1^{v_1} \cdots h_N^{v_N}$ [4]. Note that the general definition of DL-representation does not require the values $h_1, \ldots, h_N$ to be generators, nor do they need to be independent or distinct. On the other hand, every opening of a Pedersen commitment is clearly a DL-representation of the commitment with respect to the given independent generators.

Let $c = \mathrm{com}_p(u, r)$ be a commitment to a single value $u \in \mathbb{G}_q \subset \mathbb{Z}_p$ and $d = \mathrm{com}_q(v_1, \ldots, v_N, s)$ a commitment to multiple values $v_1, \ldots, v_N \in \mathbb{Z}_q$. Both c and d are publicly known. Following Au et al. [2], a proof of known *representation of a commited value* (or simply *representation proof*), denoted by

$$NIZKP[(u, r, v_1, \ldots, v_N, s) : \ c = \mathrm{com}_p(u, r) \wedge d = \mathrm{com}_q(v_1, \ldots, v_N, s)$$
$$\wedge \ u = h_1^{v_1} \cdots h_N^{v_N}],$$

demonstrates that the tuple of committed values in d is a DL-representation of the committed value in c. Note that this is a generalization of proof of knowledge of double discrete logarithms, $NIZKP\{(v) : c = g^{(h^v)}\}$, by Camenisch and Stadler [8]. A summary of the proof generation and verification is given in Fig. 2, where a security parameter K determines the soundness of the proof.

A complete proof transcript consists of $K + 1$ elements of $\mathcal{G}_p$, K elements of $\mathbb{G}_q$, $K + 2$ elements of $\mathbb{Z}_p$, and $K(N + 1)$ elements of $\mathbb{Z}_q$. Note that elements

---

[2] The number of exponentiations given in [3, Table 2] is incorrect for the verification. The correct result of $6\lfloor \log M \rfloor$ exponentiations is obtained by counting c_j^x in Step 2 and c_{j+1}^x in Step 3 as one exponentiation only. This remark together with the correct result can be found in [3, Page 11], i.e., only the table entry is incorrect. Furthermore, we cannot reproduce the result of $2M$ multiplications for the verification reported in [3, Table 2]. According to our analysis, at least $3M$ multiplications are needed.

Public Input: $c = com_p(u, r) \in \mathcal{G}_p$, $P(X) = \sum_{i=0}^{M} a_i X^i \in \mathbb{Z}_p[X]$

Secret Input: $u, r \in \mathbb{Z}_p$

Generation:

1. For $j = 1, \ldots, m$, pick $r_j \in_R \mathbb{Z}_p$ and compute $c_j = com_p(u^{2^j}, r_j)$.
2. For $j = 0, \ldots, m$, pick $\bar{a}_j, \bar{r}_j \in_R \mathbb{Z}_p$ and compute $\bar{c}_j = com_p(\bar{a}_j, \bar{r}_j)$.
3. Compute new polynomial

$$\tilde{P}(X) = \sum_{j=0}^{m} \tilde{a}_j X^j = \sum_{i=0}^{M} a_i \prod_{j=0}^{m} (u^{2^j} X + \bar{a}_j)^{i[j]} X^{1-i[j]} \in \mathbb{Z}_p[X]$$

   of degree m. For $j = 0, \ldots, m$, pick $\tilde{r}_j \in_R \mathbb{Z}_p$ and compute $\tilde{c}_j = com_p(\tilde{a}_j, \tilde{r}_j)$.

4. For $j = 0, \ldots, m-1$, compute $\hat{a}_j = u^{2^j} \bar{a}_j$, pick $\hat{r}_j \in_R \mathbb{Z}_p$, and compute $\hat{c}_j = com_p(\hat{a}_j, \hat{r}_j)$.
5. Compute $x = h(c, a_0, \ldots, a_M, c_1, \ldots, c_m, \bar{c}_0, \ldots, \bar{c}_m, \tilde{c}_0, \ldots, \tilde{c}_m, \hat{c}_0, \ldots, \hat{c}_{m-1})$.
6. For $j = 0, \ldots, m$, compute $\bar{a}'_j = \bar{a}_j + x u^{2^j}$.
7. For $j = 0, \ldots, m$, compute $\bar{r}'_j = \bar{r}_j + x r_j$.
8. For $j = 0, \ldots, m-1$, compute $\hat{r}'_j = \hat{r}_j + x r_{j+1} - b_j r_j$.
9. Compute $\tilde{r}' = \sum_{j=0}^{m} \tilde{r}_j x^j$.

Transcript:

$(c_1, \ldots, c_m, \bar{c}_0, \ldots, \bar{c}_m, \tilde{c}_0, \ldots, \tilde{c}_m, \hat{c}_0, \ldots, \hat{c}_{m-1}, \bar{a}'_0, \ldots, \bar{a}'_m, \bar{r}'_0, \ldots, \bar{r}'_m, \hat{r}'_0, \ldots, \hat{r}'_{m-1}, \tilde{r}')$

Verification:

1. Compute $x = h(c, a_0, \ldots, a_M, c_1, \ldots, c_m, \bar{c}_0, \ldots, \bar{c}_m, \tilde{c}_0, \ldots, \tilde{c}_m, \hat{c}_0, \ldots, \hat{c}_{m-1})$.
2. For $j = 0, \ldots, m$, check $c_j^x \bar{c}_j = com_p(\bar{a}'_j, \bar{r}'_j)$.
3. For $j = 0, \ldots, m-1$, check $c_{j+1}^x \hat{c}_j = c_j^{\bar{a}'_j} \cdot com_p(0, \hat{r}'_j)$.
4. Check

$$\prod_{j=0}^{m} \tilde{c}_j^{x^j} = com_p\left(\sum_{i=0}^{M} a_i \prod_{j=0}^{m} \bar{a}'_j{}^{i[j]} x^{1-i[j]}, \tilde{r}' \right).$$

Fig. 1. Non-interactive version of the polynomial evaluation proof $NIZKP[(u, r) : c = com_p(u, r) \wedge P(u) = 0]$ according to Bayer and Groth [3], using a slightly adjusted formal notation. We use $m = \lfloor \log M \rfloor = |M| - 1$ to denote the bit length of M minus 1 and a publicly known hash function $h(\cdot)$ with values in $\mathbb{Z}_p$ to compute the challenge x. The j-th bit of the binary representation of an index $i \in \{0, \ldots, M\}$ is denoted by $i[j] \in \{0, 1\}$, for $j = \{0, \ldots, m\}$. For reasons of convenience, let $c_0 = c$ and $r_0 = r$.

of $\mathbb{G}_q$ can be counted as elements of $\mathbb{Z}_p$, thus resulting in $2K + 2$ elements of $\mathbb{Z}_p$.[3] The proof generation requires $2K + 2$ exponentiations in $\mathcal{G}_p$ and $K(N + 1)$ exponentiations in $\mathbb{G}_q$. Similarly, the verification requires $2K + 1$ exponentiations in $\mathcal{G}_p$ and $K(N + 1)$ exponentiations in $\mathbb{G}_q$.

---

[3] The bandwidth requirements given in [2, Table 4] are clearly incorrect. It seems that the K elements of $\mathbb{G}_q$ have been counted falsely as elements of $\mathcal{G}_p$.

Public Input: $c = \mathrm{com}_p(u, r) \in \mathcal{G}_p$, $d = \mathrm{com}_q(v_1, \ldots, v_N, s) \in \mathbb{G}_q$
Secret Input: $u, r \in \mathbb{Z}_p$, $v_1, \ldots, v_N, s \in \mathbb{Z}_q$
Generation:
1. Pick $\bar{u}, \bar{r} \in_R \mathbb{Z}_p$ and compute $\bar{c} = \mathrm{com}_p(\bar{u}, \bar{r})$.
2. For $j = 1, \ldots, K$,
   (a) pick $\bar{v}_{1,j}, \ldots, \bar{v}_{N,j} \in_R \mathbb{Z}_q$ and compute $\bar{u}_j = h_1^{\bar{v}_{1,j}} \cdots h_N^{\bar{v}_{N,j}}$,
   (b) pick $\bar{r}_j \in_R \mathbb{Z}_p$ and compute $\bar{c}_j = \mathrm{com}_p(\bar{u}_j, \bar{r}_j)$,
   (c) pick $\bar{s}_j \in_R \mathbb{Z}_q$ and compute $\bar{d}_j = \mathrm{com}_q(\bar{v}_{1,j}, \ldots, \bar{v}_{N,j}, \bar{s}_j)$.
3. Compute $x = h(c, d, \bar{c}, \bar{c}_1, \ldots, \bar{c}_k, \bar{d}_1, \ldots, \bar{d}_k)$.
4. Compute $\bar{u}' = \bar{u} - xu$ and $\bar{r}' = \bar{r} - xr$.
5. For $j = 1, \ldots, K$,
   (a) for $i = 1, \ldots, N$, compute $\bar{v}'_{i,j} = \bar{v}_{i,j} - x[j]v_i$,
   (b) compute $\bar{r}'_j = \bar{r}_j - x[j] \cdot \mathrm{com}_q(\bar{v}'_{1,j}, \ldots, \bar{v}'_{N,j}, r)$,
   (c) compute $\bar{s}'_j = \bar{s}_j - x[j]s$.
Transcript:
$(\bar{c}, \bar{c}_1, \ldots, \bar{c}_k, \bar{d}_1, \ldots, \bar{d}_k, \bar{u}', \bar{r}', \bar{v}'_{1,1}, \ldots, \bar{v}'_{N,K}, \bar{r}'_1, \ldots, \bar{r}'_k, \bar{s}'_1, \ldots, \bar{s}'_k)$
Verification:
1. Compute $x = h(c, d, \bar{c}, \bar{c}_1, \ldots, \bar{c}_k, \bar{d}_1, \ldots, \bar{d}_k)$.
2. Check $\bar{c} = c^x \cdot \mathrm{com}_p(\bar{u}', \bar{r}')$.
3. For $j = 1, \ldots, K$,
   (a) check $\bar{d}_j = d^{x[j]} \cdot \mathrm{com}_q(\bar{v}'_{1,j}, \ldots, \bar{v}'_{N,j}, \bar{s}'_j)$,
   (b) compute $\bar{u}'_j = h_1^{\bar{v}'_{1,j}} \cdots h_N^{\bar{v}'_{N,j}}$, and check

   $$\bar{c}_j = \begin{cases} \mathrm{com}_p(\bar{u}'_j, \bar{r}'_j), & \text{if } x[j] = 0, \\ c^{\bar{u}'_j} \cdot \mathrm{com}_p(0, \bar{r}'_j), & \text{if } x[j] = 1. \end{cases}$$

Fig. 2. Non-interactive version of the representation proof $NIZKP[(u, r, v_1 \ldots, v_N, s) : c = \mathrm{com}_p(u, r) \wedge d = \mathrm{com}_q(v_1, \ldots, v_N, s) \wedge u = h_1^{v_1} \cdots h_N^{v_N}]$ according to Au et al. [2], using a slightly adjusted formal notation. We use a publicly known hash function $h(\cdot)$ with values in $\mathbb{Z}_p$ to compute the challenge x. The j-th bit of the binary representation of x is denoted by $x[j] \in \{0, 1\}$ and $K < \log p$ is the security parameter.

3 Internet Elections with Everlasting Privacy

In this section, we present our new protocol for internet elections with everlasting privacy. We start with a discussion of the adversary model and the underlying trust assumptions. In Sects. 3.2 and 3.3, which constitutes the main contribution of this paper, we provide a detailed formal description of the protocol and analyse its security properties. A compact summary of the protocol is given in Fig. 3. We round off this section with a discussion of two important side aspects and corresponding protocol extensions.

3.1 Adversary Model and Trust Assumptions

We consider two types of adversaries with different capabilities and goals. An adversary of the first type acts at the present time, before or while an election takes place, whereas an adversary of the second type acts at any point in the future. Accordingly, we call them *present adversaries* and *future adversaries*.

The goal of present adversaries is to break the integrity or secrecy of the votes during an election, for example by submitting votes in the name of someone else or by linking votes to voters. We assume present adversaries to be polynomially bounded and thus incapable of solving mathematical problems such as computing discrete logarithms in large prime order groups or breaking cryptographic primitives such as contemporary hash functions. This implies that present adversaries cannot efficiently find valid openings of Pedersen commitments or valid proof transcripts for zero-knowledge proofs of knowledge without knowing the secret inputs. We also assume that the present adversary cannot control the machines used for vote casting.[4]

For a future adversary, the only goal is breaking the secrecy of the votes of an election that took place at the present time. To avoid the problem of estimating the available computational resources far in the future, we simply assume the strongest possible adversary, one with unlimited resources in terms of computational power and time. Although contemporary cryptography will be completely useless in the presence of such an adversary, the secrets hidden in perfectly hiding commitments or in perfect zero-knowledge proofs of knowledge will never be revealed, even if they were generated today.

From the point of view of the necessary communication infrastructure, the protocol requires an authentic channel between voter and election administration during the registration process. In the basic protocol version of Sect. 3.2, voters need to re-register in every new election, but we will show later how to circumvent this limitation. Furthermore, the protocol requires a broadcast channel with memory, for example in the form of a robust append-only public bulletin board collecting the entire election data. Finally, for sending their votes to the bulletin board, voters need access to an anonymous channel. We assume that no adversary is capable of intercepting and recording the whole traffic over this channel during an election and storing the data for future vote privacy attacks [1].

3.2 Protocol Description

The first step of the protocol is the voter registration before an election. To register, voter V picks a *private credential* $(\alpha, \beta) \in_R \mathbb{Z}_q^2$ at random and computes the *public credential* $u = h_1^\alpha h_2^\beta \in \mathbb{G}_q$. Note that the private credential is a representation of the public credential with respect to (h_1, h_2). Finally, the voter sends u over an authentic channel to the election administration.[5]

---

[4] We are aware that requiring a secure platform is a strong assumption. We do not explicitly address this problem in this paper, but our protocol allows voters at least to detect a compromised platform as long as they can read the bulletin board in a secure way.

[5] To ensure that u has been computed from fresh values (α, β), the voter could be asked to prove knowledge of (α, β) by computing $NIZKP[(\alpha, \beta) : u = h_1^\alpha h_2^\beta]$. As this is not an essential step for our protocol, we omit it in our presentation.

After the registration phase, the election administration defines the list $U = ((V_1, u_1), \ldots, (V_M, u_M))$ based on the electoral roll. Each pair $(V_i, u_i) \in U$ links a public credential to the corresponding voter. Next, the coefficients $A = (a_0, \ldots, a_M)$ of the polynomial $P(X) = \prod_{i=1}^{M}(X - u_i) \in \mathbb{Z}_p[X]$ are computed to allow voters creating the set membership proof during the vote casting phase. As the computation of those coefficients is quite expensive ($\frac{1}{2}M^2$ multiplications in $\mathbb{Z}_p$), it is performed by the election administration, possibly already during the registration phase in an incremental way. Note that the coefficients can be re-computed and verified by anyone, and voters can efficiently verify the inclusion of their public credential u by checking $P(u) = 0$. Finally, an independent *election generator* $\hat{h} \in \mathbb{G}_q$ is defined in some publicly reproducible way and $(U, A, \hat{h})$ is posted to the public bulletin board.

During the election, voters create their vote e by selecting their preferred election options. We do not further specify these options and their encoding, since our protocol does not impose any restrictions. Similarly, we do not discuss vote encryption, as this is a side aspect of the protocol and only affects fairness (see Sect. 3.4). To cast the vote, the voter computes the *election credential* $\hat{u} = \hat{h}^\beta \in \mathbb{G}_q$, a commitment $c = \text{com}_p(u, r)$ to the public credential, and a commitment $d = \text{com}_q(\alpha, \beta, s)$ to the private credential, where $r \in_R \mathbb{Z}_p$ and $s \in_R \mathbb{Z}_q$. Next, the voter generates three non-interactive zero-knowledge proofs. The first proof is a set membership proof $\pi_1 = NIZKP_e[(u, r) : c = \text{com}_p(u, r) \wedge P(u) = 0]$ proving that c is indeed a commitment to one of the public credentials in U. To prevent that a voter can take just any credential from U, the voter generates $\pi_2 = NIZKP_e[(u, r, \alpha, \beta, s) : c = \text{com}_p(u, r) \wedge d = \text{com}_q(\alpha, \beta, s) \wedge u = h_1^\alpha h_2^\beta]$ to prove knowledge of the representation of the committed value in c. Finally, the voter shows by a third proof $\pi_3 = NIZKP_e[(\alpha, \beta, s) : d = \text{com}_q(\alpha, \beta, s) \wedge \hat{u} = \hat{h}^\beta]$ that β used to build d and $\hat{u}$ is the same. All three proofs are linked to e. The ballot $B = (c, d, e, \hat{u}, \pi_1, \pi_2, \pi_3)$ consisting of the two commitments, the vote, the election credential, and the three proofs is posted over an anonymous channel to the bulletin board.

The final result of the election can be derived by anyone. For this, the list $\mathcal{B}$ of submitted ballots is retrieved from the bulletin board and the proofs included in each ballot $B \in \mathcal{B}$ are verified. Then duplicate votes are determined based on identical values $\hat{u}$ and conflicts are resolved according to some policy. As we will see in Sect. 4.3, verifying the proofs can be an expensive task for a large electorate. To accelerate the publication of the final result, the election administration may verify the proofs and mark invalid ballots as soon as they appear on the bulletin board. The correctness of the result can then still be checked by anyone.

3.3   Protocol Discussion

The correctness of the protocol is based on the fact that the public credential u can be seen as a perfectly hiding commitment to β and the election credential $\hat{u}$ as a perfectly binding commitment to β. For a present adversary not in possession

---

Registration (Voter):
1. Pick private credential $\alpha, \beta \in_R \mathbb{Z}_q$.
2. Compute public credential $u = h_1^\alpha h_2^\beta \in \mathbb{G}_q$.
3. Send u over an authentic channel to the election administration.

Election Preparation (Election Administration):
1. Define $U = ((V_1, u_1), \ldots, (V_M, u_M))$ based on the electoral roll.
2. Compute coefficients $A = (a_0, \ldots, a_M)$ of $P(X) = \prod_{i=1}^M (X - u_i) \in \mathbb{Z}_p[X]$.
3. Define election generator $\hat{h} \in \mathbb{G}_q$.
4. Post $(U, A, \hat{h})$ to the bulletin board.

Vote Casting (Voter):
1. Select vote e.
2. Compute election credential $\hat{u} = \hat{h}^\beta$.
3. Pick $r \in_R \mathbb{Z}_p$ and $s \in_R \mathbb{Z}_q$ and compute commitments $c = com_p(u, r)$ and $d = com_q(\alpha, \beta, s)$.
4. Compute the following non-interactive proofs:

$$\pi_1 = NIZKP_e[(u, r) : c = com_p(u, r) \wedge P(u) = 0],$$
$$\pi_2 = NIZKP_e[(u, r, \alpha, \beta, s) : c = com_p(u, r) \wedge d = com_q(\alpha, \beta, s)$$
$$\wedge\, u = h_1^\alpha h_2^\beta],$$
$$\pi_3 = NIZKP_e[(\alpha, \beta, s) : d = com_q(\alpha, \beta, s) \wedge \hat{u} = \hat{h}^\beta].$$

5. Post ballot $B = (c, d, e, \hat{u}, \pi_1, \pi_2, \pi_3)$ to the bulletin board over an anonymous channel.

Public Tallying:
1. Retrieve the set $\mathcal{B}$ of all ballots from the bulletin board.
2. For each $B \in \mathcal{B}$, verify π_1, π_2, π_3.
3. Detect duplicate votes based on identical values $\hat{u}$ and resolve conflicts.
4. Compute final election result.

Fig. 3. Detailed protocol description.

of a private credential, there are two principle ways of creating a ballot that will be accepted in the final tally. First, the adversary may try to find (α', β') such that $u = h_1^{\alpha'} h_2^{\beta'}$ for some $u \in U$, which is equivalent to solve the discrete logarithm problem. Second, the adversary may try to fake a proof transcript without knowing such a pair (α', β'), but this is prevented by the computational soundness of the proofs. If the present adversary is an eligible voter in possession of a valid private credential, then trying to submit more than one ballot based on the same private credential will result in identical election credentials $\hat{u} = \hat{h}^\beta$. Without using the private credential, the voter is not more powerful than any other present adversary.

Everlasting Privacy. A ballot posted over an anonymous channel to the bulletin board contains no information for identifying the voter. Clearly, the future adversary will be able to determine β from $\hat{u}$ contained in the ballot, but knowing β, a suitable value α' can be found for every credential $u' \in U$ such that

$u' = h_1^{\alpha'} h_2^{\beta}$. Therefore, the adversary is unable to link $\hat{u}$ to u from knowing β. Additionally, the proofs π_1, π_2, and π_3 are perfectly zero-knowledge and therefore of no help. This implies that even the future adversary is unable to break the privacy of the vote. In other words, our protocol offers everlasting privacy.

Trust and Infrastructure Assumptions. Our protocol is based on two fundamental assumptions with regard to the available communication infrastructure. For silently casting a vote, voters require an anonymous channel, and for storing all their ballots, a robust public bulletin board must be available. Corresponding trust assumptions towards the developers and administrators of these systems are inevitable. However, no further trust assumptions are necessary in the basic version of our protocol. The election administration is the only authority involved, but the task of registering voters and publishing their public credentials can be verified by the voters themselves. The absence of further trusted authorities makes the overall election process extremely simple and allows an implementation of our protocol with almost no central infrastructure.

3.4   Extensions

In the basic version of the protocol as presented in Sect. 3.2, we have ignored some important aspects of real election systems. The following discussion of two of these aspects rounds off the description of our protocol.

Achieving Fairness. The protocol as presented is not fair. Fairness means that the published election data does not allow anyone to derive partial results during the election period. If fairness is a requirement, which is not always the case (especially in smaller elections with a very short election period), the protocol can be extended as follows. Instead of submitting the vote e in plaintext, the voter computes an encryption $E = enc_{pk}(e, t)$ using a randomized encryption scheme such as ElGamal or Paillier and generates a non-interactive proof $\pi_4 = NIZKP[(e, t) : E = enc_{pk}(e, t)]$ of knowing the plaintext vote. The public encryption key pk is generated beforehand by a group of trusted authorities in a distributed manner. When the election period is over, the authorities post their shares of the corresponding private key to the bulletin board. The encrypted votes can then be decrypted by anyone.

Multiple Elections. If the protocol as presented so far is used for multiple elections, but without requiring voters to renew their credentials, then a future adversary will be able to link the votes from the same voter by uncovering the same value β from different election credentials. This does not create a direct link to the voter's identity, but it allows creating a kind of voter profile which will eventually leak information. To overcome this problem, the protocol must be modified to ensure that a single β is used for only one election. This can be achieved by extending the private and public credentials to $(\alpha, \beta_1, \ldots, \beta_L)$

and $u = h_1^\alpha h_2^{\beta_1} \ldots h_{L+1}^{\beta_L}$, respectively, where L is the maximal number of elections the credentials can be used for. The corresponding commitment to the extended private credential, $d = \text{com}_q(\alpha, \beta_1, \ldots, \beta_L, s)$, implies that π_2 needs to be extended to a representation proof of size $N = L+1$. Finally, the modified election credential $\hat{u} = \hat{h}^{\beta_l}$ and an extended proof $\pi_3 = NIZKP_e[(\alpha, \beta_1, \ldots, \beta_L, s) : d = \text{com}_q(\alpha, \beta_1 \ldots, \beta_L, s) \wedge \hat{u} = \hat{h}^{\beta_l}]$ are computed for $l = (\varepsilon \bmod L) + 1$, where $\varepsilon = 1, 2, \ldots$ is the *election number* published beforehand by the elections administration.

4   Performance and Implementation

Given the complexity of both the set membership proof and the representation proof, we need to look closely at the computational resources required by our voting protocol. As we will see in this section, the performance is the most critical aspect of our protocol compared to others. We will first analyse the ballot size and estimate the total amount of election data that results from different electorate sizes. Then we discuss the cost of computation for creating a ballot and for verifying the entire election at the end of the election period.

4.1   Ballot Size

The size of a ballot in our protocol is mainly determined by the sizes of π_1 and π_2. In Sect. 2, we have given respective numbers. Recall that π_1 depends on M only, whereas π_2 depends on K and L. In Table 1 we recapitulate the number of group elements for $\mathcal{G}_p$, $\mathbb{Z}_p$, $\mathbb{G}_q$, and $\mathbb{Z}_q$ and sum them up. Since $\mathbb{Z}_p$ and $\mathbb{G}_q$ share the same modulo p, their elements are counted together. The table does not include corresponding numbers for the vote e and the proof of known plaintext in case of an encrypted vote.

To calculate the actual size of a ballot and estimate the total size of the election data, some of the system parameters need to be fixed. We consider the basic protocol version for a single election by setting $L = 1$. For a security parameter $K = 80$, we choose corresponding bit lengths $|q| = 160$ and $|p| = 1024$. In the light of today's recommendations for cryptographic parameters, these numbers may seem too small for offering appropriate security, but in the case of

Table 1. Ballot size as a function of M, K, and L (without encrypted vote and proof of known plaintext of the encrypted vote). Elements of $\mathbb{Z}_p$ and $\mathbb{G}_q$ are counted together.

Ballot Component	Elements of $\mathcal{G}_p$	Elements of $\mathbb{Z}_p, \mathbb{G}_q$	Elements of $\mathbb{Z}_q$
$c, d, \hat{u}$	1	2	–
π_1	$4\lfloor \log M \rfloor + 2$	$3\lfloor \log M \rfloor + 3$	–
π_2	$K + 1$	$2K + 2$	$K(L + 2)$
π_3	–	2	4
Entire Ballot	$4\lfloor \log M \rfloor + K + 4$	$3\lfloor \log M \rfloor + 2K + 9$	$KL + 2K + 3$

Table 2. Ballot size for different numbers of voters and parameters $K = 80$, $L = 1$, $|p| = 1024$, and $|q| = 160$.

$M = |U|$	Elements of $\mathcal{G}_p$	Elements of $\mathbb{Z}_p, \mathbb{G}_q$	Elements of $\mathbb{Z}_q$	Single Ballot	M Ballots
10	96	178	244	39.0 KB	0.4 MB
100	108	187	244	41.6 KB	4.1 MB
1'000	120	196	244	44.3 KB	43.2 MB
10'000	136	208	244	47.8 KB	466.5 MB
100'000	148	217	244	50.4 KB	4.8 GB
1'000'000	164	229	244	53.9 KB	51.4 GB

our protocol, the cryptography only needs to withstand vote integrity attacks by present adversaries during the election period. In other words, the cryptographic parameters can be chosen for an exceptionally short cryptoperiod.

Table 2 lists the results obtained for different electorates. The table shows that the size of a single ballot is certainly not a problem for voters to create and submit a ballot, even if M gets very large. On the other hand, if each voter submits a ballot, then the total size of the elections data sums up to more than 50 GB of data for one million voters. Given today's storage and network capacities, this amount of data should still be manageable by an ordinary server and communication infrastructure.

4.2 Cost of Computation: Ballot Generation

Let us now have a look at the cost of computation for generating a ballot. Corresponding computational resources need to be available to the voter for casting a vote. Again, generating the proofs π_1 and π_2 are the two critical tasks in this process. Recall from Sect. 2 that generating π_1 requires a logarithmic number of exponentiations in $\mathcal{G}_p$, but also a linearithmic number of multiplications in $\mathbb{Z}_p$. Since multiplications will become more expensive than exponentiations when M gets very large, they can not be neglected. Table 3 contains the number of critical operations in $\mathcal{G}_p$, $\mathbb{G}_q$, and $\mathbb{Z}_p$, and sums them up for the whole ballot. Again, we exclude the cost for encrypting the vote and generating a proof of known plaintext.

Table 3. Number of exponentiations and multiplications required to generate a single ballot (without encrypted vote and proof of known plaintext of the encrypted vote).

Ballot Component	Exponentiations in $\mathcal{G}_p$	Exponentiations in $\mathbb{G}_q$	Multiplications in $\mathbb{Z}_p$
$c, d, \hat{u}$	2	4	–
π_1	$8\lfloor \log M \rfloor + 4$	–	$2M\lfloor \log M \rfloor$
π_2	$2K + 2$	$K(L + 2)$	–
π_3	–	4	–
Entire Ballot	$8\lfloor \log M \rfloor + 2K + 8$	$KL + 2K + 8$	$2M\lfloor \log M \rfloor$

To estimate actual computation times for generating a ballot, we select the same parameters as in the previous subsection. Furthermore, we assume that the voter's computer is capable of calculating 350 exponentiations per second in $\mathcal{G}_p$, 2'000 exponentiations per second in $\mathbb{G}_q$, and 200'000 multiplications per second in $\mathbb{Z}_p$. We derive these numbers from performance tests in Java on a MacBook Pro with a 2.7 GHz Intel Core i7 processor (16GB RAM, OS X Yosemite 10.10.2, JRE 8, standard `BigInteger` class, single-threaded). The results of our analysis are shown in Table 4. The estimated cost of computation for generating a single ballot turns out to be perfectly acceptable for a medium-sized or even a large electorate. Only when M gets very large (e.g. more than 100'000 voters), the ballot generation gets delayed inappropriately. This is roughly the threshold when the multiplications start to dominate the exponentiations.

Table 4. Cost of ballot generation for different numbers of voters and parameters $K = 80$, $L = 1$, $|p| = 1024$, and $|q| = 160$. The time estimates are based on 350 exponentiations per second in $\mathcal{G}_p$, 2'000 exponentiations per second in $\mathbb{G}_q$, and 200'000 multiplications per second in $\mathbb{Z}_p$.

$M = |U|$	Exponentiations in $\mathcal{G}_p$	Exponentiations in $\mathbb{G}_q$	Multiplications in $\mathbb{Z}_p$	Estimated Time (Single Ballot)
10	192	248	60	0.7 s
100	216	248	1'200	0.7 s
1'000	240	248	18'000	0.9 s
10'000	272	248	260'000	2.2 s
100'000	296	248	3'200'000	17.0 s
1'000'000	328	248	40'000'000	3.4 min

4.3   Cost of Computation: Verification

The most expensive computational task of our protocol is clearly the public tallying, which involves the verification of all proofs included in the ballots. The values shown in Table 5 summarize the number of critical operations in $\mathcal{G}_p$, $\mathbb{G}_q$, and $\mathbb{Z}_p$ for verifying a single ballot. For very large values of M, the most expensive operations are again the $3M$ multiplications in $\mathbb{Z}_p$, which is why they cannot be neglected. As before, the results shown in the table do not contain additional operations for verifying the proof of known plaintext in case of an encrypted vote. Note that proper verification requires checking that the values included in the proof transcripts are elements of corresponding sets. In case of $\mathcal{G}_p$ and $\mathbb{G}_q$ this may require additional exponentiations. We omit them here to be consistent with the results given in [2, 3].

To conclude our performance analysis, we adopt the system parameters and the assumptions with regard to the available computation power from the previous subsection. The resulting values for different electorate sizes are shown in

Table 5. Number of exponentiations and multiplications required to verify a single ballot (without proof of known plaintext of the encrypted vote).

Ballot Component	Exponentiations in $\mathcal{G}_p$	Exponentiations in $\mathbb{G}_q$	Multiplications in $\mathbb{Z}_p$
π_1	$6\lfloor \log M \rfloor + 6$	–	$2M$
π_2	$2K + 1$	$K(L+2)$	–
π_3	–	6	–
Total	$6\lfloor \log M \rfloor + 2K + 7$	$KL + 2K + 6$	$2M$

Table 6. Cost of ballot verification for different numbers of voters and parameters $K = 80$, $L = 1$, $|p| = 1024$, and $|q| = 160$. The time estimates are based on 350 exponentiations per second in $\mathcal{G}_p$, 2'000 exponentiations per second in $\mathbb{G}_q$, and 200'000 multiplications per second in $\mathbb{Z}_p$.

$M = |U|$	Exponentiations in $\mathcal{G}_p$	Exponentiations in $\mathbb{G}_q$	Multiplications in $\mathbb{Z}_p$	Estimated Time (Single Ballot)	Estimated Time (M Ballots)
10	185	166	30	0.6 s	6.1 s
100	203	166	300	0.7 s	1.1 min
1'000	221	166	3'000	0.7 s	12.2 min
10'000	245	166	30'000	0.9 s	2.6 h
100'000	263	166	300'000	2.3 s	64.8 h
1'000'000	287	166	3'000'000	15.9 s	4417.5 h

Table 6. By multiplying the time estimates for verifying a single ballot by the total number of votes, we obtain time estimates for the full verification process.

From the given results, we conclude again that our protocol works reasonably well for a medium-sized or even a large electorate. Note that the verification of the ballots can already start during the vote casting phase, and since it can be executed in parallel, there is a huge potential for distributing the total amount of work to arbitrarily many and possibly more powerful machines. While this is in principle a solution for reducing the 4'400 hours of computation for an election with one million ballots to a more reasonable value, it restricts somewhat the idea of a *public* tallying process.

4.4 Implementation and Optimizations

In course of developing the protocol presented in this paper, we implemented both the set membership and the representation proof in UniCrypt [17]. This is an open-source Java library developed for the purpose of simplifying the implementation of cryptographic voting protocols.[6] The library consist of a mathematical and a cryptographic layer. The two implemented proofs extend the proofsystem package, which is a central component of the cryptographic layer. The same package also contains classes for generating all sorts of preimage or equality proofs, which we need for computing π_3. Other packages in the cryptographic layer provide implementations of Pedersen commitments and various encryption schemes. The library provides therefore the full functionality for a straightforward implementation of our protocol.

In order to check the accuracy of the calculated time estimates of the previous subsections, we used UniCrypt to generate and verify ballots for different electorate sizes and measured the times of computation. The results of these measurements are shown in Table 7. We used the same machine for the tests as in the previous subsection, a MacBook Pro with a 2.7 GHz Intel Core i7 processor, and the current UniCrypt version from the project's development branch on April 1, 2015. In general, the measured running times are quite consistent with the time estimates from the previous section, for example 18.2 instead of 17.0 seconds for generating a ballot with 100'000 voters. This difference can be explained by the overhead for other less expensive operations and for Java's memory and object management. Note that for 1'000'000 voters, the actual running times are even slightly better than the estimates (3.3 instead of 3.4 min). An explanation for this is the fact, that $2M\lfloor \log M \rfloor$ is an upper approximation for the number of multiplications in $\mathbb{Z}_p$.

To conclude the discussion about our implementation and the results of the performance analysis, we need to stress that the prototype implementation has not been optimized in any way. To speed up the ballot generation, we may pre-compute the proofs in a background process of the vote preparation software, and we may distribute the computations to all available cores of the given machine, or to the machine's graphics processing unit. In the final verification of all ballots, the potential of executing tasks in parallel—possibly on many different machines—is even higher. Furthermore, techniques like multi-exponentiation

Table 7. Actual running times for generating and verifying a single ballot using the UniCrypt library.

$M = |U|$	Ballot generation	Ballot verification
10	1.3 s	0.9 s
100	1.4 s	1.0 s
1'000	1.6 s	1.1 s
10'000	3.0 s	1.3 s
100'000	18.2 s	2.9 s
1'000'000	3.3 min	18.8 s

---

[6] UniCrypt is publicly available on GitHub under a dual AGPLv3/commercial licence, see https://github.com/bfh-evg/unicrypt.

and fixed-base exponentiation may bring considerable performance improvements, especially for small elections, where the exponentiations predominate the multiplications. For very large elections, we should consider replacing the set membership proof as described in this paper by an approach by Brands et al. [5], which requires $8\sqrt{M}$ exponentiations but only $2M + 8\sqrt{M}$ multiplications for generating a proof.

5   Conclusion

In this paper, we have introduced a new approach for a cryptographic voting protocol. Its underlying mechanism is very different compared to mainstream approaches based on mixing and homomorphic tallying. In our protocol, the distinction between valid and invalid ballots is strictly based on perfectly hiding commitments and perfect zero-knowledge proofs of knowledge. This prevents computationally bounded adversaries from submitting illegitimate votes during the election. At the same time, even a computationally unbounded adversary in the future will never be able to link votes to voters. Our protocol offers therefore a solution to the everlasting privacy problem. Compared to other protocols offering everlasting privacy, we do not require any trusted authorities. This makes our protocol particularly attractive for straightforward implementation in a practical system. The relatively high computational costs for generating and verifying the ballots is a clear disadvantage of our approach, but we have demonstrated that with today's technology, this is only a drawback for very large electorates.

Acknowledgments. We thank the anonymous reviewers for their thorough reviews and appreciate their comments and suggestions. This research has been supported by the Swiss National Science Foundation (project No. 200021L_140650).

References

1. Arapinis, M., Cortier, V., Kremer, S., Ryan, M.: Practical everlasting privacy. In: Basin, D., Mitchell, J.C. (eds.) POST 2013 (ETAPS 2013). LNCS, vol. 7796, pp. 21–40. Springer, Heidelberg (2013)
2. Au, M.H., Susilo, W., Mu, Y.: Proof-of-knowledge of representation of committed value and its applications. In: Steinfeld, R., Hawkes, P. (eds.) ACISP 2010. LNCS, vol. 6168, pp. 352–369. Springer, Heidelberg (2010)
3. Bayer, S., Groth, J.: Zero-knowledge argument for polynomial evaluation with application to blacklists. In: Johansson, T., Nguyen, P.Q. (eds.) EUROCRYPT 2013. LNCS, vol. 7881, pp. 646–663. Springer, Heidelberg (2013)
4. Brands, S.: Rethinking Public Key Infrastructures and Digital Certificates: Building in Privacy. MIT Press, Cambridge (2000)
5. Brands, S., Demuynck, L., De Decker, B.: A practical system for globally revoking the unlinkable pseudonyms of unknown users. In: Pieprzyk, J., Ghodosi, H., Dawson, E. (eds.) ACISP 2007. LNCS, vol. 4586, pp. 400–415. Springer, Heidelberg (2007)

6. Buchmann, J., Demirel, D., van de Graaf, J.: Towards a publicly-verifiable mix-net providing everlasting privacy. In: Sadeghi, A.-R. (ed.) FC 2013. LNCS, vol. 7859, pp. 197–204. Springer, Heidelberg (2013)

7. Camenisch, J.L., Chaabouni, R., Shelat, A.: Efficient protocols for set membership and range proofs. In: Pieprzyk, J. (ed.) ASIACRYPT 2008. LNCS, vol. 5350, pp. 234–252. Springer, Heidelberg (2008)

8. Camenisch, J.L., Stadler, M.A.: Efficient group signature schemes for large groups. In: Kaliski Jr., B.S. (ed.) CRYPTO 1997. LNCS, vol. 1294, pp. 410–424. Springer, Heidelberg (1997)

9. Canard, S., Traoré, J.: List signature schemes and application to electronic voting. In: Augot, D., Charpin, P., Kabatianski, G. (eds.) WCC'03, 3rd International Workshop on Coding and Cryptography, Versailles, France, pp. 81–90 (2003)

10. Chaum, D.: The dining cryptographers problem: unconditional sender and recipient untraceability. J. Cryptol. 1(1), 65–75 (1988)

11. Demirel, D., Henning, M., van de Graaf, J., Ryan, P.Y.A., Buchmann, J.: Prêt à voter providing everlasting privacy. In: Heather, J., Schneider, S., Teague, V. (eds.) Vote-ID 2013. LNCS, vol. 7985, pp. 156–175. Springer, Heidelberg (2013)

12. Demirel, D., van de Graaf, J., Araújo, R.: Improving Helios with everlasting privacy towards the public. In: Halderman, J.A., Pereira, O. (eds.) Electronic Voting Technology Workshop/Workshop on Trustworthy Elections, EVT/WOTE 2012, Bellevue, USA (2012)

13. Fiat, A., Shamir, A.: How to prove yourself: practical solutions to identification and signature problems. In: Odlyzko, A.M. (ed.) CRYPTO 1986. LNCS, vol. 263, pp. 186–194. Springer, Heidelberg (1987)

14. Fujioka, A., Okamoto, T., Ohta, K.: A practical secret voting scheme for large scale elections. In: Seberry, J., Zheng, Y. (eds.) ASIACRYPT 1992. LNCS, vol. 718, pp. 244–251. Springer, Heidelberg (1992)

15. Groth, J.: Efficient maximal privacy in boardroom voting and anonymous broadcast. In: Juels, A. (ed.) FC 2004. LNCS, vol. 3110, pp. 90–104. Springer, Heidelberg (2004)

16. Kiayias, A., Yung, M.: Self-tallying Elections and Perfect Ballot Secrecy. In: Naccache, D., Paillier, P. (eds.) PKC 2002. LNCS, vol. 2274, pp. 141–158. Springer, Heidelberg (2002)

17. Locher, P., Haenni, R.: A lightweight implementation of a shuffle proof for electronic voting systems. In: Plödereder, E., Grunske, L., Schneider, E., Ull, D. (eds.) INFORMATIK 2014. Lecture Notes in Informatics, Stuttgart, Germany, pp. 1391–1400. Gesellschaft für Informatik, Bonn (2014)

18. Moran, T., Naor, M.: Receipt-free universally-verifiable voting with everlasting privacy. In: Dwork, C. (ed.) CRYPTO 2006. LNCS, vol. 4117, pp. 373–392. Springer, Heidelberg (2006)

19. Moran, T., Naor, M.: Split-ballot voting: everlasting privacy with distributed trust. In: Ning, P., de Capitani di Vimercati, S., Syverson, P. (eds.) CC 2007, 14th ACM Conference on Computer and Communications Security, Alexandria, USA, pp. 246–255 (2007)

20. Moran, T., Naor, M.: Split-ballot voting: everlasting privacy with distributed trust. ACM Trans. Inf. Syst. Secur. 13(2), 16:1–16:43 (2010)

21. van de Graaf, J.: Voting with unconditional privacy by merging Prêt à Voter and PunchScan. IEEE Trans. Info. Forensics Secur. 4(4), 674–684 (2009)

Vote Validatability in Mix-Net-Based eVoting

Pedro Bibiloni[1]([✉]), Alex Escala[2,3], and Paz Morillo[3]

[1] Departament de Matemàtiques i Informàtica,
Universitat de Les Illes Balears, Palma, Spain
pedro@bibiloni.es
[2] Scytl Secure Electronic Voting, Barcelona, Spain
alex.escala@ma4.upc.edu
[3] Departament de Matemàtica Aplicada IV,
Universitat Politècnica de Catalunya, Barcelona, Spain
paz@ma4.upc.edu

Abstract. One way to build secure electronic voting systems is to use Mix-Nets, which break any correlation between voters and their votes. One of the characteristics of Mix-Net-based eVoting is that ballots are usually decrypted individually and, as a consequence, invalid votes can be detected during the tallying of the election. In particular, this means that the ballot does not need to contain a proof of the vote being valid.

However, allowing for invalid votes to be detected only during the tallying of the election can have bad consequences on the reputation of the election. First, casting a ballot for an invalid vote might be considered as an attack against the eVoting system by non-technical people, who might expect that the system does not accept such ballots. Besides, it would be impossible to track the attacker due to the anonymity provided by the Mix-Net. Second, if a ballot for an invalid vote is produced by a software bug, it might be only detected after the election period has finished. In particular, voters would not be able to cast a valid vote again.

In this work we formalize the concept of having a system that detects invalid votes during the election period. In addition, we give a general construction of an eVoting system satisfying such property and an efficient concrete instantiation based on well-studied assumptions.

Keywords: Electronic voting systems · Mix-Nets · Formal definitions

1 Introduction

Even though many electronic voting schemes have been proposed, we could argue that two of the most important conceptual categories are *Homomorphic Tallying* based voting schemes and *Mix-Net* based voting schemes. Both types of schemes consist on having the voter encrypt her selected voting option on her voting device and having an electoral authority decrypting these encrypted voting options, after

P. Bibiloni was partially supported by the Spanish project TIN 2013-42795-P and the fellowship FPI/1645/2014, which was cofinanced by the European Social Fund.

© Springer International Publishing Switzerland 2015
R. Haenni et al. (Eds.): VoteID 2015, LNCS 9269, pp. 92–109, 2015.
DOI: 10.1007/978-3-319-22270-7_6

some anonymization procedure. This anonymization procedure is what defines each category and has implications on the whole voting system.

In *Homomorphic Tallying* based voting systems [8], the anonymization procedure consists on homomorphically aggregating the encryptions of the voting options from different voters to obtain the encryption of the aggregated selections. For instance, if each voter computes as many encryptions as voting options exist in the election, the aggregate would be the encryption of the number of votes for the first voting option, the encryption of the number of votes for the second voting option and so on. This would imply that electoral authorities only need to compute one decryption operation per voting option in the election, whereas each voter would need as many encryptions.

This does not fit well within our paradigm, since electronic voting is an extremely asymmetric scenario: the computational power of a single voter's device is much smaller than the computational power of the electoral authority. This is due to two factors. First, the resources available to a single voter (personal computers, smartphones or tablets) are usually considerably lower than those available to electoral authorities (multiple servers with many cores per server), specially in big elections. Second, the recent trend seems to be to implement the voting client in JavaScript, which performance is orders of magnitude lower than Java or C, the languages in which the back-end of the system is usually implemented. There are technologies which improve the performance of JavaScript but they are not available in all web browsers. Finally, the time it takes to tally an election is less critical than the time it takes to cast a vote. As estimated in [2], encrypting a single candidate in the JavaScript implementation of Helios, the most popular implementation of a Homomorphic Tallying-based voting system, takes up to 1 s. This clearly does not scale well when hundreds or thousands of candidates are eligible.

On the other hand, in *Mix-Net* based voting systems [7], the computational cost for the voter is much smaller than the computational cost for the electoral authority and even smaller than the computational cost in a Homomorphic Tallying-based scheme. This is achieved by changing the anonymization procedure, which consists on shuffling the encrypted voting options to break any correlation between the ballot and the voter. In this case, the voter only needs to encrypt an encoding of her selected voting options, which might be as efficient as computing a single encryption. On the other hand, the electoral authority will need to decrypt all the ciphertexts individually, but that's a reasonable trade-off.

To have a fair comparison between these two categories of voting systems, one has to consider how many voting options exist in an election. If the election is a single referendum answer, there will be usually three answers (yes, no, blank), which implies that using a Homomorphic Tallying-based system is more than reasonable. However, there are elections where a voter might choose between close to a thousand candidates. We find such an example in elections where tens of parties are eligible in an election, each party having close to a hundred candidates and a voter being able to choose candidates from any party, in which case the benefits of using a Mix-Net-based system outweight its disadvantages.

Lastly, it should be noted that the Damgård Jurik cryptosystem [9] allows encrypting several candidates in a single ciphertext, pushing the boundaries of Homomorphic Tallying-based voting systems. However, only a certain number of candidates can be encrypted, which depends on the number of voters. Above this number, more than one ciphertext needs to be computed and casting a ballot becomes more costly. Determining at which point Mix-Net-based systems outperform Homomorphic Tallying-based systems (with respect to the voting client) is outside the scope of this paper.

1.1   The Problem of Invalid Votes

When building a Homomorphic Tallying based voting system, a technical requisite is that the voter must construct a proof that her vote conforms to the election rules. Otherwise, the homomorphic aggregation of invalid votes could produce completely unreasonable results. Current Homomorphic Tallying based systems consider this requirement, so we can consider it a solved problem.

Mix-Net-based systems do not have this requirement. As votes are individually decrypted, it can be checked whether each decrypted vote conforms to the election rules and, in case it does not, consider it an invalid vote. From a technical perspective this is completely reasonable, we do not need to ask voters for a proof of her vote conforming to the election rules in order to have a secure Mix-Net-based system. Indeed, this is how paper voting systems work nowadays.

Despite proofs of ballot well-formedness not being necessary to implement a secure eVoting system, the lack of such proofs might affect the reputation of the system. Firstly, from a non-technical voter's perspective, it is reasonable to assume that if the voting interface does not allow for an invalid vote to be cast then invalid votes should be impossible to cast. Therefore, modifying the voting client to cast an invalid vote might be seen as an attack against the system, *even if it has no effect on the result on the election*. Besides, it would be impossible to track the attacker due to the anonymity provided by the Mix-Net. The paper voting scenario is slightly different: in paper voting the voting interface allows voters to easily cast an invalid ballot. In addition, should there be a software bug which created invalid votes inadvertently, this would be only detected at the tallying phase. Depending on the amount of invalid votes, the election might even have to be restarted – with the reputation loss that it represents.

1.2   Introducing Vote Validatability

In this work we introduce the concept of *vote validatability*, which attempts to solve the problem mentioned above. We consider that an electronic voting system has vote validatability if it can be *publicly verified* that a ballot contains a vote conforming to the election rules – we want to be able to detect whether a vote is invalid before it is decrypted. This means that (a) no invalid votes will appear during the tallying of the election and (b) any software bug in the voting devices will be detected during the election period, so it can be quickly fixed, providing the voters another attempt to vote before the end of the election.[1]

As we discussed above, Homomorphic Tallying systems have vote validatability since it is a requisite in order to have a secure voting system, in contrast with Mix-Net-based systems. Adding this property to a Mix-Net-based scheme is not a theoretical problem: there are inefficient cryptographic tools such as general-purpose zero-knowledge proofs which can be used to achieve it. The challenge is thus using appropriate proofs to retain low computational cost from the voters' side, which is one of the advantages of using a Mix-Net-based system.

There is a trivial approach to achieve vote validatability: considering all possible contents of a ballot as valid. This can be done by defining an encoding for all-but-one eligible candidates and assigning any other encoding to the last candidate. However, this has some drawbacks. First, having several encodings for the same candidate opens the door to facilitating vote selling by making it possible to introduce the voter's identity in the encoding of the candidate. In addition, requiring a specific encoding might limit the amount of features of the eVoting system, such as the so called return codes [11], which require that each candidate has only one encoding, or using special encodings to aggregate encryptions before the tallying, as also done in [11]. Therefore, we prefer a modular solution to vote validatability which does not require a specific encoding of the candidates.

In this work, we introduce a formal definition for the concept of vote validatability in Sect. 3. Then, we give a general construction of a Mix-Net-based scheme achieving vote validatability and privacy. This construction is based on basic cryptographic primitives and is given in Sect. 4, along with its security properties. Finally, we give a concrete, efficient instantiation of a Mix-Net-based system with vote validatability in Sect. 5.

2   Preliminaries

2.1   Encryption Schemes

An encryption scheme consists of three probabilistic polynomial time (p.p.t.) algorithms: KeyGenEnc, Enc, Dec. On input a security parameter 1^k, the KeyGenEnc algorithm outputs a public key pk and a secret key sk, implicitly defining a message space M_e. The Enc algorithm takes as input the public key pk and a message $m \in M_e$ and outputs a ciphertext C. Dec takes as input a secret key sk and a ciphertext C and outputs a message $m \in M_e$ or halts outputting $\perp$.

An encryption scheme is NM-CPA (Non-Malleability under a Chosen Plaintext Attack) if, loosely speaking, no adversary can find a non-trivial relation between the plaintexts hidden in some ciphertexts generated by him, querying the encryption oracle as in the IND-CPA experiment [5].

---

[1] There could be bugs in the software which verifies vote validatability. However, this verification can be done in parallel by different implementations done by different entities, leveraging this risk.

2.2   Signature Schemes

A signature scheme consists of three p.p.t. algorithms KeyGenSign, Sign, VerifySign. On input a security parameter 1^k, the KeyGenSign algorithm outputs a public key pk and a secret key sk, implicitly defining a message space M_s. The Sign algorithm takes as input the secret key sk and a message $m \in M_s$ and outputs a signature σ. The VerifySign algorithm takes as input a public key pk and a signature σ and outputs success (1) or reject (0).

One usual notion of security for a signature scheme is EUF-CMA [13]. In such a scheme, no adversary is able to forge a new valid signature for any message not already signed, regardless the number of signatures issued.

2.3   Pseudo-Random Permutations

A Pseudo-Random Permutation family [15] is a family of efficient functions $F_{(.)} : \mathcal{X} \to \mathcal{X}$ parametrized by a key $k \in K_{PRP}$.

The pseudo-random property of a PRP family states that it is difficult to distinguish the outputs of a function F_k for a random key $k \in K_{PRP}$ from those of a function f chosen at random from the space of random permutations of $\mathcal{X}$.

2.4   Non-Interactive Zero-Knowledge Proof of Knowledge

Let R be a relation, containing pairs (x, w) such that, given (x, w) it can be verified in polynomial time whether $(x, w) \in R$. We call x the statement and w the witness. We define the language L_R as the set of statements x for which there exists a witness w such that $(x, w) \in R$.

A non-interactive zero-knowledge proof of knowledge (NIZKPK) for a language L_R consists of three p.p.t. algorithms: GenCRS, Prove, VerifyProof. GenCRS takes as input a security parameter 1^k and outputs a common reference string crs. Prove takes as input the common reference string crs, a statement x and a witness w such that $(x, w) \in R$ and outputs a proof π. VerifyProof takes as input a common reference string crs, a statement x and a proof π and outputs 1 if it accepts the proof or 0 if it rejects it.

A NIZKPK must satisfy the properties of completeness, witness extraction and zero-knowledge (see, for instance, [16]). Intuitively, completeness states that VerifyProof will always return 1 on correctly generated proofs. Witness extraction states that (a) there exists an algorithm ExtGenCRS which outputs a common reference string c͂rs, indistinguishable from a common reference string output by GenCRS, and a trapdoor key tk; and (b) that there exists an algorithm Extract that, on input the trapdoor key tk, a statement x and a valid proof π it returns a witness w such that $(x, w) \in R$. Finally, zero-knowledge states that (a) there exists some SimGenCRS which outputs a common reference string c͂rs, indistinguishable from a common reference string output by GenCRS, and a simulation key fk; and (b) that there exists an algorithm SimProve that, on input a statement x and the simulation key fk it can generate a proof indistinguishable from a proof generated using the Prove algorithm with a valid witness.

3   Definitions

In this section we present the syntactical definition of an eVoting scheme and we define some security properties. We have not considered all the desirable security properties of an eVoting scheme – all the end-to-end verifiability properties, including the handling of voters' credentials, are considered to be out of the scope of this paper. However, the solution given in this paper can be combined with the usual techniques for achieving end-to-end verifiability.

3.1   Syntactical Definition

We now give the syntax of a voting scheme. We will consider single-pass voting schemes as defined in [5], which are characterized by the fact that voters interact with the system only by submitting their ballots.

We will consider the following entities regarding an election. First, *election authorities* are in charge of defining the election parameters, generating any required cryptographic keys and tallying the result of the elections. The *bulletin board* is a repository of information containing public keys and ballots. It can be read by any entity but only the *bulletin board manager* and the election authorities can write to it. *Voters* participate in the election by choosing their preferred voting options and submitting their ballots. For the sake of simplicity, we will assume that there is only one election authority. This assumption can be avoided with well-known tools such as multi-party computation.

A voting scheme is parametrized by the set of possible votes $\mathbb{V}$, a result space R and a result function $\rho : (\mathbb{V} \cup \{\bot\})^* \to R$, where $\bot$ denotes an invalid vote.

The result function states how votes should be tallied, i.e., which counting function should be applied to votes. One such result function which we are interested in is the *multiset function*. As defined in [4], the multiset function discloses the sequence of all the cast votes, in a random order. In this case, an invalid vote is treated as any other vote.[2]

A voting scheme is defined by the following p.p.t. algorithms:

- Setup(1^λ) on input a security parameter 1^λ it outputs an election public key pk and an election secret key sk.
- Vote(pk, v) on input the election public key pk and a vote $v \in \mathbb{V}$, outputs a ballot b.
- ValidateBallot(BB, b) takes as input a bulletin board BB and a ballot b. It outputs either success (1) or reject (0).
- Tally(sk, BB) on input the election secret key sk and the bulletin board BB. It outputs the tally $r \in R$ together with a proof of correct tabulation Π.
- VerifyTally(BB, r, Π) takes as input the bulletin board BB, the tally r and a proof of correct tabulation Π. It outputs either success (1) or reject (0).

A single-pass protocol is executed in three phases.

---

[2] As in [4], the result function can be used to model revote policies. In this work we just consider the scenario where each voter can only cast one vote.

1. In the *setup* phase, the election authority runs the Setup algorithm. It publishes the election public key pk in the bulletin board BB and keeps the election secret key sk.
2. In the *voting* phase, each voter can vote. To vote, the voter chooses a vote v and retrieves the public key pk from the bulletin board. Both v and pk are used to create a ballot b using the Vote algorithm, which is sent to the bulletin board manager. The bulletin board manager then executes the ValidateBallot algorithm on the ballot. If the algorithm returns 1, then the bulletin board manager adds the ballot to the bulletin board. Otherwise, it rejects the ballot and notifies both the voter and the electoral authority for auditability purposes.
3. In the *counting* phase, the election authority runs the Tally algorithm on the bulletin board using the election secret key. The output of the Tally algorithm, which consists of the result r and the correct tabulation proof Π, is published to the bulletin board. The proof Π can then be verified by any entity using the VerifyTally algorithm.

A voting system as defined above is *correct* if, when the three phases are run with all the participants behaving correctly, then (a) the result r output by the Tally algorithm is equal to the evaluation of the result function ρ on the voting options corresponding to the ballots cast by the voters and (b) the algorithm VerifyTally on input the result of the Tally algorithm returns success.

3.2 Privacy

Intuitively, a voting system has ballot privacy if an adversary with access to all the ballots and the public key of the election is not able to get any information about the voters' preferences. Formalizing this intuition turns out to be non-straightforward, and it is not until recently that *good* definitions have been given. We adopt the formalization given in [4], a game-based definition of ballot privacy, proven to be equivalent to the intuitive simulation-based security notion.

Ballot privacy is defined by using two experiments between an adversary $\mathcal{A}$ and a challenger $\mathcal{C}$. As usual, the goal of the adversary is to distinguish between the two experiments. In both experiments, the adversary may corrupt voters and submit ballots on their behalf. In addition, for each honest voter the adversary can specify two votes to be used for casting her ballot. However, the electoral authority is assumed to remain honest. Depending on the experiment, the challenger will cast a ballot containing either of those two votes. To prevent trivial attacks, the same tally is always shown to the adversary regardless of which experiment is being played.

For compactness, we present the two experiments as a single experiment which depends on a bit $\beta \in \{0, 1\}$. Both experiments assume given the set of voting options $\mathbb{V}$, the result space R, the result function ρ and use an algorithm SimProof(BB, r) which, given a bulletin board and a result, simulates a correct tabulation proof. The experiment Exp_β is run in these phases:

1. **Setup phase.** The challenger sets up two empty bulletin boards BB_L and BB_R. It runs the Setup(1^λ) protocol to obtain the election public key pk and the election private key sk. It then posts pk on both bulletin boards. The adversary is given read access to either BB_L if $\beta = 0$ or BB_R if $\beta = 1$.

2. **Voting phase.** The adversary may make two types of queries:
   - **Vote**(v_L, v_R) queries. The adversary provides two votes $v_L, v_R \in \mathbb{V}$. The challenger runs Vote(pk, v_L) and Vote(pk, v_R) obtaining two ballots b_L and b_R respectively. $\mathcal{C}$ then obtains new versions of the boards BB_L and BB_R by running ValidateBallot(BB_L, b_L) and ValidateBallot(BB_R, b_R) and updating the boards accordingly.
   - **Ballot**(b) queries, which model queries made on behalf of corrupt voters. The adversary provides a ballot b, with which ValidateBallot(BB_L, b) is run by the challenger. If the algorithm returns 1, BB_L is updated and ValidateBallot(BB_R, b) is executed, updating BB_R accordingly. Otherwise, if the algorithm returns 0, it does nothing.

3. **Tallying phase.** The challenger evaluates Tally(sk, BB_L) obtaining the result r and the proof of correct tabulation Π. If $\beta = 0$, the challenger publishes (r, Π) on the bulletin board BB_L. If $\beta = 1$, the challenger runs SimProof(BB_R, r) obtaining a simulated proof Π' and posts (r, Π') on the bulletin board BB_R.

4. **Output.** The adversary $\mathcal{A}$ outputs a bit α, which depends on $\mathcal{A}$, $\mathbb{V}$, R, ρ and SimProof.

We say that a voting protocol for $(\mathbb{V}, R, \rho)$ as defined in Sect. 3.1 provides ballot privacy if there exists an algorithm SimProof such that for any p.p.t. adversary $\mathcal{A}$ the following advantage is negligible in the security parameter λ.

$$\mathbf{Adv}^{priv}_{\mathbb{V}, R, \rho, \mathsf{SimProof}}(\lambda) := |\Pr[\alpha = 1 | \beta = 1] - \Pr[\alpha = 1 | \beta = 0]|$$

We remark that honest voters are assumed to generate the ballots correctly (i.e., proper randomness is used and it is not leaked to the adversary).

3.3 Strong Consistency

In order to define *vote validatability* we will first define the notion of strong consistency. Strong consistency states that the tally of the bulletin board must correspond to the result of applying the result function to the *contents* of the ballots in the bulletin board. As shown in [4], this property is needed to avoid having leaky tallying algorithms.

In our case, we also use it to define what a meaningful content extractor is. This content extractor will be useful to define the concept of vote validatability.

Strong consistency is given by the following game, where we assume given election parameters $(\mathbb{V}, R, \rho)$ and uses an algorithm Extract(sk, b) which takes the election secret key and a ballot and outputs either a vote or the error symbol $\perp$ denoting an invalid vote.

1. **Setup Phase.** The challenger runs $\mathsf{Setup}(1^\lambda)$ to obtain the election public key pk and the election secret key sk. It gives both pk and sk to the adversary $\mathcal{A}$.
2. **Bulletin Board**(BB). The adversary submits a bulletin board BB to the challenger.
3. **Output.** The challenger runs $\mathsf{Tally}(sk, BB)$ to obtain a result r and a correct tabulation proof Π. The output of the game is a bit γ, which depends on $\mathcal{A}$, $\mathbb{V}$, R, ρ and SimProof. This bit is defined as 1 if $r \neq \rho(\mathsf{Extract}(sk, BB))$ and 0 otherwise, where Extract is applied on the bulletin board by applying it to each individual ballot.

We say that a voting protocol for $(\mathbb{V}, R, \rho)$ as defined in Sect. 3.1 has strong consistency with respect to an extract algorithm Extract if the following conditions are satisfied:

(i) For any (pk, sk) in the image of Setup, for any vote $v \in \mathbb{V}$ it is satisfied that $\mathsf{Extract}(\mathsf{Vote}(pk, v)) = v$

(ii) For any p.p.t. adversary $\mathcal{A}$, the following advantage is negligible in the security parameter λ:

$$\mathbf{Adv}^{s-const}_{\mathbb{V},R,\rho,\mathsf{SimProof}}(\lambda) := \Pr[\gamma = 1]$$

3.4   Vote Validatability

We now present the definition of vote validatability, which is the first contribution of this paper. Simply stated, vote validatability states that a ballot which passes all validations *must* correspond to a valid vote. This is modeled by stating that the algorithm Extract, the one from the strong consistency property, never returns the error symbol $\bot$ on ballots for which ValidateBallot returns 1.

Vote validatability is given by the following game, which assumes that the election parameters $(\mathbb{V}, R, \rho)$ are given and uses an algorithm $\mathsf{Extract}(sk, b)$, which takes the election secret key and a ballot and outputs either a vote or the error symbol $\bot$ denoting an invalid vote.

1. **Setup phase.** The challenger runs $\mathsf{Setup}(1^\lambda)$ to obtain the election public and private keys (pk, sk), giving both of them to the adversary.
2. **Ballot**(b). The adversary submits a ballot b to the challenger.
3. **Output.** The output of the game is a bit δ, which depends on $\mathcal{A}$, $\mathbb{V}$, R, ρ and SimProof. This bit is defined as 1 if $\mathsf{Extract}(sk, b) = \bot$ and ValidateBallot $= 1$, and as 0 otherwise.

We say that a voting protocol for $(\mathbb{V}, R, \rho)$ as defined in Sect. 3.1 has vote validatability with respect to an extract algorithm Extract if the following conditions are satisfied:

(i) The voting protocol for $(\mathbb{V}, R, \rho)$ is strongly consistent with respect to Extract

(ii) For any p.p.t. adversary $\mathcal{A}$, the following advantage is negligible in the security parameter λ:

$$\mathbf{Adv}^{val}_{\mathbb{V},R,\rho,\mathsf{SimProof}}(\lambda) := \Pr[\delta = 1]$$

One implication of the definition given above is that, if the protocol has vote validatability, then it must be satisfied that, for any honestly-generated keys and any adversarially generated bulletin board, the result output by the tally can be obtained with only valid votes, $r \in \rho(\mathbb{V}^*)$.

We want to remark that vote validatability does not depend on the secrecy of the election secret key. However, it assumes that the Setup is run honestly. Even though this can be achieved by distributing the trust among multiple authorities, we have decided to give the definition assuming that there is only one authority for the sake of simplicity.

4 General Construction

4.1 Core Idea

In an electronic voting system, voters might be able to vote for more than one candidate, so we will consider a generic scenario in which votes are subsets of n distinct candidates from a larger but specified list of them. Treating the set of votes as the set of combinations of candidates would result in a terribly inefficient system. Therefore, each of the selected candidates will be encrypted independently. To prove that each candidate hidden in its respective encryption belongs to the list of candidates, we will use a set membership protocol based on digital signatures. In addition, we will use another technique to demonstrate that the candidates hidden in these encryptions are distinct.

The main idea of our new construction is inspired by the set membership protocol proposed by Camenisch et al. [6]. In that work, the authors construct a protocol for proving that a value is a commitment to a member of a pre-defined set. Their protocol works as follows. First, there is a trusted third party which produces signatures on each element of the set. Then, the prover constructs a zero-knowledge proof that she knows a signature on the committed value which verifies under the trusted third party's secret key. When the encryption scheme and the signature scheme being used have *nice* structural properties, the size of the proof is small and constant on the size of the set. In our case, the electoral authority will sign all candidates, and the voter will prove that she knows a signature on each selected candidate. However, this would still allow the voter to choose repeated candidates.

To detect this last situation, we use a technique inspired by the compact e-cash scheme given in [3]. In e-cash, detecting double-spending is essential, and this problem is similar to detecting repeated candidates in a vote. We will ask the voter to choose a pseudo-random permutation key and to publish the image of each chosen candidate under the pseudo-random permutation defined by such key. Given that the pseudo-random permutation is deterministic, if the voter chooses the same candidate more than once this will be detected by any entity. Finally, the prover needs to prove that the images of the pseudo-random permutation correspond to the candidates which she encrypted and that she knows a signature for each candidate.

In Sect. 4.2 we describe a generic protocol built on the mentioned crypto-graphic primitives. In general, computing non-interactive proofs of knowledge for such statements might be inefficient. In Sect. 5 we show that by instantiating the cryptographic primitives with adequate schemes the resulting protocol can be made as efficient as currently deployed e-voting systems.

4.2   Detailed Protocol

We begin by characterizing the set of allowed votes $\mathbb{V}$. Given a set of candidates $\mathcal{V}$, we define the set of votes as $\mathbb{V} = \{v \mid v \subset \mathcal{V} \wedge |v| = n\}$ for some fixed value of n. Here, we are assuming that a voter must vote for n candidates. We can handle blank votes and undervotes by designating n different blank candidates.

Our voting scheme uses a common setup generation algorithm, ComSetupGen, in order to generate some common information that might be shared among the rest of algorithms like, for instance, the description of a mathematical group. This will be useful for efficiency reasons.

It also uses, as building blocks, an encryption scheme (KeyGenEnc, Enc, Dec), a signature scheme (KeyGenSign, Sign, VerifySign), a PRP family $F_{(.)}$ and a NIZK proof system (GenCRS, Prove, VerifyProof) for the relation R defined as:

$$R = \{(x, w) \mid x = (C_1, \ldots, C_n, p_1, \ldots, p_n, pk_e, pk_s) \wedge$$
$$w = (\nu_1, \ldots, \nu_n, r_1, \ldots, r_n, \sigma_1, \ldots, \sigma_n, k) \wedge$$
$$(C_1, \ldots, C_n) = (\mathsf{Enc}(pk_e, \nu_1, r_1), \ldots, \mathsf{Enc}(pk_e, \nu_n, r_n)) \wedge$$
$$(\mathsf{VerifySign}(pk_s, \sigma_1, \nu_1), \ldots, \mathsf{VerifySign}(pk_s, \sigma_n, \nu_n)) = (1, \ldots, 1) \wedge$$
$$(p_1, \ldots, p_n) = (F_k(\nu_1), \ldots, F_k(\nu_n))\}$$

The algorithms are then defined as follows:

Setup(1^λ) starts by running the ComSetupGen algorithm to generate the common setup information cs, which will be used by GenCRS, KeyGenEnc and KeyGenSign. Then the algorithm runs GenCRS to generate the common reference string crs, KeyGenEnc to generate a pair of public/private encryption keys (pk_e, sk_e) and KeyGenSign to generate a pair of public/private signing keys (pk_s, sk_s), all of which may depend on the common setup information cs. This implicitly defines the message space for the encryption scheme M_e and the message space for the signature scheme M_s. We require that there exist two injective mappings η_1, η_2 such that $\eta_1(\mathcal{V}) \subset M_e$ and $\eta_2(\mathcal{V}) \subset M_s$. For the sake of simplicity we will assume that $\mathcal{V} = M_e = M_s$. Then, for each $\nu \in \mathcal{V}$, the algorithm produces a signature on it, $\sigma_\nu = \mathsf{Sign}(sk_s, \nu)$. The election public key is defined as $pk = (\mathsf{crs}, pk_e, pk_s, \{\sigma_\nu\}_{\nu \in \mathcal{V}})$ and the election secret key is defined as $sk = (pk, sk_e)$.

Vote(pk, v) parses pk as $(\mathsf{crs}, pk_e, pk_s, \{\sigma_\nu\}_{\nu \in \mathcal{V}})$ and v as $(\nu_1, \ldots, \nu_n)$. It then samples fresh randomness $(r_1, \ldots, r_n)$ and runs the $(\mathsf{Enc}(pk_e, \nu_1, r_1), \ldots, \mathsf{Enc}(pk_e, \nu_n, r_n))$ obtaining ciphertexts $C = (C_1, \ldots, C_n)$. Next, it selects a fresh random PRP key $k \in K_{PRP}$ and computes $(p_1, \ldots, p_n) = (F_k(\nu_1), \ldots, F_k(\nu_n))$ Finally, it computes a NIZK proof π for the statement $x = (C_1, \ldots, C_n,$

$p_1, \ldots, p_n, pk_e, pk_s)$ and witness $w = (\nu_1, \ldots, \nu_n, r_1, \ldots, r_n, \sigma_{\nu_1}, \ldots, \sigma_{\nu_n}, k)$. The ballot is defined as $b = (C, \pi, \{p_i\}_{i=1}^n)$.

ValidateBallot(BB, b) recovers pk from the bulletin board BB and parses it as $pk = (\text{crs}, pk_e, pk_s, \{\sigma_\nu\}_{\nu \in \mathcal{V}})$. Upon reception of a ballot b, which parses it as $b = (C, \pi, \{p_i\}_{i=1}^n)$, it is checked if in the bulletin board there is another ballot b' such that $C'_j = C_i$ for any $i, j \in \{1, \ldots, n\}$. If any such ballot is found, the algorithm stops and returns 0. Otherwise, the algorithm checks that the values $(p_1, \ldots, p_n)$ are distinct, returning 0 if they are not. If the values are distinct, the algorithm returns the output of VerifyProof using the statement $x = (C_1, \ldots, C_n, p_1, \ldots, p_n, pk_e, pk_s)$.

Tally(sk, BB) after individual ballot b ballot has been processed with ValidateBallot, during the tallying algorithm they are *decrypted* and the result function is computed. The *decryption procedure* is defined as follows.

1. $(\tilde{\nu}_1, \ldots, \tilde{\nu}_n) = (\text{Dec}(sk_e, C_1), \ldots, \text{Dec}(sk_e, C_n))$ is computed.
2. It is checked that $\tilde{\nu}_1, \ldots, \tilde{\nu}_n \in \mathcal{V}$.
3. It is checked that $(\tilde{\nu}_1, \ldots, \tilde{\nu}_n)$ are pairwise different.
4. If any of such checks fail, v is assigned the value $\perp$. Otherwise, v is assigned the value $(\tilde{\nu}_1, \ldots, \tilde{\nu}_n)$.

Then, ρ is applied to the resulting decryptions $\{v\}$. Note that, for each v, either $v \in \mathbb{V}$ or $v = \perp$, so ρ can be applied. The output of ρ is defined as the result and the proof of correct tabulation is defined to be the empty string ϵ

Note that, as the proof of correct tabulation is the empty string ϵ, VerifyTally can be the algorithm which returns 1 on any input.

Security of Our Scheme. Finally, we give the security properties fulfilled by our scheme. Let (KeyGenEnc, Enc, Dec) be a NM-CPA secure encryption scheme, let $F_{(.)}$ be a PRP family, let (GenCRS, Prove, VerifyProof) be a NIZK proof system, and let (KeyGenSign, Sign, VerifySign) be an EUF-CMA signature scheme. Let ρ be the counting function which outputs its inputs randomly permuted and let Extract be the *decryption procedure* of the Tally algorithm. Then, the protocol defined above (i) has ballot privacy, and (ii) has vote validatability for any $\mathbb{V}$, with respect to ρ, Extract. These two results are formally stated in Theorems 1 and 3, which are found along with their proof in Appendix A.

5   Concrete Instantiation

We now give a concrete instantiation of the voting protocol given above. In order to give the concrete instantiation, we just need to define which encryption scheme, signature scheme, pseudo-random permutation family and non-interactive zero-knowledge proof of knowledge scheme the protocol will use. With regard to our instantiation, the candidates will be encoded as n *randomly sampled* elements of $\mathbb{G}_1$.

The ComSetupGen algorithm will output a type-III bilinear group as a common setup cs, i.e., a tuple $(p, \mathbb{G}_1, \mathbb{G}_2, \mathbb{G}_T, e, G, H)$, where p is a prime, $\mathbb{G}_1, \mathbb{G}_2, \mathbb{G}_T$

are groups of order p, G, H generate $\mathbb{G}_1, \mathbb{G}_2$ respectively, e is a non-degenerate bilinear map and there is no efficiently computable homomorphism from $\mathbb{G}_1$ to $\mathbb{G}_2$ or viceversa. Besides, the Decisional Diffie-Hellman assumption [18] holds in $\mathbb{G}_1$ and in $\mathbb{G}_2$.

Encryption Scheme. The protocol will use the Signed ElGamal [17] encryption scheme in $\mathbb{G}_1$, which is NM-CPA secure [5].

Signature Scheme. The signature scheme that we will use is the structure-preserving signature scheme given in [1]. A structure-preserving signature scheme is characterized by having messages, signatures and verification keys to be group element and having a verification procedure that only consists on evaluating product-pairing equations.

The signature works as follows. On a common setup $(p, \mathbb{G}_1, \mathbb{G}_2, \mathbb{G}_T, e, G, H)$, an extra random element $X \in \mathbb{G}_1$ is added to the public parameters. The secret key is a value $v \in \mathbb{Z}_p$ and the public key is computed as $V = H^v$. The signature on $M \in \mathbb{G}_1$ is then $(R, S, T) = (H^r, M^{\frac{v}{r}}, S^{\frac{v}{r}} G^{\frac{1}{r}})$ for a random r. To verify a signature it is checked if $e(S, R) = e(M, V)e(X, H)$ and $e(T, R) = e(S, V)e(G, H)$.

Pseudo-Random Permutation Family. We will define the set of candidates, $\mathcal{V}$, as a set containing n randomly sampled group elements from $\mathbb{G}_1$. This allows us to define the pseudo-random function $F_k : \mathbb{G}_1 \rightarrow \mathbb{G}_1$ where $F_k(g) = g^k$ and $k \in \mathbb{Z}_p^*$. As we assume that the Decisional Diffie-Hellman assumption holds in $\mathbb{G}_1$, this function family is pseudo-random when we restrict the input to $\mathcal{V}$.[3]

Non-Interactive Zero-Knowledge Proof of Knowledge. Finally, we have to give the NIZKPK scheme that we will use. We will use the Groth-Sahai Proof System [14] but we will frame it as a Commit-and-Prove scheme as done in [10]. A Commit-and-Prove scheme is similar to a NIZKPK scheme with the difference that a Commit-and-Prove scheme explicitly splits the process of committing to secret values and proving statements related to such values. In addition, [10] introduces *type-based* commitments, where the type indicates how the commitment should be computed. For example, the type "encryption" indicates that the secret value should be encrypted, as opposed to using the more expensive commitment operation.

We first remark that the encryption and signature schemes must use the same algebraic groups that the NIZKPK scheme. Therefore, at the beginning of the Setup algorithm, the common setup $(p, \mathbb{G}_1, \mathbb{G}_2, \mathbb{G}_T, e, G, H)$ is generated and will be used to generate the crs and the keys of the encryption and signature schemes. There is no loss of generality since the groups are generated in the same way in ComSetupGen and, respectively, in GenCRS, KeyGenEnc and KeyGenSign.

In addition, the Commit-and-Prove scheme given in [10] allows us to treat the ElGamal encryption of a value as a commitment of type "encryption", where the

---

[3] Technically, it is a Pseudo-Random Function [12] from $\mathcal{V}$ to $\mathbb{G}_1$ where $F_{(\cdot)}$ is injective for any $k \in \mathbb{Z}_p^*$. Therefore, an adversary restricted to only evaluate the function in points from $\mathcal{V}$ can not distinguish those evaluations from randomly sampled elements, which is sufficient for the security reduction to work.

randomness used for the encryption is the randomness used for the commitment. The encryption scheme is thus embedded into the NIZKPK scheme, instead of being an independent scheme, as assumed in the general construction. However, we can still adapt the security proof to keep it sound as we now describe.

We will consider the conjunction of two proofs. The first one is a zero-knowledge proof for the language defined by the relation

$$R_1 = \{(x,w)|\, x = (C_1, \ldots, C_n, pk_e, pk_s) \wedge$$
$$w = (\nu_1, \ldots, \nu_n, r_1, \ldots, r_n, \sigma_1, \ldots, \sigma_n) \wedge$$
$$(C_1, \ldots, C_n) = (\mathsf{Enc}(pk_e, \nu_1, r_1), \ldots, \mathsf{Enc}(pk_e, \nu_n, r_n)) \wedge$$
$$(\mathsf{VerifySign}(pk_s, \sigma_1, \nu_1), \ldots, \mathsf{VerifySign}(pk_s, \sigma_n, \nu_n)) = (1, \ldots, 1)\}$$

For this proof, the prover computes a commitment to each value of the signature and builds proofs for satisfiability of the verification equations.

We now need to see that the Commit-and-Prove scheme in [10] is Zero-Knowledge for the language defined by R_1. In other words, we need to see that exists a simulator. As seen in [10], this reduces to check that there are no terms in pairing product equations which prevent simulation. Those terms are pairings where in each side of the pairing there is either a public, non-equivocable value[4] or a value which commitment type is "encryption". Going back to the verification equations of the signature scheme, we see that there are none of these terms. Therefore, there exists a simulator for the statement defined by R_1.

The second zero-knowledge proof is defined by the relation

$$R_2 = \{(x,w)|\, x = (C_1, \ldots, C_n, p_1, \ldots, p_n, pk_e) \wedge$$
$$w = (\nu_1, \ldots, \nu_n, r_1, \ldots, r_n, k) \wedge$$
$$(C_1, \ldots, C_n) = (\mathsf{Enc}(pk_e, \nu_1, r_1), \ldots, \mathsf{Enc}(pk_e, \nu_n, r_n)) \wedge$$
$$(p_1, \ldots, p_n) = (F_k(\nu_1), \ldots, F_k(\nu_n))\}$$

For the proof for the relation R_2, we will consider the multi-exponentiation equations $\nu_i^k = p_i$, where ν_i and k are secret values. The prover computes a commitment on k and builds a proof for satisfiability of this equation using C_i as a commitment to ν_i. Both the commitments on the signatures and the proofs will be included in π. As noted in [10], multi-exponentiation equations are always simulatable.

Note that Groth-Sahai proofs are not extractable for exponents such as k. However, the proof of our scheme having vote validatability only needs to extract the values $\nu_1, \ldots, \nu_n$ and their corresponding signatures.

5.1 Efficiency

Each Signed ElGamal encryption consists of 2 elements in $\mathbb{G}_1$ and 2 elements in $\mathbb{Z}_p$. Each value p_i consists of a single element in $\mathbb{G}_1$.

---

[4] In [10] the authors define equivocable values as the generators of the group. However, it can be seen that values for which the simulator knows the discrete logarithm w.r.t. the generator of the group are also equivocable.

When looking at the proof π, we have to consider both the proof for the language defined by R_1 and the language defined for R_2. For the proof for the language defined by R_1, we have that in the structure-preserving signature of [1] each signature consists of three elements. A Groth-Sahai commitment on a single element consists on 2 elements in $\mathbb{G}_1$. As we have to commit to n signatures, the number of elements is $6n$ elements in $\mathbb{G}_1$. Furthermore, there are two verification equations per signature and a Groth-Sahai proof for a single of such equation consists of 4 elements in $\mathbb{G}_1$ and 4 elements in $\mathbb{G}_2$. Therefore, the proofs for all the verification equations consist on $8n$ elements in $\mathbb{G}_1$ and $8n$ elements in $\mathbb{G}_2$.

When considering the proof for the language defined by R_2, we have to commit to k, which has a cost of 2 elements in $\mathbb{G}_2$, and compute the Groth-Sahai proofs. A Groth-Sahai proof for an equation of the form $\nu^k = p$ consists on 2 elements in $\mathbb{G}_1$ and 4 elements in $\mathbb{G}_2$, and we have to compute n of them.

In total, we get that a ballot consists of $19n$ elements in $\mathbb{G}_1$, $12n+2$ elements in $\mathbb{G}_2$ and $2n$ elements in $\mathbb{Z}_p$. The cost is linear in n (the number of candidates encoded in each vote). Moreover, the constant factor is relatively small.

6   Conclusions

We have formalized the definition of vote validatability in order to give an accurate meaning to *avoid voters from casting invalid votes*, both if done in purpose or as a consequence of a software bug. Besides creating a construction based on generic building blocks and general-purpose zero-knowledge proofs, we have provided a concrete instantiation. We have shown that its efficiency fits into the device's computational capacity of voters in current elections.

There are other alternatives which may improve the performance of our construction achieving the same security properties. First, a cryptographic accumulator could be used to prove that candidates are valid. This approach could reduce the length of the ballot but would make the scheme to rely on the Random Oracle Model. Second, much of the cost of the ballot comes from the NIZKPK proof for the language defined by R_1. A choice of a different structure-preserving signature scheme might improve the efficiency of our system.

A   Proofs of Security Theorems

We prove the security for the construction given in Sect. 4.2.

Theorem 1. *Let* (KeyGenEnc, Enc, Dec) *be a NM-CPA secure encryption scheme, let* $F_{(.)}$ *be a PRP family and let* (GenCRS, Prove, VerifyProof) *be a NIZK proof system. Then, the protocol defined in Sect. 4.2 has ballot privacy.*

Proof. Recall that privacy is defined as the indistinguishability of two experiments which depend on a bit β. We will refer to them as Exp_β for $\beta \in \{0, 1\}$.

Let $\mathsf{SimVote}_1(pk, v)$ be the Vote algorithm of the protocol given in Sect. 4.2 but, instead of using the Prove algorithm to generate π it uses the SimProve algorithm. Moreover, let $\mathsf{SimVote}_2(pk, v)$ to be the $\mathsf{SimVote}_1$ algorithm but, instead of using a PRP it uses a truly random permutation.

Consider experiments $\mathsf{Exp}_{\beta,0} = \mathsf{Exp}_{\beta}$, $\mathsf{Exp}_{\beta,1}$ to be the experiment which are the same as $\mathsf{Exp}_{\beta,0}$ but the challenger runs SimGenCRS instead of GenCRS and it runs SimProve instead of Prove. Finally, let $\mathsf{Exp}_{\beta,2}$ be the experiments which are identical to $\mathsf{Exp}_{\beta,1}$ but in which the challenger uses a truly random function instead of a PRP in order to cast ballots.

Due to the zero-knowledge property of the NIZK proof system, $\mathsf{Exp}_{\beta,0}$ and $\mathsf{Exp}_{\beta,1}$ are indistinguishable for $\beta \in \{0, 1\}$. Besides, $\mathsf{Exp}_{\beta,1}$ and $\mathsf{Exp}_{\beta,2}$ are indistinguishable for $\beta \in \{0, 1\}$ due to the pseudo-randomness of the PRP. Now the only thing left is to prove that $\mathsf{Exp}_{0,2}$ and $\mathsf{Exp}_{1,2}$ are indistinguishable.

Consider the Enc2Vote scheme [5], where the result function ρ is the multiset function. The scheme is defined as follows: the Setup algorithm runs KeyGenEnc to produce a public key pk_e and a secret key sk_e. Then, pk is set to be pk_e and sk is set to be (pk_e, sk_e). The Vote algorithm takes as input a vote v and a public key pk_e and outputs b defined by $b = \mathsf{Enc}(pk_e, v, r)$ for some fresh randomness r. ValidateBallot looks if the ballot b already appears on the bulletin board BB: it returns 1 if it does already appear and 0 otherwise. Tally decrypts all ballots b on the bulletin board obtaining votes v and evaluates $r = \rho(v)$, outputting an empty proof of correct tabulation. Observe that Enc2Vote implicitly assumes that $\mathbb{V} = M_e$, the message space of the encryption scheme. As shown in [5], the following is satisfied:

Theorem 2. *Let* (KeyGenEnc, Enc, Dec) *be an NM-CPA secure encryption scheme. Then,* Enc2Vote *has ballot privacy.*

Finally, we reduce the privacy of our scheme to the privacy of Enc2Vote.

Lemma 1. *Let* $\mathcal{A}^1$ *be a p.p.t. adversary that interacts which challenger* $\mathcal{C}$ *and outputs a bit* $\alpha^{\mathcal{A}^1}$ *such that* $|\Pr[\alpha^{\mathcal{A}^1} = 1|\mathsf{Exp}_{0,2}] - \Pr[\alpha^{\mathcal{A}^1} = 1|\mathsf{Exp}_{1,2}]|$ *is non-negligible. Then, there exists an adversary* $\mathcal{A}^2$ *that breaks the ballot privacy property of the* Enc2Vote *scheme.*

In our reduction, $\mathcal{A}^1$ will interact with $\mathcal{A}^2$, which will act as the challenger for $\mathcal{A}^1$. At the same time, $\mathcal{A}^2$ will interact with the privacy challenger $\mathcal{C}$. The reduction is as follows:

In the **Setup** phase, $\mathcal{C}$ will run ComSetupGen, outputing cs and posting it to the bulletin board. It will also run KeyGenEnc, keeping the private key for itself and publishing the public key pk_e to the bulletin board. Then, A^2 will run the GenCRS and the KeyGenSign algorithms and will produce signatures on each voting option, posting all the information to the bulletin board.

In the **Voting** phase, when $\mathcal{A}^1$ submits a **Vote** query, A^2 will submit n **Vote** queries to $\mathcal{C}$, one for each pair of candidates. The challenger $\mathcal{C}$ will answer with n pairs of ciphertexts $(C_{0,1}, \ldots, C_{0,n})$ and $(C_{1,1}, \ldots, C_{1,n})$. A^2 will then sample two pairs of random values $(p_{0,1}, \ldots, p_{0,n})$ and $(p_{1,1}, \ldots, p_{1,n})$ of the target space of the PRP. Finally, it will create ballots $b_0 = (C_{0,1}, \ldots, C_{0,n}, p_{0,1}, \ldots, p_{0,n}, \pi_0)$ and $b_1 = (C_{1,1}, \ldots, C_{1,n}, p_{1,1}, \ldots, p_{1,n}, \pi_1)$ where π_0 and π_1 will be simulated. $\mathcal{A}^2$ will post these ballots to the respective bulletin boards. Finally, when $\mathcal{A}^1$ submits a **Ballot**(b) query, $\mathcal{A}^2$ will run the ValidateBallot algorithm and will create a **Ballot**(b') for $\mathcal{C}$ with $b' = (C_1, \ldots, C_n)$ from b.

It is straightforward to see that the output of $\mathcal{A}^2$ in its interaction with $\mathcal{A}^1$ is correctly distributed, which implies that the reduction is sound.

Theorem 3. *Let ρ be the counting function which outputs its inputs randomly permuted. Let* (GenCRS, Prove, VerifyProof) *be a NIZKPK proof system and let* (KeyGenSign, Sign, VerifySign) *be an EUF-CMA signature scheme. Let* Extract *be the decryption procedure of the* Tally *algorithm of the protocol defined in Sect. 4.2. Then, the protocol defined in Sect. 4.2 has vote validatability for any* $\mathbb{V}$, *with respect to ρ,* Extract.

Proof. Strong consistency of the protocol follows by construction. Therefore we only need to show that, on correctly generated (pk, sk) no adversary can construct a ballot b such that ValidateBallot returns 1 but Extract returns $\perp$.

Let Exp_0 be the vote validatability experiment and let Exp_1 be identical to Exp_0 but instead of using GenCRS the challenger uses ExtGenCRS. These two experiments are indistinguishable by the properties of the NIZKPK. Now assume that an adversary $\mathcal{A}^1$ is able to output a ballot b in the experiment Exp_1 such that ValidateBallot $= 1$ and Extract$(sk, b) = \perp$. Then, we build an adversary $\mathcal{A}^2$ which breaks the EUF-CMA of the signature scheme.

The reduction is straightforward: $\mathcal{A}^2$, interacting with an EUF-CMA challenger asks for signatures on $\{\nu\}_{\nu \in \mathcal{V}}$. Then, it interacts with $\mathcal{A}^1$, posing as a vote validatability challenger. It runs all the algorithms as in the protocol but uses ExtGenCRS, keeping the trapdoor key tk for itself, and using the answers from the EUF-CMA challenger as the signatures on the voting options. When $\mathcal{A}^1$ outputs a ballot b, $\mathcal{A}^2$ uses Extract on π to obtain a witness $w = (\tilde{\nu}_1, \ldots, \tilde{\nu}_n, r_1, \ldots, r_n, \sigma_{\tilde{\nu}_1}, \ldots, \sigma_{\tilde{\nu}_n}, k))$ such that $(x, w) \in R$. This means that VerifySign$(pk_s, \sigma_{\tilde{\nu}_i}, \tilde{\nu}_i) = 1$ for $i \in \{1, \ldots, n\}$. Extract(sk, b) might return $\perp$ either because (i) some $\mathsf{Dec}(sk_e, C_i) = \perp$, (ii) some $\tilde{\nu}_i = \tilde{\nu}_j$ for $i \neq j$ or (iii) some $\tilde{\nu}_i \notin \mathcal{V}$. However, (i) and (ii) are ruled out due to w being a valid witness, so the only possibility is (iii). Then, $\mathcal{A}^2$ can submit $(\tilde{\nu}_i, \sigma_{\tilde{\nu}_i})$ as its EUF-CMA forgery.

References

1. Abe, M., Groth, J., Ohkubo, M., Tibouchi, M.: Unified, minimal and selectively randomizable structure-preserving signatures. In: Lindell, Y. (ed.) TCC 2014. LNCS, vol. 8349, pp. 688–712. Springer, Heidelberg (2014)
2. Adida, B.: Encrypting your vote in javascript. Electronic Voting Technology Workshop - EVT/WOTE, August 2011. http://assets.adida.net/presentations/2011-08-08-helios-evt-rump.pdf
3. Belenkiy, M., Chase, M., Kohlweiss, M., Lysyanskaya, A.: Compact E-Cash and simulatable VRFs revisited. In: Shacham, H., Waters, B. (eds.) Pairing 2009. LNCS, vol. 5671, pp. 114–131. Springer, Heidelberg (2009)

4. Bernhard, D., Cortier, V., Galindo, D., Pereira, O., Warinschi, B.: A comprehensive analysis of game-based ballot privacy definitions. IACR Cryptology ePrint Archive 2015, 255 (2015). http://eprint.iacr.org/2015/255

5. Bernhard, D., Pereira, O., Warinschi, B.: On necessary and sufficient conditions for private ballot submission. IACR Cryptology ePrint Archive 2012, 236 (2012). http://dblp.uni-trier.de/db/journals/iacr/iacr2012.html#BernhardPW12. Informal Publication

6. Camenisch, J.L., Chaabouni, R., shelat, a: Efficient protocols for set membership and range proofs. In: Pieprzyk, J. (ed.) ASIACRYPT 2008. LNCS, vol. 5350, pp. 234–252. Springer, Heidelberg (2008)

7. Chaum, D.: Untraceable electronic mail, return addresses and digital pseudonyms. In: Gritzalis, D. (ed.) Secure Electronic Voting, Advances in Information Security, vol. 7, pp. 211–219. Springer, New York (2003). http://dx.doi.org/10.1007/978-1-4615-0239-5_14

8. Cramer, R., Gennaro, R., Schoenmakers, B.: A secure and optimally efficient multi-authority election scheme. Eur. Trans. Telecommun. 8(5), 481–490 (1997). http://dx.doi.org/10.1002/ett.4460080506

9. Damgård, I., Jurik, M., Nielsen, J.B.: A generalization of Paillier's public-key system with applications to electronic voting. Int. J. Inf. Secur. 9(6), 371–385 (2010)

10. Escala, A., Groth, J.: Fine-tuning Groth-Sahai proofs. In: Krawczyk, H. (ed.) PKC 2014. LNCS, vol. 8383, pp. 630–649. Springer, Heidelberg (2014)

11. Gjøsteen, K.: Analysis of an internet voting protocol. Cryptology ePrint Archive, Report 2010/380 (2010). http://eprint.iacr.org/

12. Goldreich, O., Goldwasser, S., Micali, S.: How to construct random functions. J. ACM 33(4), 792–807 (1986). http://doi.acm.org/10.1145/6490.6503

13. Goldwasser, S., Micali, S., Rivest, R.L.: A digital signature scheme secure against adaptive chosen-message attacks. SIAM J. Comput. 17(2), 281–308 (1988). http://dx.doi.org/10.1137/0217017

14. Groth, J., Sahai, A.: Efficient noninteractive proof systems for bilinear groups. SIAM J. Comput. 41(5), 1193–1232 (2012)

15. Luby, M., Rackoff, C.: How to construct pseudo-random permutations from Pseudo-random functions. In: Williams, H.C. (ed.) CRYPTO 1985. LNCS, vol. 218, pp. 447–447. Springer, Heidelberg (1986)

16. Santis, A.D., Persiano, G.: Zero-knowledge proofs of knowledge without interaction (extended abstract). In: FOCS, pp. 427–436. IEEE Computer Society (1992)

17. Schnorr, C.-P., Jakobsson, M.: Security of signed ElGamal encryption. In: Okamoto, T. (ed.) ASIACRYPT 2000. LNCS, vol. 1976, p. 73. Springer, Heidelberg (2000)

18. Tsiounis, Y., Yung, M.: On the security of ElGamal based encryption. In: Imai, H., Zheng, Y. (eds.) PKC 1998. LNCS, vol. 1431, p. 117. Springer, Heidelberg (1998)

Making Code Voting Secure Against Insider Threats Using Unconditionally Secure MIX Schemes and Human PSMT Protocols

Yvo Desmedt[1,2]($\boxtimes$) and Stelios Erotokritou[1,3]

[1] Department of Computer Science, The University of Texas at Dallas, Richardson, USA
{y.desmedt,s.erotokritou}@cs.ucl.ac.uk
[2] Department of Computer Science, University College London, London, UK
[3] CaSToRC, The Cyprus Institute, Nicosia, Cyprus

Abstract. It is clear to the public that when it comes to privacy, computers and "secure" communication over the Internet cannot fully be trusted. Chaum introduced code voting as a solution for using a possibly infected-by-malware device to cast a vote in an electronic voting application. He trusted the mail system. However, a conspiracy between the mail system and the recipient of the cast ballots breaks privacy. Considering a t-bounded passive adversary, we remove the trust in the mail. We propose both single and multi-seat elections, using PSMT protocols (SCN 2012) where with the help of visual aids, humans can carry out mod10 addition correctly with a 99 % degree of accuracy. We introduce an unconditionally secure MIX based on the combinatorics of set systems.

Keywords: Voting systems · Internet voting · Information theoretic anonymity · Private and secure message transmission · Computer system diversity

1 Introduction

Electronic voting over the Internet enables to cast votes from *any* computer connected to physical Internet accessible location. There is no need to be physically present at a polling station, a disadvantage of booth based electronic voting systems developed by the cryptographic community [8].

Even though secure Internet voting is in its infancy, many countries and organizations are considering adoption or have already done so, such as Switzerland [1] and Estonia [27] where participation increased by 17 % [28]. Similarly, after IACR used the Helios Internet voting system [24], voting increased from 20 % to around 30 %–40 %.

Home computers are vulnerable to security attacks and are easy to hack. So, experts agree that achieving secure Internet voting will be even more difficult

---

A part of this work was done while being, part time, at RCIS/AIST, Japan.

© Springer International Publishing Switzerland 2015
R. Haenni et al. (Eds.): VoteID 2015, LNCS 9269, pp. 110–126, 2015.
DOI: 10.1007/978-3-319-22270-7_7

than booth-based electronic voting (see e.g., [2,22]). Modern browsers are vulnerable to attacks - as demonstrated against Helios 2.0 Internet voting in [19]. Already in 2001 Chaum proposed a breakthrough solution called "code voting" [6], where one can use a possibly hacked computer.

In code voting, a voter receives through the *postal mail* a long enough unique code for every candidate. Voters just enter the code corresponding to the candidate of their choice. Chaum's approach assumes the postal mail to be secure from a reliability and privacy viewpoint. Unfortunately, a collaboration of the postal service with the returning officer[1] may allow for the anonymity of all votes to be broken by divulging the identity of voters to whom specific voting codes were delivered. Other problems that relate to active attacks against code voting are described in [14].

In Chaum [7] MIX-networks, proposed for anonymity, senders input encrypted messages. The MIX-network outputs each message to all recipients (see Sect. 2.1 for a survey). Their security is conditional. No conditional secure cryptosystem designed so far has withstood cryptanalysis for more than 300 years. Quantum computers will undermine computational voting schemes cryptographers have proposed, in particular these based on ElGamal. This motivates an unconditionally secure voting scheme. Note that for many goals other than voting, unconditionally secure solutions have already been proposed.

The importance of requiring unconditional vote security is further highlighted with the following example:

> In 2020 Alice turns 18 and votes using a popular ElGamal based electronic voting scheme. 50 years later, Alice is a candidate for president of the USA. Imagine that in 2070 USA politics is going through a new McCarthy witch hunt. Unfortunately for Alice, ElGamal security has since been broken. The newspapers find that Alice voted for the what is then considered the "*wrong*" party!

We propose an *unconditional secure* MIX construction with t insiders corrupted by a passive adversary, which cannot cause deviation of protocol execution in any way. Our solution considering an active adversary will be presented in a future full version of this paper.

To deal with foreign governments who might have hacked hardware and software, we employ a *diversity of computing systems*. We consider the t-bounded computationally unlimited adversary to be capable of taking control of a total of at most t nodes between the vote authority and the voters which includes nodes in the MIX-network, nodes in the communication network or voters computational devices (through malware).

Considering a t-bounded adversary we emphasize the following:

Important Statement 1. *As shown in [20], when the number of corrupted nodes is at most t, the minimum number of disjoint paths to allow for private communication between a sender and a receiver is $t + 1$.*

---

[1] A returning officer oversees elections in one or more constituencies [34].

Corollary 1. *Because of the above, voters will have to use a number of computing devices to securely receive (or dually send) their voting codes.*

Note that *nowadays, many people in developed countries can have effortless access to more than one device* such as PC's, laptops, smartphones and tablets. These devices could be owned or from friends and relatives, or available to the public (such as at libraries). These devices can be connected to a communication network in a different manner (Internet or cellular), using different providers and run different operating systems.

The protocols in [4] use humans and avoid relying on a fully trusted computer (see also [18]). We follow a similar approach in the context of Internet voting. We propose unconditionally secure Internet code voting solutions for single seat and multi-seat elections, both user friendly, to guarantee high accuracy.[2]

Our solution can also be used for other established code voting schemes as it is a way of removing the use of a possibly untrusted mail system and transmitting the voting codes securely, reliably and anonymously to voters.

The text is organized as follows. Background and relevant previous work are presented in Sect. 2. In Sect. 3 a high level description of the protocol is given and we identify the required cryptographic tools. In Sect. 4 we provide a simplified version of the MIX private and anonymous communication protocol. This is used in Sect. 5 in a more efficient manner where we present private and anonymous communication protocols for the transmission of voting codes to voters for single seat and multi seat elections. Section 6 presents the electronic code voting protocol.

2 Background and Previous Related Work

2.1 Previous Related Work

MIX-networks can be constructed using a shuffle (permutation). One way of achieving this [26,32] is by using approaches which are based on zero-knowledge arguments [21,35]. In [15] the use of zero-knowledge was avoided. MIX-networks based on zero-knowledge arguments can be used in electronic voting protocols - as proposed in [23]. Earlier work [31] similarly used shuffles in electronic voting based on zero-knowledge proofs. Other work on MIX-networks includes the work of Abe in [3]. Such constructions are based on computational assumptions which only allow for *conditional security*. The work we present is based on the stronger model of *unconditional security*.

Anonymity in practice is difficult to achieve. One proposed implementation was that of [25] but it was shown to be insecure in [33].

In EVOTE2014, [30] addressed a similar problem to our work. The solution though achieves conditional security and the authors consider the adversary to be present in the MIX network only. This does not take into account the possible

---

[2] The work of [5] is independent and their MIX servers are different. For a further comparison, see [14].

presence of malware upon the tablets with which voters will use to cast their votes. Passive malware could possibly identify to an adversary how someone voted, whereas active malware could alter the way someone votes - thus rigging the result of an election.

A voting scheme similar to the one we propose which achieves information theoretic security and requires the voter to carry out modular addition is that presented in [29]. Contrary to the voting scheme proposed in this paper, the work of [29] is *not* an Internet voting scheme as it requires voters to cast their votes at a polling station.

The work of [11] describes an election scheme which requires computational modular exponentiation operations to be carried out by voters. These operations require software or hardware. Furthermore, public key-cryptography is used, meaning that the security properties achieved are computational and not information theoretic - as achieved in our scheme.

2.2 Message Transmission Security Properties

We define security properties considering a setting where a single receiver S is connected to m number of senders $(r_1, \cdots, r_m)$ over a possibly corrupt underlying network. For formal definitions, see [17].

(Perfectly) Correct - When the receiver accepts a message, it was sent by a sender S.

(Perfectly) Reliable - When a sender S transmits a message, this message will be received by the receiver with probability 1.

(Perfectly) Private - Only the designated receiver(s) can read a message transmitted by S. i.e., for any coalition of t parties, their probability of correctly determining a message is the same whether the coalition is given their transmission view or not.

(Perfect) Security - Means perfect correctness, perfect reliability and perfect privacy.

(Perfectly) Anonymous - Considering the single receiver wants to receive m different messages - one from each m number of senders, perfect anonymity is achieved when for any coalition of t parties, their probability of correctly determining the sender of *any* message is the same whether the coalition observes the transmission view or not. In the context of Internet voting, perfect anonymity is achieved when the voting protocol used does not facilitate any party in the voting process to correlate any cast vote to a specific voter with greater probability than any other.

2.3   Existential Honesty

Some of our ideas use concepts of *existential honesty*, defined in [15] as:

> "It is possible to divide the MIX servers into blocks, which guarantee that one block is free of dishonest MIX servers, assuming the number of dishonest MIX servers is bounded by t."

To achieve this, [15] defined and used the following[3]:

Definition 1 [10]. *A set system is a pair* $(X, \mathcal{B})$*, where* $X \triangleq \{1, 2, \ldots, m\}$ *and* $\mathcal{B}$ *is a collection of blocks* $B_i \subset X$ *with* $i = 1, 2, \ldots, b$.

Definition 2 [15]. $(X, \mathcal{B})$ *is an* (m, b, t)*-verifiers set system if* $|X| = m$*,* $|B_i| = t + 1$ *for* $i = 1, 2, \ldots, b$ *and for any subset* $F \subset X$ *with* $|F| \leq t$*, there exists a* $B_i \in \mathcal{B}$ *such that* $F \cap B_i = \emptyset$.

We *assume that private channels* connect respective MIX servers of corresponding blocks (i.e. MIX server $MIX_{k,i}$ and $MIX_{k+1,j}$ are connected with a private channel). We also assume such channels between the receiver and $MIX_{1,i}$ and similarly, between $MIX_{b,i}$ and the sender.

2.4   Human Perfectly Secure Message Transmission Protocols

Perfectly secure message transmission (PSMT) protocols where the sender or receiver is a human were introduced in [18]. In such protocols it is assumed that the human receiver does *not* have access to a trusted device since these may be faulty and/or infected with malware. Because the receiver is a human, such protocols aim to achieve perfectly secure message transmission (PSMT) in a computationally efficient and computationally simple manner. It is also important that the amount of information and operations the human receiver should process be kept to a minimum.

Addition mod10 was used by humans in these protocols [18] to reconstruct the secret message of the communication protocol from received shares through addition mod10. The idea of using addition mod10 for human computable functions was also used in [4] but within a different security context. By regarding in [18] $Z_{10}(+)$ as a subgroup of S_{10} the operation became very reliable for humans to perform. Experiments have shown that given clear, correct and precise instructions, coupled with visual aids, allowed for the correct usage of these protocols by a very high percentage of human participants.

2.5   Secure Multiparty Computation in Black-Box Groups

Black box multiparty computation protocols against a passive adversary for non-Abelian group have been presented in [9] and in [13] through the use of a

---

[3] See also [18, Sect. 2.3] for an extensive description of set systems and how these relate to covering designs.

t-reliable n-coloring admissible planar graph. These papers studied in particular the existence of secure n-party protocols to compute the n-product function $f_G(x_1, \cdots, x_n) := x_1 \cdot \ldots \cdot x_n$ where each participant is given the private input x_i from some non-Abelian group G where $n \geq 2t + 1$. It was assumed that the parties are only allowed to perform black-box operations in the finite group G, i.e., the group operation $((x, y) \mapsto x \cdot y)$, the group inversion $(x \mapsto x^{-1})$ and the uniformly random group sampling $(x \in_R G)$.

3 Secure Code Voting with Distributed Security

Assuming the reader is familiar with [6] we present a high level description of the secure code voting protocol we will present in this paper.

3.1 High Level Description

We call Code Generation Entity (CGE) the entity which is responsible for creating the codes with which voters will cast their votes. These codes are unique and are sent to the voters so that each of these codes is used only once for the *whole* election. For single seat elections each voter receives as many codes as there are candidates. For multi-seat elections each voter receives a single permutation - which is a permutation of the alphabetical ordering of the candidates. After these codes pass through a MIX network, they will be sent to voters using PSMT. Voters will receive each share using a different device, identify the shares which correspond to the candidate of their choice and reconstruct using human computation this voting code. To cast their vote, voters will send this code back to the CGE via the MIX servers, which perform inverse operations. For each of the received cast codes, the CGE will identify the candidate the code corresponds and will tally up the cast votes for each candidate.

Our protocol does *not* use the mail system for the delivery of voting codes to voters, but instead these are sent by the CGE to voters over a MIX network and using PSMT. Similarly, cast votes will be sent by voters to the CGE over a network as explained in Sect. 6.3.

3.2 Required Cryptographic Tools

The process *should not* facilitate the CGE (or any t other passive parties) to identify that a specific voter cast a particular vote given that *a number of underlying network nodes may be corrupt*. The use of secret sharing should also allow any protocol to prevent any t parties (apart from voters) learning voting codes, otherwise anonymity of votes could be broken.

Human PSMT protocols as presented in [18] are employed. We rely on the feasibility tests performed which confirm that humans can perform these basic operations. We use the secret sharing scheme friendly to humans as presented in [18, Sect. 2.2] which guarantees perfect privacy unconditionally. Except for the voters computing the codes from the shares they receive, all other computations are carried out by computers.

4 Transmit and Reply Protocol

In this section we present the first of the required primitives - a perfectly private and perfectly anonymous network communication protocol. For didactic purposes, the simplest form of our proposed protocol will be presented - with more efficient constructions described later.

Suppose that we have a single receiver and v senders each of whom needs to receive a secret one time pad so as to send a secret back to the receiver in an interactive anonymous way[4].

We assume the passive adversary controls at most t MIX servers with each MIX server being involved in one mixing. $t + 1$ blocks of MIX servers will be required - denoted as $B_1, \ldots, B_{t+1}$, with each block consisting of $t + 1$ MIX servers and we use $B_k = \{MIX_{k,1}, MIX_{k,2}, \ldots, MIX_{k,t+1}\}$ to identify MIX servers of the kth block and call $MIX_{k,1}$ "B_k's leader".

4.1 Protocol Main Idea

The receiver will share each of the v one-time pads into $t + 1$ shares using XOR with each share given to a corresponding MIX server (i.e. one of the $t+1$ servers) in B_1. The shares of the ith one-time pad and those of the jth one-time pad might be transposed and will also be altered. To guarantee shares of the same pad stay together, the transpositions and alterations are chosen by the block leader.

After the last MIX operation, the final block of MIX servers delivers the shares to the senders which reconstruct the received and altered one-time pad sent by the receiver. Each sender will then XOR a secret message with the received altered one-time pad and send the result to the receiver over the MIX network. During this reverse transmission, the inverse alterations will be applied by each block leader.

By XOR'ing the one time pad initially sent out by the receiver, the secret message sent by each sender can be obtained by the receiver.

4.2 The MIX Communication Protocol - 1A: Receiver to Sender Transmission

We now present the steps in the MIX communication protocol for the transmission of the one-time pads from the receiver to the set of senders.

Protocol 1. *Private and Anonymous Communication Protocol.*

Step 1. Let π_i^1 be the ith one-time pad (where $1 \leq i \leq v$). The receiver shares each π_i^1 into $t + 1$ shares $\pi_{i,j}^1 \in F_{2^l}$ using XOR (where $1 \leq j \leq t + 1$) and privately sends $\pi_{i,j}^1$ to the corresponding MIX $MIX_{1,j}$ in block B_1.

---

[4] The dual problem is that instead of having v senders, we have v receivers and one sender. Obviously a solution for the first provides a similar solution for the second.

Step 2. The *leader* of B_1 (we call $MIX_{1,1}$) informs all others MIX servers in B_1 how they have to permute the i-index of all above $\pi_{i,j}^1$. This permutation is defined by $\rho_1 \in_R S_v$.

Step 3. On the i indices all MIX servers in B_1 apply the permutation ρ_1. So, $\pi_{i,j}^1 := \pi_{\rho_1(i),j}^1$.

Step 4. The *leader* of B_1 chooses $t + 1$ random bit string modifiers $\omega_{i,j}^1 \in_R F_{2^l}$ and privately sends $\omega_{i,j}^1$ to parties in B_1.

Step 5. For each (i, j) the $t+1$ values $\pi_{i,j}^1$ are regarded as shares of π_i^1. Similarly, the $t + 1$ values $\omega_{i,j}^1$ are regarded as shares of ω_i^1.

The MIX server in B_1 computes $\pi_{ij}^2 = \omega_{ij}^1 + \pi_{ij}^1$. $\pi_{i,j}^2$ are regarded as shares of π^2, the $\rho_1(i)$ permuted and modified one time pad.

Step 6. Steps 2–5 are repeated, incrementing by one the indices of B_1 and B_2 until the last block B_b is reached.

Step 7. Shares held by MIX-servers of block B_{t+1} are denoted as $\phi_{i,j}$. $MIX_{t+1,j} \in B_{t+1}$ then sends $\phi_{i,j}$ to the ith sender.

4.3 The MIX Communication Protocol - 1B: Sender to Receiver Transmission

Upon the end of the first phase, each sender reconstructs their respective altered one-time pad using XOR over all received shares.

Using XOR, senders encrypt their secret and send this to the *leader* of block B_{t+1}. These are sent back to the receiver in much the same way as transmitted from receiver to sender. This time though data are sent between *leaders* of MIX blocks, with the inverse permutations ρ_b^{-1} and XOR invalidation of modifiers using $-\omega_i^k$ being applied.

The data sent back to the receiver correspond to encrypted messages transmitted by senders. By applying XOR using the respective one-time pad, the secret message transmitted by senders can be obtained.

4.4 Security Proof

In this section we present the security proof for Protocol 1.

Theorem 1. *Protocol 1 is a reliable, private and anonymous message transmission protocol.*

Proof. The protocol achieves perfect reliability due to the passive nature of the adversary. Perfect privacy is achieved as each one-time pad or encrypted message is "shared" over $t + 1$ shares. As each MIX server is used only once and as the adversary can control at most t MIX servers, secrecy of these transmitted data is retained.

We now prove the perfect anonymity of the protocol - for simplicity of the proof we assume that there are only two messages (two one time pads). As $t + 1$ blocks of MIX servers are used and each MIX server is used only once, there exists a block B_i - $1 \le i \le b$, free from adversary controlled MIX servers.

Because of this, the adversary is unable to learn the modifiers and permutation which are added and implemented respectively to the shares of the messages.

Assuming the adversary is present in B_{i+1} and absent from B_i, the view of the adversary of a share for both messages can be one of the following two possibilities: $(\omega_1^i + \pi_1^{i-1}, \omega_2^i + \pi_2^{i-1}), (\omega_2^i + \pi_2^{i-1}, \omega_1^i + \pi_1^{i-1})$

Obviously, the adversary cannot distinguish between the first and the second possibility as the modifiers and permutation used in block B_i are random and unknown to the adversary. Indeed, there exists an (ω_1', ω_2') such that $(\omega_2^i + \pi_2^{i-1}, \omega_1^i + \pi_1^{i-1}) = (\omega_1' + \pi_1^{i-1}, \omega_2' + \pi_2^{i-1})$. So, the adversary cannot distinguish whether the messages have been interchanged or not.

Without loss of generality, the proof can be extended to any number v of messages.   □

5   Reducing the Number of MIX Servers

In this section we improve on the "Transmit and Reply Protocol" presented in Sect. 4 presenting a solution for the single seat election case where an Abelian group is used.

Our solution uses Chaum's code voting and considers a single receiver (e.g., CGE) and v human voters who each need to receive voting codes (one code per candidate) in a non-interactive anonymous way. We consider the CGE as the receiver and the human voters as the senders of the communication because at the end of the combined protocol, the human voters will send back to the CGE the voting code which corresponds to the candidate of their choice. We regard codes intended for the same receiver as a long string and the MIX servers MIX the strings (i.e. those intended for different receivers).

A more efficient network of MIX servers is used as our solution is not confined to using each MIX server only once, thus the total number of MIX operations done is b. We denote the set of MIX servers by X and assume we have an $(X, \mathcal{B})$ set system, which is an (m, b, t)-verifiers set system set system as defined in [15]. We let $B_k = \{MIX_{k,1}, MIX_{k,2}, \ldots, MIX_{k,t+1}\}$ and call $MIX_{k,1}$ "B_k's leader".

The main idea of the protocol is very similar to the communication protocol of the previous section. This time, the receiver (e.g., CGE) will share each of the v messages to transmit using an appropriate secret sharing scheme (and not using XOR). In a similar fashion, messages are permuted and altered as they are transmitted within the MIX network. After the last MIX operation, the final block of MIX servers delivers the shares of messages to the senders, with each sender reconstructing the secrets (voting codes) sent by the receiver. We will assume the transmission of the shares of these secrets uses the human friendly method presented in [18]. Similarly, since a code is only used once, it can be modified using addition over a finite Abelian group. To be compatible with [18] one such example is addition mod10 over the group used. Senders will then transmit back to the receiver the voting code corresponding to their choice.

5.1 Virtual Directed Acyclic Graphs

When an Abelian group is used and when blocks of the (m, b, t)-verifiers set system can share common MIX servers between them, we define the construction of a *virtual* vertex-labeled Directed Acyclic Graph (DAG). The set of vertices of the DAG is composed of parties participating in the protocol (which is similar to Protocol 3), with the source of the graph being the receiver of the protocol and the sink being a sender.

The directed edges of the DAG identify the transmission of messages from one party to another *amongst different levels* in the DAG. We define levels of the DAG as the receiver, a sender and the different blocks of MIX servers used. Considering block B_i as a tuple (ordered set), when B_i is a block where $|B_i| = l$ and $b \in B_i$, at *location* k in this tuple, we say that b is at position k. With the above definition, directed edges of the DAG will occur (i) from the receiver to all b_j in B_1 ($1 \leq j \leq l$), (ii) from each b_j in block B_b to the sender, (iii) moreover, we have edges between nodes in B_i and nodes in B_{i+1}. The following is required:

1. If a unique color was to be assigned to each party of the protocol, based on the results of [16], the sender and receiver can privately communicate, if when choosing any t colors and removing the vertices of the DAG with those t colors the sender and receiver remain connected - meaning that there still exists a directed path from the sender to the receiver on the reduced DAG.
2. We require that if at level k the parties in B_k receive shares of π_i^k, the parties in B_{k+1} (i.e., at level $k + 1$) receive shares of $\pi_i^{k+1} = \omega_i^k + \pi_{\rho(i)}^k$.

Two methods can be used to achieve the above requirements. One uses re-sharing - such as the redistribution scheme described in [12]. The other uses a large set of MIX servers X to guarantee the following property.

Definition 3. *We say that set X of MIX servers is under t-confinement if all members of set T where $|T| = t$ appear in at most t positions over all blocks of MIX servers used and this for all $T \subseteq X$ where $|T| = t$.*

It is easy to see that the above satisfies the DAG requirements.

5.2 The MIX Protocol

In the case of Internet voting this is used as a pre-voting protocol for the transmission of voting codes to voters and it is used to achieve anonymity of voting codes. We assume S to be a finite Abelian group and denote with v the number of senders, and thus the number of messages (sets of voting codes) that need to be transmitted. In the following, we only describe the required difference when compared to Protocol 1.

Protocol 2. *Private and Anonymous Random Communication Protocol.*

Step 1. Let s_i be the ith message (where $1 \leq i \leq v$). The sender shares each s_i by choosing l shares $\pi_{i,j}^1 \in_R S$ (using an appropriate secret sharing scheme over an Abelian group where $1 \leq j \leq l$) and privately sends $\pi_{i,j}^1$ to the corresponding party $B_{1,j}$ in B_1.

     – As an (m, b, t)-verifiers set system is used, $l = t + 1$ denotes the number of shares.

Step 2. Same as in Protocol 1.

Step 3. Same as in Protocol 1.

Step 4. The *leader* of B_1 chooses modifiers $\omega_{i,j}^1 \in_R S$ and privately sends $\omega_{i,j}^1$ to parties in B_1.

Step 5. Similar as in Protocol 1. Only:
The MIX servers in B_1 compute shares of $\pi_i^2 = \omega_i^1 + \pi_i^1$, i.e. party $P_j \in B_i$ adds the modifiers it receives from the leader of B_i to the share(s) it holds. The shares of the π_i^2 are denoted as $\pi_{i,j}^2$.

Step 6. If the concept of t-confinement is not used, re-sharing of shares $\pi_{i,j}^2$ is carried by out by parties in B_1 using the redistribution scheme described in [12]. That means that each party in B_2 receives $l = t + 1$ values, which they then compress.

Step 7. Steps 2–5 are repeated incrementing by one the indices of B_1 and B_2 until the last block B_b is reached. For all iterations - except when the last block B_b is reached, Step 6 is also repeated (except if t-confinement is used).

Step 8. If t-confinement is not used, shares held by the MIX-servers of block B_b are re-shared.

Step 9. Shares held by MIX-servers of block B_b are denoted as $\phi_{i,j}$. $MIX_{b,j} \in B_b$ then sends $\phi_{i,j}$ to the ith voter using [18].

It should be noted, that as in [18], MIX servers will send shares to voters using network disjoint paths, as the communication network cannot be trusted with the adversary capable of listening to at most t of these paths. The way voters cast their vote will be described in Sect. 6.

5.3   Security Proof

Corollary 2. *Protocol 2 is a reliable, private and anonymous message transmission protocol.*

Proof. Formally, we have:

Perfect Reliability - This is the same as in Theorem 1.

Perfect Privacy - The protocol achieves perfect privacy as each message is "shared" over $l = t + 1$ shares. In the case of t-confinement, the view of the adversary will consist of at most t shares. This number is one less that the number required to reconstruct a secret and thus perfect privacy is achieved. In the case of re-sharing, the re-sharing guarantees that shares at level i are independent of those at level $i+1$ (note that the adversarial parties are passive). The rest follows from [16] and through the use of re-sharing or t-confinement. When using re-sharing we ensure that there is no cut of t vertices (colors) that can disconnect the sender and the receiver. This is because the resharing of shares makes certain that the parties in block b_i receive shares from $t+1$ parties in block b_{i-1}. So, any adversarial t parties in block b_{i-1} will not allow to cut the graph. It is easy to see that the condition of [16] (i.e. no t parties are able to cut a graph) is satisfied when using t-confinement thus allowing for secure solutions.

Perfect Anonymity - This is very similar to the anonymity proof of Theorem 1. The only difference is that now where a lower number of MIX servers are used, due to Property 3 from the definition of verifier set systems, there exists a block b_i - $1 \leq i \leq b$, free from adversary controlled MIX servers. Because of this, the adversary is unable to learn the modifiers and permutation which are added and implemented respectively to the shares of the messages.   □

5.4   Use of non-Abelian Group - Multi-seat Election Case

When a non-Abelian group is used, the protocol is similar to that presented in Sect. 5.2. Due to the non-Abelian nature of the group, alternative additional techniques will have to be employed to manage the fact that dealing with shares cannot be done locally (due to the multiplication) thus this needs to be shared and securely computed among many parties using techniques presented in [13].

Suppose we have an election in which we have s seats in which every voter can vote for up to s of the c candidates - where $s \leq c$. To enable *blinding* of the code, we give to each voter a secret permutation $\pi \in S_c$, where S_c is the symmetric group. For each favourite candidate i the voter wants to vote for, $\pi(i)$ is transmitted to the returning officer.

Note that π is *not* necessarily unique to the election, as opposed to Chaum's code voting. The protocol is organized to avoid that this creates a problem. In the case of Internet voting, the following protocol is used as a pre-voting protocol, for the transmission of v number of voting "codes" (i.e. permutations) to v number of voters and it is used to achieve anonymity of voting codes. We assume $S = S_c$ to be a finite non-Abelian group.

It should be noted that the protocol to be presented is only useful for the private and anonymous transmission of permutations with which receivers can cast their vote.

Protocol 3. Private and Anonymous Random Communication Protocol

Step 1. Same as in Protocol 2 only now a non-Abelian group is used and per-mutations are transmitted.
Step 2. The *leader* of B_2 chooses modifiers $\omega_{i,j}^2 \in_R S_c^l$ and privately sends $\omega_{i,j}^2$ to parties in B_2 such that the l values $\omega_{i,j}^2$ are regarded as shares of ω_i^2.[5]
Step 3. For each (i, j) the l values $\pi_{i,j}^1$ are regarded as shares of π_i^1.
The MIX servers in $X'_{1,2} \subseteq X$ where $|X'_{1,2}| \geq 2t + 1$ and $B_1 \cup B_2 \subseteq X'_{1,2}$ compute shares of $\pi_i^2 = \omega_i^2 \circ \pi_i^1$ using a black box non-Abelian

---

[5] As shown in [13], to securely compute π and ω where π is chosen by one party and ω by another, we need $2t + 1$ parties with t curious parties. To mimic as closely as possible the working of [13], the leader of B_2 chooses $\omega_{i,j}^1$ and *not* the leader of B_1.

multiparty computation protocol[6] (see Sect. 2.5). This is done so that ω_i^2 blinds π_i^1. The shares of the product are denoted as $\pi_{i,j}^2$ and are obtained by the parties[7] in B_2.

Step 4. The *leader* of B_2 informs all other MIX servers in B_2 how they have to permute the i-index of all shares they hold from the above operations. This permutation is defined by $\rho_2 \in_R S_v$. On the i indices the MIX servers in B_2 apply the permutation ρ_2. So, $\pi_{i,j}^2 := \pi_{\rho_2(i),j}^2$.

Step 5. The above three steps are repeated by incrementing by one the indices of B_1 and B_2 (thus $B_k \neq B_{k+1}$). After parties in B_k permute the i indices of $\pi_{i,j}^k$ using ρ_k - where $2 \leq k \leq b-1$, the *leader* of B_{k+1} chooses modifiers $\omega_{i,j}^3 \in_R S_c^l$ which are given to parties in B_k, the black box non-Abelian multiparty computation sub-protocol is executed by parties in $X_{k,k+1}' \subseteq X$ where $B_k \cup B_{k+1} \subseteq X_{k,k+1}'$ $|X_{k,k+1}'| \geq 2t+1$ and the process continues till the final block of servers B_b is reached.

Step 6. After parties in B_b permute the i indices of $\pi_{i,j}^b$ using ρ_b, the *leader* of B_1 chooses modifiers $\omega_{i,j}^1 \in_R S_c^l$ which are given to parties in B_1, the black box non-Abelian multiparty computation sub-protocol is executed between parties in block B_b and B_1 and the output of which is held by parties in B_1. $MIX_{1,j} \in B_1$ sends the output it holds to the ith voter using [18].

It should be noted, that as in [18], MIX servers will send shares to voters using network disjoint paths, as the communication network cannot be trusted with the adversary capable of listening to at most t of these paths. The way voters will use what they receive to cast their vote will be described in Sect. 6.

Theorem 2. *Provided Protocol 3 together with the appropriate black box non-Abelian multiparty computation sub-protocol is used, then Protocol 3 is a reliable, private and anonymous random transmission protocol.*

The proof of the above theorem is similar to the proof of Theorem 1, but relying on either [9, 13].

6   Electronic Code Voting Protocol

We now outline how components of previous sections are combined.

6.1   Preparation, Mixing and Transmission of Voting Codes

As described in Sect. 3.1 the CGE is responsible for creating the codes with which voters will cast their votes. We first explain this for the single-seat election.

---

[6] Note that the MIX servers in $B_1 \cup B_2$ can also be a in $X_{1,2}'$ where $|X_{1,2}'| \geq 2t+1$. Additionally, the efficiency of black box non-Abelian multiparty computation protocols is better when $|X_{1,2}'| >> 2t+1$.

[7] Note that [13] allows to organize the computation such that the output, i.e. shares of π_i^2, are received by parties in B_2.

Considering an election has c number of candidates and that there are v number of voters, the CGE will create v random *initial* codes for each of the c candidates. In total, $c \times v$ unique number of codes will be generated. The CGE will then group these codes to form v number of $c - tuples$, with each tuple containing a single code for each of the c candidates.

Each of these codes will then be transmitted as one-time pads to the voters in the same way as described by Protocol 2. It should be noted that Protocol 2 describes the transmission of only v codes as opposed to $c \times v$ required by the voting protocol. To transmit all the voting codes, c executions of Protocol 2 will be executed at the same time. These executions should *not be independent between them but instead should use the same permutations* ($\rho \in_R S_v$ in Step 2) and modifiers ($\omega_{i,j}$ in Step 4) used throughout all executions of the protocol, i.e. the same modifier is used for all codes the same voters will receive and they remain bundled together (i.e. by reusing ρ). These c executions can be carried out either in parallel or sequentially, as long as each voter receives c voting codes.

In the case of multi-seat elections, each voter will receive a single permutation over S_c - which is a permutation of the alphabetical ordering of the candidates. Moreover, Protocol 3 will be used.

6.2   Receiving and Reconstructing Voting Codes

We first explain the single-seat case. Each voter will receive $l = t + 1$ shares for each voting code, receiving each one using a *different* computational device. It should be noted that the ith share of each of the c voting codes will be received upon the *same* computational device.

A voter can then identify the code for their chosen candidate. Once all pieces of each code are received, the code corresponding to their choice can be reconstructed in a similar manner as described in Sect. 2.4.

In the multi-seat election, instead of receiving a c-tuple, a single permutation is received - which is a permutation of the alphabetical ordering of the candidates. Similar to the single seat case, $t + 1$ shares of this permutation will be received by the voter who will reconstruct the permutation as described in [18, Sects. 4.2 and 4.3]. This will allow the voter to identify the candidates of their choice. Supposing the voter wants to vote for candidate c and candidate c', the reconstruction of the permutation will help the voter identify $\pi(c)$ and $\pi(c')$ which correspond to the candidates of their choice. To cast their vote, voters will have to send back to the CGE these $\pi(c)$ and $\pi(c')$ values.

6.3   Transmission, Mixing and Counting of Cast Votes

We first explain for the single-seat case. A voter identifies the code corresponding to their chosen candidate and sends this code back to the CGE by transmitting this code *to the leader* of the last block of MIX.

To transmit voter codes in the reverse direction (towards the CGE), *the leaders* of each block of MIX servers will have to carry out the reserve operations on the codes. Thus the inverse permutations (ρ_b^{-1}) and modifiers $(-\omega_i^k)$ are used. Once a code arrives to the CGE, it will identify the candidate it corresponds to and the vote will be counted.

The multi-seat case is similar. Voter identify the $\pi(c)$ corresponding to one of their chosen candidates and send this $\pi(c)$ to the leader of the last block of MIX servers. Similar to the single-seat case, the reverse operations on the codes will be carried out. Once a voter's $\pi(c)$ arrives to the CGE, the CGE will apply π^{-1} and identify the candidate the voting corresponds to and the vote will be counted.

Acknowledgments. The authors would like to thank the anonymous referees for their valuable comments on improving the presentation and clarity of this paper. We thank Rebecca Wright for having co-invented the concept of having anonymous communication allowing a receiver to reply anonymously to the sender. The authors would also like to thank Juan Garay and Amos Beimel for expressing their interests in PSMT in which one cannot trust the equipment used by the receiver.

References

1. E-voting. https://www.ch.ch/en/online-voting/
2. Four Grand Challenges in Trustworthy Computing. In: CRA Conference on Grand Research Challenges in Information Security and Assurance, Warrenton, Virginia, 16–19 November 2003
3. Abe, M.: Universally verifiable mix-net with verification work independent of the number of mix-servers. In: Nyberg, K. (ed.) EUROCRYPT 1998. LNCS, vol. 1403, pp. 437–447. Springer, Heidelberg (1998)
4. Blocki, J., Blum, M., Datta, A.: Human computable passwords. CoRR (2014)
5. Buchmann, J., Demirel, D., van de Graaf, J.: Towards a publicly-verifiable mix-net providing everlasting privacy. In: Sadeghi, A.-R. (ed.) FC 2013. LNCS, vol. 7859, pp. 197–204. Springer, Heidelberg (2013)
6. Chaum, D.: SureVote: technical overview. In: Proceedings of the Workshop on Trustworthy Elections, Tomales Bay, CA, USA, 26–29 August 2001
7. Chaum, D.: Untraceable electronic mail, return addresses, and digital pseudonyms. Commun. ACM **24**(2), 84–88 (1981)
8. Chaum, D., Essex, A., Carback, R., Clark, J., Popoveniuc, S., Sherman, A.T., Vora, P.L.: Scantegrity: end-to-end voter-verifiable optical-scan voting. IEEE Secur. Priv. **6**(3), 40–46 (2008)
9. Cohen, G., Damgård, I.B., Ishai, Y., Kölker, J., Miltersen, P.B., Raz, R., Rothblum, R.D.: Efficient multiparty protocols via log-depth threshold formulae. In: Canetti, R., Garay, J.A. (eds.) CRYPTO 2013, Part II. LNCS, vol. 8043, pp. 185–202. Springer, Heidelberg (2013)
10. Colbourn, C.J., Dinitz, J.H.: Handbook of Combinatorial Designs. Discrete Mathematics and Its Applications, 2nd edn. Chapman & Hall/CRC, Boca Raton (2006)
11. Cramer, R., Franklin, M.K., Schoenmakers, B., Yung, M.: Multi-authority secret-ballot elections with linear work. In: Maurer, U.M. (ed.) EUROCRYPT 1996. LNCS, vol. 1070, pp. 72–83. Springer, Heidelberg (1996)
12. Desmedt, Y., Jajodia, S.: Redistributing secret shares to new access structures and its applications. Technical Report ISSE-TR-97-01, George Mason University

13. Desmedt, Y., Pieprzyk, J., Steinfeld, R., Sun, X., Tartary, C., Wang, H., Yao, A.C.-C.: Graph coloring applied to secure computation in non-abelian groups. J. Cryptol. **25**(4), 557–600 (2012)
14. Desmedta, Y., Erotokritou, S.: Making Code Voting Secure against Insider Threats using Unconditionally Secure MIX Schemes and Human PSMT Protocols. https://www.cyi.ac.cy/images/ResearchProjects/SteliosE/voteID2015FinalShort.pdf
15. Desmedt, Y.G., Kurosawa, K.: How to break a practical MIX and design a new one. In: Preneel, B. (ed.) EUROCRYPT 2000. LNCS, vol. 1807, pp. 557–572. Springer, Heidelberg (2000)
16. Desmedt, Y.G., Wang, Y., Burmester, M.: A complete characterization of tolerable adversary structures for secure point-to-point transmissions without feedback. In: Deng, X., Du, D.-Z. (eds.) ISAAC 2005. LNCS, vol. 3827, pp. 277–287. Springer, Heidelberg (2005)
17. Dolev, D., Dwork, C., Waarts, O., Yung, M.: Perfectly secure message transmission. J. ACM **40**(1), 17–47 (1993)
18. Erotokritou, S., Desmedt, Y.: Human perfectly secure message transmission protocols and their applications. In: Visconti, I., De Prisco, R. (eds.) SCN 2012. LNCS, vol. 7485, pp. 540–558. Springer, Heidelberg (2012)
19. Estehghari, S., Desmedt, Y.: Exploiting the client vulnerabilities in internet e-voting systems: Hacking Helios 2.0 as an example. In: EVT/WOTE 2010 (2010)
20. Franklin, M.K., Yung, M.: Secure hypergraphs: privacy from partial broadcast. SIAM J. Discrete Math. **18**(3), 437–450 (2004)
21. Furukawa, J.: Efficient and verifiable shuffling and shuffle-decryption. IEICE Trans. **88–A**(1), 172–188 (2005)
22. Gerck, E., Neff, C.A., Rivest, R.L., Rubin, A.D., Yung, M.: The business of electronic voting. In: Syverson, P.F. (ed.) FC 2001. LNCS, vol. 2339, p. 234. Springer, Heidelberg (2002)
23. Groth, J., Ishai, Y.: Sub-linear zero-knowledge argument for correctness of a shuffle. In: Smart, N.P. (ed.) EUROCRYPT 2008. LNCS, vol. 4965, pp. 379–396. Springer, Heidelberg (2008)
24. Helios. Helios Voting. http://heliosvoting.org/
25. Katti, S., Cohen, J., Katabi, D.: Information slicing: anonymity using unreliable overlays. In: Proceedings of the 4th USENIX Symposium on NSDI, Cambridge, Massachusetts, U.S.A., 11–13 April 2007, pp. 43–56 (2007)
26. Khazaei, S., Moran, T., Wikström, D.: A mix-net from any CCA2 secure cryptosystem. In: Wang, X., Sako, K. (eds.) ASIACRYPT 2012. LNCS, vol. 7658, pp. 607–625. Springer, Heidelberg (2012)
27. Maaten, E.: Towards remote e-voting: Estonian case. In: Electronic Voting in Europe - Technology, Law, Politics and Society, 7th-9th July 2004. LNI, vol. 47, pp. 83–100. GI, Bregenz (2004)
28. Malkopoulou, A.: Lost voters: participation in eu elections and the case for compulsory voting. CEPS Working Document No. 317, 24 July 2009
29. Moran, T., Naor, M.: Split-ballot voting: everlasting privacy with distributed trust. ACM Trans. Inf. Syst. Secur. **13**(2), 16:1–16:43 (2010)
30. Rabin, M.O., Rivest, R.L.: Efficient end to end verifiable electronic voting employing split value representations. In: EVOTE 2014, Bregenz, Austria (to appear)
31. Sako, K., Kilian, J.: Secure voting using partially compatible homomorphisms. In: Desmedt, Y.G. (ed.) CRYPTO 1994. LNCS, vol. 839, pp. 411–424. Springer, Heidelberg (1994)
32. Sampigethaya, K., Poovendran, R.: A survey on mix networks and their secure applications. Proc. IEEE **94**, 2142–2181 (2006)

33. Tran, A., Hopper, N., Kim, Y.: Hashing it out in public: common failure modes of DHT-based anonymity schemes. In: Proceedings of WPES 2009, Chicago, Illinois, USA, 9 November, pp. 71–80 (2009)
34. Wikipedia. Returning officer. http://en.wikipedia.org/wiki/Returning_officer
35. Wikström, D.: The security of a mix-center based on a semantically secure cryptosystem. In: Menezes, A., Sarkar, P. (eds.) INDOCRYPT 2002. LNCS, vol. 2551, pp. 368–381. Springer, Heidelberg (2002)

Other Topics

Other Topics

Document Analysis Techniques for Automatic Electoral Document Processing: A Survey

J. Ignacio Toledo[1]([✉]), Jordi Cucurull[1], Jordi Puiggalí[1],
Alicia Fornés[2], and Josep Lladós[2]

[1] Scytl Secure Electronic Voting, Barcelona, Spain
{JuanIgnacio.Toledo,Jordi.Cucurull,Jordi.Puiggali}@scytl.com
[2] Computer Vision Center, Universitat Autònoma de Barcelona, Barcelona, Spain
{afornes,josep}@cvc.uab.es

Abstract. In this paper, we will discuss the most common challenges in electoral document processing and study the different solutions from the document analysis community that can be applied in each case. We will cover Optical Mark Recognition techniques to detect voter selections in the Australian Ballot, handwritten number recognition for preferential elections and handwriting recognition for write-in areas. We will also propose some particular adjustments that can be made to those general techniques in the specific context of electoral documents.

Keywords: Document image analysis · Computer vision · Paper ballots · Paper based elections · Optical scan · Tally

1 Introduction

While remote or poll-site electronic voting is gaining more and more acceptance worldwide, many elections are still paper based. Be it for tradition, for its simplicity, because it leaves a physical evidence of the vote or because of a restrictive electoral law, there are several countries that are not willing to abandon paper based elections yet. However, this does not mean that they are not willing to use modern technology in elections.

Countries with complex electoral systems, like the US, have been exploring how to automate the tally for paper based elections for decades. Mark sense scanners, first developed for educational testing, have been used for ballot processing since the 1950's. They were based on a ballot printed with a special ink, that was invisible to the sensor, and the use of index marks to define the position of the voting targets. In the 1990's, devices using imaging technology were developed. They used fiducial marks that allowed the scanner to interpolate the voting targets and counted the number of dark pixels in each area. More recently, in 2006, a patent was granted to a device based on edge detection, which could detect empty voting targets (ovals) and filled voting targets.

We can see a trend moving from solutions requiring specific hardware to more generic hardware-independent solutions using computer vision techniques.

© Springer International Publishing Switzerland 2015
R. Haenni et al. (Eds.): VoteID 2015, LNCS 9269, pp. 129–141, 2015.
DOI: 10.1007/978-3-319-22270-7_8

However, there are still a lot of challenges to be able to support more complex elections. In the document analysis field, techniques have been developed to process different kind of documents. To our knowledge, the work specifically applied to electoral documents has mainly dealt with Optical Mark Recognition. In this paper we will discuss several of the techniques developed in the document analysis community that can be applied in the electoral document context, while pointing out some improvements that can be done using knowledge of the electoral process.

This paper is organized as follows: In Sect. 2 we will discuss the more relevant preprocessing steps applied in document image analysis. In Sect. 3 we will deal with ballots, starting with the most common issue, detecting filled voting targets. We will also deal with preferential voting, where voters have to sort candidates according to their preferences by assigning them a number, and the hardest problem we can find in ballots, write-ins, where voters can write in the name of the candidate in a designated area will be discussed. In Sect. 4, we will see how we can apply most of the techniques previously discussed in another kind of electoral document, the ballot statement. In Sect. 5 we show a few small security enhancements that can be easily implemented. Finally we draw some conclusions and outline some possible lines of future work.

2   Preprocessing

In image processing, before trying to understand a document image, we can try to simplify the problem by removing some sources of variance. The same intensity value can sometimes represent a black pixel or white (background pixel) depending on the acquisition device. It is also very common to find different skews on each scan, due to small misalignments when feeding the paper sheet into the scanner. Finally the image can be noisy. We will discuss techniques to address each of these problems.

A key preprocessing step in most document analysis tasks is image binarization. That is, determining if a pixel of the image should be considered "black/foreground" or "white/background" depending on whether its darker or brighter than a certain threshold value. If the image acquisition is done in a very controlled environment, a global threshold value can be predefined. This is the less flexible approach and it can fail if you have to use scanners from different manufacturers or with different contrast response. There are also several different methods to automatically find optimum global thresholds. One of the most widely used method is Otsu's method [17]. This method is based on iterating through the 256 possible threshold values of a typical 8-bit gray level image finding the value that minimizes the intra-class variance (which is equivalent to maximizing the inter-class variance). This kind of methods would allow us more flexibility in the requirements of a particular scanner configuration.

There are also adaptive threshold methods like Niblack [16], Bernsen [4] or Sauvola [21]. In this kind of methods, instead of selecting a single threshold value for the whole image, the threshold value is determined for each individual pixel,

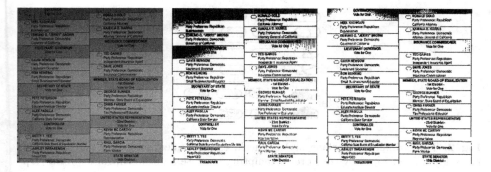

Fig. 1. The original ballot image acquired with a camera (left). The image thresholded with Otsu's Method (center) and with Sauvola's Method (right). We can see how using Otsu's method the darker areas of the ballot become black while voting targets in the lighter areas disappear, showing the limitations of setting a global threshold.

taking into account its neighbors in a local area of a predefined size. In the case of Sauvola, a widely used method for documents, the mean and the standard deviation in the local area are calculated. Then each pixel is classified as dark, if it is at least k times (a parameter) the standard deviation darker than the mean in that area. This kind of binarization methods are specially interesting if there are illumination changes (as for instance when the ballot images are acquired using a camera), noise in the image, or stains or folding marks in the ballot. A very interesting survey on both global and local thresholding algorithms can be found in [19,23] showing that despite being a mature research area, there is still interest in the community for binarization techniques. See Fig. 1.

Another key preprocessing step is the removal of the skew; there are also several approaches to do this. One of the most common approaches [13], is based on rotating the document in all allowed skews (i.e., from −10 to 10 degrees with a precision of 1 degree), trying to find the right orientation. There are several ways to find out the correct orientation. Assuming an horizontal writing, the document will have the correct orientation when the horizontal projection histogram has a higher variance. Also, if there is a long horizontal line separating two areas, the correct orientation would be the one that produces the highest peak value for a specific line in the horizontal projection histogram. Another common approach would be to use the Hough Transform [3,9,24]. Using the Hough Transform we get the equation of all the lines $y = ax + b$ that we can find in a document, making it trivial to find the skew of the document. Nevertheless, mainly because of the computational cost of the Hough Transform, methods based on the horizontal projection are more commonly used.

In some cases, after thresholding and skew correction, some noise removing algorithms can be applied. For instance, the median filter can be useful to remove "salt and pepper" noise (isolated black or white pixels). Mathematical morphology operators [22] (opening, closing, erosion, etc.) can also be used in case we need to remove artifacts with a specific shape/size or connect some broken shapes.

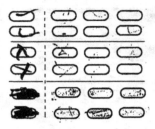

Fig. 2. Three different marking styles: check, ex, and filled, and their corresponding noisy inputs generated by the voter attempting to erase a mark. Extracted from [29].

3 Ballots

The most common election document is the ballot. Ballot design can have a high variability depending on the electoral system of each country or state. The kind of challenges we can find in ballots can be divided in three big groups: mark recognition, preferential voting and write-ins. We will review each of them in the following subsections.

3.1 Mark Recognition

The ballots used in most of the elections consist of a grid where a voter selects k out of n candidates for each contest by filling in empty voting targets in predefined locations. In the most simple case, there will only be one ballot model. In this case, the recognition software will only require a mapping from a filled voting target (dark pixels in a certain area) to a candidate name.

However, in most complex elections we usually have to deal with different ballot models (in different languages, or different districts with different contests). The first step that the software will perform (after the preprocessing step) is to identify the ballot model. The most popular solutions use QR-codes or barcodes to identify each model. After reading the barcode and identifying the ballot model, the configuration for that particular model can be loaded, that is, the position of the pixels of each voting target and the candidate it is associated to. If there are enough dark pixels in that area, it means that the voter cast a vote for that candidate. This kind of approach looks very efficient and simple, but it has problems because some voters do not fill the voting target completely or place their mark near but not inside the voting target. What kind of marks are considered a valid vote depends on the electoral law, and traditional approaches like this are lacking in flexibility.

An alternative approach could allow us to perform both the ballot model and mark detection at the same time, avoiding the need of barcodes. To do that, we need a template image of an empty ballot of each ballot model. The process would consist in computing the difference of the ballot (after preprocessing) and each of the templates. The actual ballot model will have the smaller difference, and that difference would be the marks made by the voter. This difference will usually have an amount of noise due to small misalignments, dust or different scanning conditions. To obtain a mark detector that is less sensitive to noise, several approaches are discussed in [25, 27], like using a distance transform to detect safe and unsafe zones, depending on their distance to black pixels, using Gaussian filters to smooth the images before performing the subtraction or using morphological filters. Some authors try to detect a grid for possible positions of marks by analyzing the geometry of the ballot [26]. Other authors simply require user collaboration to tag a blank voting target and locate the rest using pattern matching techniques. Once they know where voting targets are, they search for filled in targets in that region [12, 28].

One drawback of the approaches described above is that they mainly rely on the size of the mark. Usually, some voters do not follow exactly the instructions to completely fill the voting target area, and use marks like X or ✓ (see Fig. 2). Since most electoral laws define a vote in terms of voter intent, we have to be able to detect these marks. A possibility suggested in [29], assuming that the voter makes consistent marks, is to train classifiers taking into account the style of the marks, improving mark detection.

3.2   Preferential Voting

In some elections the voter is allowed to perform preferential voting. In that scenario detecting a mark in a voting target is not enough. In preferential voting, the voter assigns a number to each candidate indicating their preference, so we have to classify the marks we find as belonging to a particular class (i.e. "1", "2", etc.).

The problem of identifying the particular class of an image among a possible set of classes is one of the big challenges in computer vision. Fortunately, in handwritten numbers, the number of different classes is small (only ten different classes) and there have been free datasets available for years. The main challenge is the huge difference in writing styles. Classifying handwritten isolated digits has been tackled by computer vision for the last three decades and there is now a wide variety of techniques that allow us to perform the recognition of individual digits with less than a 2 % error rate [15] on the popular MNIST dataset [14]. See Fig. 3 for some examples.

Fig. 3. Some examples from the MNIST dataset. It's a common benchmark for isolated handwritten digit recognition consisting of 60,000 digit images from approximately 250 different writers.

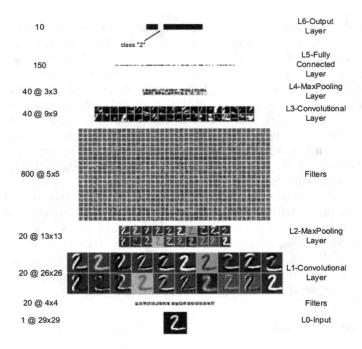

Fig. 4. The architecture of one column of the convolutional neural network that achieved the best scores so far in handwritten digit recognition on the MNIST dataset. The response for each neuron to the input image is also shown as an image. Extracted from [5]

Recently, a multicolumn convolutional deep neural network trained for weeks with several GPU has surpassed human performance in this task, achieving an error rate of 0.23 % [5]. Convolutional neural networks combine the ability to learn low level features (convolutional layers) with the invariance to translation and scale given by max-pooling layers. Deep neural networks try to emulate the hierarchical representations of the human brain, where the first layers learn low level features, and the layers above learn higher level features (non-linear combination of the low level ones). The last layer is the actual classifier (a non-linear multiclass logistic regression) that outputs the probability of each class given that particular input image (Fig. 4).

In practice, these "deep learning" systems are still difficult to train because they require long training times, huge amounts of data, careful tuning of network parameters, and expertise in GPU programing. For that reason, traditional systems using handcrafted features like Histogram of Oriented Gradients (HOG) [11] and classifiers like Support Vector Machines (SVM) are still a very popular approach [6]. SVM also output the probability of the observation belonging to each specific class. This is very important because it gives us not only a most probable label, but also a confidence on that prediction.

In electoral documents there is additional context information that can be used to further reduce the error rate. Usually a number cannot be repeated within the same contest (there cannot be two candidates with the same preference in the same contest) and usually they have to be correlative (i.e. a voter cannot assign a preference "3" without previously assigning preferences "1", and "2"). Instead of individual classifications, we are facing a problem of a set of observations with some restrictions that can help us lower our error rate even more. Finally, the number of preferences a single voter can choose is probably less than ten, that would reduce the number of classes (which has a great impact in error rates). For example, usually the digit 1 is mistaken by a 7, or the digit 3 with a 5 or an 8, so if we have less than 7 preferences to assign, the error rate would drastically decrease. Finally, since these techniques also provide a confidence level on the classification result, this confidence level can be used to discard an ambiguous ballot and ask for a human decision if the confidence is below a certain threshold. This approach of combining Intelligent Character Recognition techniques with human inspection of dubious ballots has been used successfully in several elections in the Australian Capital Territory [2].

3.3   Write-In

Recognizing the text in write-in areas is the most difficult problem we can find in electoral documents. Handwriting recognition can be performed with online or offline information. In online systems, the temporal sequence of the handwriting is available whereas in offline scenarios, we only have an scanned image available. While the recognition rate is better in the online scenario, we discarded its usage in our systems because: (1) it requires special hardware (a digital pen or digitizing board that records the (x, y) position of the pentip at each timestep) and (2) it has security implications because it detaches the voter input from the ballot background, forcing to perform audits on the physical ballots to avoid ballot tampering.

Offline cursive handwriting recognition, with open vocabularies in a multi-writer scenario is still an open problem, the state of the art [8] character error rates are around 18–19%. Probably the main reason that can explain why this is a hard problem is the so called 'Sayre's Paradox'. This paradox states that handwriting recognition is a "chicken-egg" problem. In order to segment a cursive word into characters you need to recognize the characters first, but to recognize the characters you first need to segment them out. A way to circumvent this problem is to use segmentation-free techniques. Also we have to keep in mind that cursive handwriting has huge variability, thus most of the approaches include a preprocessing step trying to normalize the slant, horizontal and vertical size of the characters and, in some cases, even the stroke width.

The key idea is to model the handwritten text line or word like a temporal series of observations with a "sliding window approach". See the example of the sliding window approach on a previously normalized handwritten text line in Fig. 5. That is, we focus our attention only in a column of a few pixels wide at a time and extract some representative features in that window. There are different

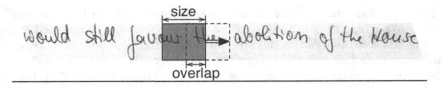

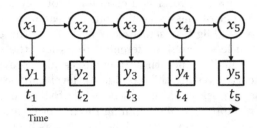

Fig. 5. The "sliding window". Extracted from [7]

Fig. 6. In Hidden Markov Models, the data is modeled as a series of observations generated by a hidden state that is only dependent on the state at the previous time step.

set of features that are used in the literature, like statistical moments, the slope of the upper and lower contour, image derivatives, the number of black and white transitions, etc. Once we have the handwritten text represented as a series of features, the correct alignment with the ground truth character sequence has to be found. Since the character sequence and the feature sequence have different lengths the alignment is not trivial.

Since the 90s, technologies like Hidden Markov Models [7,20] have been used to address this problem [18]. Hidden Markov Models are generative models that have been adapted from the speech recognition area. According to this model, each observation(x_t) in every timestep is conditionally dependent only from a latent unobserved variable (hidden state x_t), which in turn depends only on the hidden state of the previous timestep (Markov process). Given a number of states (x), a matrix T of allowed transitions among them $p(x_t|x_{t-1})$, and a parametric probability distribution P for $p(y|x)$, the Baum-Welch algorithm can be used to train the system, that is, finding the parameters for T and P that better fit our observations. A graphical representation of the HMM can be seen in Fig. 6.

In 2009 a new algorithm was developed that allows us to use neural networks for segmentation free handwriting recognition. The algorithm, called Connectionist Temporal Classification (CTC) allows us to align two sequences of different lengths and return a differentiable error for each timestep. With the output from the CTC algorithm, and using the traditional backpropagation algorithm, it is possible to train a recurrent neural network to map the image feature representation with the character sequence. However, traditional recurrent neural networks have problems learning long sequences, because of a problem known as the vanishing gradient. After several timesteps, because the activation function of each neuron is smaller than 1, the error gradient fades into the network, making it unable to learn long range dependencies. This problem can be solved with the Long Short-Term Memory (LSTM) cells (Fig. 7), that incorporate input, output and forget gates, that the cell can learn to open or close depending on the input and the current state, thus allowing the network to learn arbitrarily long sequences.

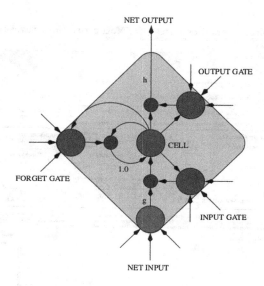

Fig. 7. A Long Short Term Memory Cell with multiplicative input, output and forget gates. Extracted from [8]

The easier way to dramatically improve the recognition rate would be to change the write-in areas so that they are expected to be filled with a set of isolated capital letters. Also, in electoral documents we can assume that the content of the write-in area will be a name. We can then use a reduced vocabulary, consisting of the 5,000 most common surnames in that country, to improve the accuracy of the system in both the original connected handwriting and isolated character recognition scenarios. Finally, since the number of voters who actually use the write-ins area is usually low, there is also the option to simply detect the presence of write-in text, and mark the ballot for human inspection. This approach would still be better than current optical scan technologies, since they require the voter to fill in a mark associated to the write-in in order to process it. Requiring to fill-in that mark does not seem intuitive since, according to a study performed by Ji [10], a 49 % of the voters who used write-ins forgot to fill the associated mark.

138   J.I. Toledo et al.

4   Ballot Statements

In some elections, with very simple ballot designs (e.g. Partisan Ballot), processing the ballot is extremely easy, you just have to identify the party corresponding to each ballot. In that case, human tally at precinct level is feasible. After performing the tally, the electoral officials have to fill in a report or 'ballot statement' with the election results for that precinct. We can see an example of such a document in Fig. 8.

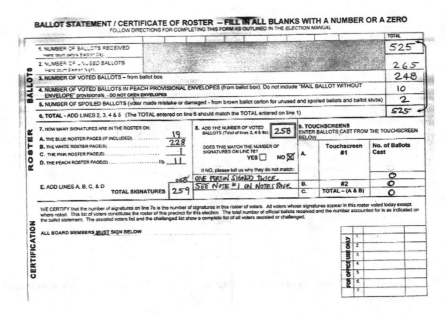

Fig. 8. Example of a ballot statement. Extracted from [1]

These ballot statements usually contain handwritten numbers that represent the number of votes for a specific party, the number of eligible voters, etc. The same techniques as the one described above for "Preferential Voting" in ballots can be used. In the case of ballot statements, some integrity checks could also be performed when recognizing the digits that can help to reduce even more the classification errors (o even help to detect election official errors). Spatial grammars can be defined for a ballot statement document, that is, numbers recognized in a certain area must meet some requirements. For instance, the sum of the recognized votes of all the parties and blank votes must match the number recognized as total votes cast, which in turn has to match the number recognized as number of voters, which has to be smaller than the number of eligible voters, etc.

Some ballot statements can also contain connected handwriting. Usually the numbers are also written in text form (like the courtesy amount in cheques).

We can recognize this text with high accuracy because of the very restricted vocabulary and syntax. Since recognizing the text "thirty four" and the number '34' use different techniques to analyze different data, they can be considered independent probabilities, which can be easily combined to boost the confidence of the recognition.

To finish, usually, there is also an "observations" field, where the election officers can write free text to explain some anomaly during the election. As we explained above, unconstrained offline handwriting recognition is still an open problem. Since that field is usually empty, simply detecting if there are any observations, and asking a human operator for a transcription seems the best option.

5   Security

With traditional mark detection scanners, it may be feasible to tamper elections by replacing the original ballots by ballots with candidates in permuted order, easily affecting the election results, or by changing the configuration of the machine. Also, mark sense scanners can't detect any kind of identification mark, thus allowing vote-coercion and vote buying by corrupt election officials. If coercion or vote-buying are a concern for that particular election, we could detect possible identification marks anywhere on the ballot using document analysis techniques like the ones described above, based on the difference with a template ballot image. These same techniques would be able to detect a false ballot. In the case that we wanted to go even further (or if for some reason we can't have an image of an empty ballot for every ballot model) we could perform an OCR on the printed text to further validate the authenticity of the ballot. Knowing the font used in the ballot, the OCR can be done with almost perfect accuracy. These techniques cannot prevent pattern based marking or deliberate mismarking as way of identification. The document analysis community has also worked on signature verification. Given enough training samples from the election officers, we could verify that the signatures in a ballot statement are not forgeries.

6   Conclusions

We have reviewed the most relevant document analysis techniques that can be applied to ballot processing in all of the possible configurations: mark detection, preferential voting and write-ins. We also proposed some small improvements to the general techniques that can be applied in the specific context of ballots, like using the fact that numbers cannot be repeated in a same contest in preferential voting or that there may be less than ten different classes of numbers to improve the accuracy, or in write-ins, where we can use a vocabulary of common surnames. Using the techniques described in this paper we can go beyond the traditional Optical Mark Recognition systems and support most complex election types, dramatically reducing the need of human intervention. Finally, we have also shown that advanced techniques for mark detection also lead to improved security. As a possible future line of research, we would like to study if it would be possible to develop a system that, by using layout detection, OCR and prior knowledge of electoral processes, could be able to interpret most common ballot designs without requiring a manual configuration for each ballot model.

Acknowledgements. We thank the reviewers for their suggestions and comments. This work has been partially supported by the Spanish project TIN2012-37475-C02-02 and the European project ERC-2010-AdG-20100407-269796 and by the Secretaria d'Universitats i Recerca del Departament d'Economia i Coneixement de la Generalitat de Catalunya.

References

1. Citizen's oversight projects (2009). www.copswiki.org/Cops/BallotStatements
2. Elections ACT: Scanning of ballot papers (2015). http://www.elections.act.gov. au/elections_and_voting/scanning_of_ballot_papers
3. Amin, A., Fischer, S.: A document skew detection method using the hough transform. Pattern Anal. Appl. **3**(3), 243–253 (2000)
4. Bernsen, J.: Dynamic thresholding of grey-level images. In: International Conference on Pattern Recognition (ICPR), pp. 1251–1255 (1986)
5. Ciresan, D.C., Meier, U., Schmidhuber, J.: Multi-column deep neural networks for image classification. In: IEEE Conference on Computer Vision and Pattern Recognition CVPR 2012 (2012), long preprint arXiv:1202.2745v1 [cs.CV]
6. Ebrahimzadeh, R., Jampour, M.: Efficient handwritten digit recognition based on histogram of oriented gradients and svm. Int. J. Comput. Appl. **104**(9), 10–13 (2014)
7. Fischer, A., Frinken, V., Bunke, H.: Hidden markov models for off-line cursive handwriting recognition. In: Govindaraju, V., Rao, C.R. (eds.) Handbook of Statistics: Machine Learning: Theory and Applications, vol. 31, p. 421. Elsevier, Amsterdam (2013)
8. Graves, A., Liwicki, M., Fernández, S., Bertolami, R., Bunke, H., Schmidhuber, J.: A novel connectionist system for unconstrained handwriting recognition. IEEE Trans. Pattern Anal. Mach. Intell. (PAMI) **31**(5), 855–868 (2009)
9. Hinds, S.C., Fisher, J.L., D'Amato, D.P.: A document skew detection method using run-length encoding and the hough transform. In: 10th International Conference on Pattern Recognition (ICPR), 1990, vol. 1, pp. 464–468. IEEE (1990)
10. Ji, T., Kim, E., Srikantan, R., Tsai, A., Cordero, A., Wagner, D.: An analysis of write-in marks on optical scan ballots. In: Proceedings of the 2011 Conference on Electronic Voting Technology/Workshop on Trustworthy Elections, EVT/WOTE 2011. USENIX Association, Berkeley (2011)
11. Keysers, D., Gollan, C., Ney, H.: Local context in non-linear deformation models for handwritten character recognition. In: 17th International Conference on Pattern Recognition (ICPR), 2004, vol. 4, pp. 511–514. IEEE (2004)
12. Kim, E., Carlini, N., Chang, A., Yiu, G., Wang, K., Wagner, D.: Improved support for machine-assisted ballot-level audits. In: Presented as part of the 2013 Electronic Voting Technology Workshop/Workshop on Trustworthy Elections. USENIX, Berkeley (2013). https://www.usenix.org/conference/evtwote13/ workshop-program/presentation/Kim

13. Le, D.S., Thoma, G.R., Wechsler, H.: Automated page orientation and skew angle detection for binary document images. Pattern Recogn. **27**(10), 1325–1344 (1994)
14. Lecun, Y., Cortes, C.: The MNIST database of handwritten digits. http://yann.lecun.com/exdb/mnist/
15. Liu, C.L., Nakashima, K., Sako, H., Fujisawa, H.: Handwritten digit recognition: benchmarking of state-of-the-art techniques. Pattern Recogn. **36**(10), 2271–2285 (2003)
16. Niblack, W.: An Introduction to Digital Image Processing. Strandberg Publishing Company, Birkerod (1985)
17. Otsu, N.: A threshold selection method from gray-level histograms. Automatica **11**(285–296), 23–27 (1975)
18. Plötz, T., Fink, G.A.: Markov models for offline handwriting recognition: a survey. Int. J. Doc. Anal. Recogn. **12**(4), 269–298 (2009)
19. Pratikakis, I., Gatos, B., Ntirogiannis, K.: ICDAR 2013 document image binarization contest (DIBCO 2013). In: 12th International Conference on Document Analysis and Recognition (ICDAR), 2013, pp. 1471–1476. IEEE (2013)
20. Rabiner, L., Juang, B.H.: An introduction to hidden markov models. IEEE ASSP Mag. **3**(1), 4–16 (1986)
21. Sauvola, J., Pietikäinen, M.: Adaptive document image binarization. Pattern Recogn. **33**(2), 225–236 (2000)
22. Serra, J.: Introduction to mathematical morphology. Comput. Vis. Graph. Image Process. **35**(3), 283–305 (1986)
23. Sezgin, M., et al.: Survey over image thresholding techniques and quantitative performance evaluation. J. Electron. Imaging **13**(1), 146–168 (2004)
24. Singh, C., Bhatia, N., Kaur, A.: Hough transform based fast skew detection and accurate skew correction methods. Pattern Recogn. **41**(12), 3528–3546 (2008)
25. Smith, E.H.B., Lopresti, D.P., Nagy, G.: Ballot mark detection. In: ICPR, pp. 1–4. IEEE (2008)
26. Smith, E.H.B., Lopresti, D.P., Nagy, G., Wu, Z.: Towards improved paper-based election technology. In: International Conference on Document Analysis and Recognition (ICDAR), pp. 1255–1259. IEEE (2011)
27. Smith, E.H.B., Nagy, G., Lopresti, D.P.: Mark detection from scanned ballots. In: Berkner, K., Likforman-Sulem, L. (eds.) DRR. SPIE Proceedings, vol. 7247, pp. 1–10. SPIE (2009)
28. Wang, K., Kim, E., Carlini, N., Motyashov, I., Nguyen, D., Wagner, D.: Operator-assisted tabulation of optical scan ballots. In: Presented as part of the 2012 Electronic Voting Technology Workshop/Workshop on Trustworthy Elections. USENIX, Berkeley (2012)
29. Xiu, P., Lopresti, D.P., Baird, H.S., Nagy, G., Smith, E.H.B.: Style-based ballot mark recognition. In: International Conference on Document Analysis and Recognition (ICDAR), pp. 216–220. IEEE (2009)

Machine-Checked Reasoning About Complex Voting Schemes Using Higher-Order Logic

Jeremy E. Dawson, Rajeev Goré$^{(\boxtimes)}$, and Thomas Meumann

Research School of Computer Science,
Australian National University, Canberra, Australia
rajeev.gore@anu.edu.au

Abstract. We describe how we first formally encoded the English-language Parliamentary Act for the Hare-Clark Single Transferable Vote-counting scheme used in the Australian state of Tasmania into higher-order logic, producing SPECHOL. Based on this logical specification, we then encoded an SML program to count ballots according to this specification inside the interactive theorem prover HOL4, giving us IMPHOL. We then manually transliterated the program as a real SML program IMP. We are currently verifying that the formalisation of the implementation implies the formalisation of the specification: that is, we are using the HOL4 interactive theorem prover to prove the implication IMPHOL $\rightarrow$ SPECHOL.

1 Introduction

Two fundamental principles in tallying an election are the transparency and trustworthiness of the process. Strict protocols are enforced when dealing with the ballot boxes and interested parties are provided with the opportunity to scrutinise the tally while it is being undertaken. Thus traditional manual vote-counting methods are designed to ensure trustworthiness via scrutiny.

Despite these measures, manually counting ballots is still error-prone. During the 2013 Senate election, the Australian Electoral Commission (AEC) was required to recount the Western Australian (WA) ballots after a close result. During the recount, approximately 1370 ballots were found to be missing. It is unclear whether these ballots were present in the first count and then mislaid, or whether the original tallies were wrong. The error had the capacity to influence the outcome of the election, so the AEC was forced to re-run the election for the WA seats in its entirety at a cost of approximately AUD 20 million [1]. The electoral commissioner of the AEC itself subsequently resigned.

Paper ballots and manual counting methods in modern elections are therefore increasingly seen as archaic, especially as cash-strapped electoral bodies seek cheaper alternatives. Indeed, numerous electoral bodies are ploughing ahead with electronic vote-casting and vote-counting of preferential votes using computers and the most recent state election in New South Wales in Australia even used an internet voting system which was shown to be vulnerable to vote-tampering [22]. Alarmingly, many of these software systems are not open to scrutiny and some

© Springer International Publishing Switzerland 2015
R. Haenni et al. (Eds.): VoteID 2015, LNCS 9269, pp. 142–158, 2015.
DOI: 10.1007/978-3-319-22270-7_9

are even officially deemed to be "commercial in confidence" and are deliberately kept from researchers like us who wish to scrutinise the code for correctness. Given the importance of the task of electing a government, this state of affairs is totally unacceptable.

The ideal of course is to use some form of end-to-end verifiable system which provides strong evidence that electronic ballots are cast-as-intended, transported-without-tampering and that all electronic ballots are included in the final tally *without having to blindly trust the underlying computer code*. Unfortunately, such systems do not guarantee that the electronic ballots are counted correctly according to complex vote-counting schemes such as single-transferable voting (STV) and methods for extending them to STV are in their infancy [7].

A "voting scheme" is a method that spells out the structure of a ballot, how to cast a vote using such a ballot, and how to count such votes regardless of whether these activities are carried out using pen and paper, hand-counting or electronically. We describe a methodology for formally reasoning about complex vote-counting schemes. Specifically, we describe how we first formally encoded the English-language description of the Hare-Clark Single Transferable Vote-counting scheme used in the Australian state of Tasmania into higher-order logic, giving a formula called SPECHOL. We then created a more algorithmic version using the syntax of the functional programming language Standard ML (SML) to give a formula called IMPHOL. We manually transliterated this formula into an actual SML program IMP to count ballots. We are currently verifying that the formalisation of the implementation logically implies the formalisation of the specification: that is, we are using the HOL4 interactive theorem prover to machine-check the implication IMPHOL → SPECHOL.

2   Hare-Clark Single Transferable Voting

Farrell and McAllister [12] provide a definitive study of preferential electoral systems in Australia. Wen [23] provides an engineering perspective of preferential systems, legislation and verifiable cryptographic schemes for preferential voting and counting. Here, we briefly describe STV and Hare-Clark STV.

STV for Electing Multiple Candidates. We assume that there are more candidates than seats, as otherwise, there is no need for an election. Voters order the candidates on the ballot paper in order of preference, usually by placing a number next to each candidate's name. To become elected, a candidate must reach a quota of votes, as opposed to an absolute majority. This quota is set according to the number of seats available. There are several ways of calculating a quota.

The votes are all initially allocated according to their first preference. A candidate who reaches the quota is elected, or else, if no candidate reaches the quota, then one "weakest" candidate is eliminated. There are several ways to choose the "weakest" candidate. If a candidate is elected by reaching the quota, each surplus ballot for that candidate is transferred to the next continuing (un-elected and un-eliminated) candidate on that ballot. There are many different ways to choose a surplus ballot, and many ways to choose its new, possibly fractional, value. If a candidate is eliminated, all of the ballots currently counted as being for that candidate are transferred to their next (continuing) preference, again possibly with a fractional transfer value. The election is complete either when all seats are filled, or the number of vacant seats equals the number of continuing candidates, in which case all these candidates are elected.

The transfer of votes is key to ensuring that candidates with particular political views are elected in proportion to their support within the community, so the complexity resulting from surplus calculations and transfers cannot be removed without seriously crippling the system. As we shall see, there are many subtleties in the naive description above.

The Hare-Clark Scheme. Hare-Clark is an instance of the proportional representation scheme that uses single transferable vote as described above and has been used to elect members of Tasmania's House of Assembly since 1907 [8,17]. A slightly different version has also been used to elect members of the Legislative Assembly in the Australian Capital Territory (ACT) since 1995 [3]. Hand-counting according to Hare-Clark is notoriously difficult and error-prone with some ballots examined in excess of 50 times before a result is declared. Thus a formally verified program for either version is likely to have practical benefits almost immediately. We already have a formal specification of Hare-Clark ACT [2], so we decided to concentrate on Hare-Clark Tasmania as this will allow us to compare and contrast the properties of these two variants of Hare-Clark.

3   Related Work

Various authors have attempted to apply formal methods to algorithms for STV counting, starting from early work using only pen-and-paper proofs, and ending with more recent work using light-weight computer-based tools. We present them in order of the amount and rigour of machine-checking involved in each. As far as we know, the only other work on using heavy-weight verification is our own previous work on reasoning about the first-past-the-post voting scheme [14].

Hill *et al.* [15] give a pen-and-paper proof of various properties of an algorithm to count votes using the Meek's method. It's correctness relies totally on these pen-and-paper proofs, which presumably were checked by the referees.

Poppleton [19] takes a step towards machine-checked proofs by writing a specification for STV vote-counting in the logic-based specification language Z, but does not verify an implementation using computer tools based on Z [20].

Kiniry *et al.* [10] formalised the STV scheme used for proportional representation elections in Ireland using the Alloy tool. They automatically generated test cases that covered every possible scenario using breadth-first search. Finally, they tested an implementation of the Irish vote-counting scheme, which had been developed using light-weight formal methods, and found two errors. They conclude that *"this level of coverage (100 % statement and condition coverage) does not prove that the system is error-free. ... But what it does do is (a) provide strong evidence, especially when combined with a rigorous development method and formal verification, that the system is correct, and (b) raise the state-of-the-art for election tally system testing enormously"* [10].

Cochran conducted a comprehensive study of verifying STV counting using light-weight (automatic) formal methods [9] by attempting to formally verify a Java program for the Irish proportional representation single-transferable voting scheme against its English natural language description using the ESC/Java tool. Most proofs were completed automatically, but in some, *"ESC/Java2 could neither verify the loop invariants nor the post-condition"* [9, p. 46]. Moreover, lightweight formal methods, such as ESC/Java, are not guaranteed to be sound or complete since their code base is huge. Cochran concludes with *"Despite the use of a verification-centric process, and 100 % statement coverage of the code, the following issues are outstanding, representing a potential inconsistency in the JML specifications."* [9, p. 63].

Recent attempts by Beckert et al. [5] show that even state-of-the-art light-weight verification techniques such as bounded model-checking do not scale to realistic elections for even simple voting schemes such as first-past-the-post.

The move to using interactive theorem proving technology based upon (higher-order) logic is apparent in the work of De Young and Schurmann [11]. Rather than translating English prose into higher-order logic, they express the vote-counting scheme itself as a linear logic program. Read purely declaratively, this logic program specifies what the algorithm should do. It can also be executed to count actual ballots, although tests showed that it did not scale to real-world elections. The logical framework they utilise is not able to capture formal reasoning about the logic program itself: thus there is no correctness proof.

The related work described above is mostly about verifying algorithms against specifications. Thus there is no ability to formally compare and contrast two variants of the same voting scheme. Light-weight methods allow us to specify two variants of an STV voting scheme (say) and compare them by specifying different post-conditions. But recall that such tools are not guaranteed to be sound or complete. Recent work of Beckert *et al.* [6] shows other pen-and-paper methods for reasoning about voting schemes using first-order and linear logic.

Our methodology goes beyond all of these efforts in the following senses:

Formal specifications: the specification is encoded as a formula of higher-order logic inside the HOL4 theorem prover. Thus it is type-checked and we can be sure that it actually is a well-formed formula of higher-order logic;

Formal termination: the SML program is encoded into HOL4 as IMPHOL and HOL4 will only accept the program if we can create a proof inside HOL4 that the program will terminate for all inputs;

Proof Objects: both the implementation and the specification are encoded as formulae of higher-order logic inside the theorem prover HOL4. Thus we can construct a proof that IMPHOL $\rightarrow$ SPECHOL which can be exported and checked by others using their own favourite theorem prover;

Correctness: the HOL4 theorem prover checks all steps in this proof are correct so we can be certain that the proof is mathematically correct.

Our methodology has three inherent weaknesses. As with all formal methods, there is no guarantee that SPECHOL correctly captures the English prose that makes up the Hare-Clark method of STV counting since it is merely one person's interpretation of the English-language prose of the relevant Parliamentary Act. We mitigated the risks of errors in interpretation by using two people to complete the formalisation: Meumann wrote the initial SPECHOL and IMPHOL but Dawson carried out all the proofs. Thus, Dawson first had to check whether these formulae accurately captured the Hare-Clark act and Meumann's implementation. In so doing, Dawson found some errors, as discussed in Sect. 8.3. Second, we have no formal model of the programming language SML, so we cannot prove that the final SML code meets its formal programming language semantics. As we point out previously [14], the CakeML [16] project will allows us to provide such proofs in the future. Finally, our approach is very labour-intensive: it took Dawson at least six months of full-time work to complete these proofs and he has over 20 years of experience in using higher-order logic theorem provers!

4   Higher-Order Logic and the HOL4 Theorem Prover

The rigorousness of our approach stems from the use of HOL4 to construct the proofs. HOL4 is an interactive theorem proving assistant based upon Dana Scott's "Logic for Computable Functions" (LCF), a mathematically rigorous logic engine consisting of 8 primitive inference rules which have been proven to be mathematically correct [13]. HOL4 implements this logic engine using approximately 3000 lines of ML code and this code has been scrutinised by experts in LCF to ensure that it correctly implements the 8 inference rules. Any complex inference rules must be constructed as a programmatic combination of the core primitive rules only. Thus its code base is small and trusted.

Our verification process falls under the rubric of "heavy-weight verification" since it requires a person to direct the process in an interactive fashion. As such, it is very labour intensive. It involves producing a logical formalisation of both the program's requirements and the program itself in the HOL4 theorem proving assistant (http://hol.sourceforge.net/), then constructing a formal proof showing that the program matches the requirements. Producing the program using a strictly functional programming style ensures the program can be readily represented in higher order logic with minimal alterations. We used Standard ML (SML), the same language in which HOL4 is itself implemented.

When applied to electoral systems, the requirements are usually informed by the relevant legislation. As we shall show, translating complex legislation into rigorous formal logic can be a non-trivial task. Our methodology involves producing the following:

SPECHOL: a hand-encoding of the English-language description of the vote-counting process into higher-order logic;

IMPHOL: a hand-translation of SPECHOL into the HOL4 rendering of SML;

IMP: a hand-transliteration of IMPHOL into SML;

Formal Proof: a proof acceptable to the HOL4 theorem prover that IMPHOL logically implies SPECHOL which guarantees that the <u>translation</u> of the implementation meets the <u>translation</u> of the Parliamentary Act.

When applying this methodology to vote counting schemes, the counting program is represented in higher-order logic (as IMPHOL). It thus becomes possible to prove various results about the program. We can also verify various desiderata of the voting scheme (SPECHOL) itself. Our methodology is particularly suited to the verification of new voting schemes against the presence of desired properties or the avoidance of objectionable ones. For example it would be possible to prove that the voting scheme in question adheres to the independence of irrelevant alternatives (see [4]). It is also possible to prove comparative results between different voting schemes: for instance that voting scheme A differs from voting scheme B in only x specific situations.

The specification (in this case the translation of the legislation into HOL4's logic) is performed *prior* to the implementation of a counting program. This is intended to ensure the specification remains as independent of the implementation as possible. Thus ensuring any shortcuts or misconceptions adopted during the implementation process are not carried through to the specification.

Rather than producing an SML program and translating that to HOL4, the program is produced first in HOL4's formal logic, then translated to SML. Programming directly in HOL4's formal logic also helps to ensure that the non-functional features of SML are avoided.

The astute reader may notice there are certain gaps in this methodology that cannot be filled: there is no *proof* that the SML program (IMP) is the same as the HOL4 translation (IMPHOL), and there is no *proof* that the HOL4 encoding of the legislation (SPECHOL) is logically the same as the legislation itself.

5   Translating Legislation into Higher-Order Logic

The following list of HOL4 syntax may be helpful.

HOL4	\x y. A	T	F	~t	t_1 \/ t_2	t_1 /\ t_2	t_1 ==> t_2	t_1 = t_2	!x.t	?x.t
Logic	$\lambda xy.\ A$	verum	falsum	$\neg t$	$t_1 \vee t_2$	$t_1 \wedge t_2$	$t_1 \rightarrow t_2$	$t_1 = t_2$	$\forall x.t$	$\exists x.t$

The translation of the Tasmanian House of Assembly vote counting legislation is a non-trivial task. Theoretically, if there is only one way to interpret the legislation logically, then higher-order logic is expressive enough to capture the legislation's meaning. When examined closely, however, the legislation contains various ambiguities and contradictions that prevent a direct "translation". In many cases the intended *meaning* of the legislation must be encoded in HOL4 rather than a direct logical translation of each predication.

For example, clause 12 deals with the case in which there is a tie amongst the weakest candidates and one of them must be eliminated. The legislation specifies that the tie is to be broken by deferring to *"the last count or transfer at which [the candidates involved in the tie] had an unequal number of votes"*. When more than two candidates are concerned, there are three different ways of interpreting which candidate should be excluded:

(a) the candidate who has the lowest count at the last count or transfer at which all of the candidates concerned had pairwise unequal counts;
(b) the candidate who has the lowest count at the last count or transfer at which one candidate had a count less than all of the other candidates concerned;
(c) the candidate who has the lowest count in a lexicographical ordering of all of the previous counts for the candidates concerned (with the most recent count being the first element of the lexicographical combination and the next-most recent count being the next element of the lexicographical combination etc.).

Option (a) appears to most closely mirror the wording of the legislation, but causes deferral to counts older than the other two options. This one is the most likely to defer all the way back to the initial count and result in a lot-based elimination. Option (b) causes deferral to counts more recent than option (a), but may result in the exclusion of a candidate who had a higher count than some or all of the other candidates concerned at a more recent count. Option (c) is the intuitively fairest option, but appears to reflect the legislation least. The ACT has a similar issue with their Hare-Clark legislation, in which the clauses regarding tie breaking are similarly worded. The ACTEC interprets their legislation according to option (c), so we also used this option.

Ambiguities such as this increase the difficulty of the formalisation process. Nevertheless, it is a testament to the rigorousness of our approach that it results in ambiguities such as this being discovered and properly questioned. This is a positive outcome if it results in a tightening of the legislation.

Another issue encountered whilst formalising the legislation is that the legislation is written in a procedural manner. In particular, the legislation makes regular reference to various "stages" of the count, and what should happen if certain conditions are met at various stages. This implies a mutable representation of the count, where the state changes over time (at each stage of the count) and is a side-effect of the legislation specifying *how* the votes should be counted, not what the result of the count should be. This is in direct contradiction with the ideal of functional programming, which is to have a declarative representation of computation (effectively stateless).

The procedural nature of the legislation forces SPECHOL to make statements about IMPHOL's "state". In lieu of an existing IMPHOL, the SPECHOL must be built based on assumptions about IMPHOL's structure. This results in a certain level of coupling between SPECHOL and IMPHOL, but cannot be avoided when the legislation is written in a procedural manner.

5.1 Assumptions About the Implementation

To have a concrete conceptualisation about which to build the logical statements of SPECHOL, some assumptions must be made about the form of IMPHOL. The initial assumptions are explained below. Note that some of the assumptions now need revision due to unforeseen technical restrictions on IMPHOL. The revision process is yet to be undertaken, but the intention is to combine it with a general review of SPECHOL to remove any inconsistencies.

Inputs and Outputs. The inputs and outputs of the counting procedure must be defined. This is fairly straightforward. At a minimum, the procedure must take the set of ballots and the set of running candidates as input. These are assumed to be provided using lists: a mainstay of functional programming. The procedure is assumed to take as input a list of candidates and a list of ballots. Each ballot itself is assumed to be a list of candidates in order of preference (the head of the list being the first preference). It is also assumed the function takes as input the number of candidates to be elected since the number of seats per electorate has changed multiple times in Tasmania. The output of the function is assumed to be a list of elected candidates. Let us call the function COUNT_HCT, so we have the following type-definition to work with:

```
COUNT_HCT: num -> 'a list -> 'a list list -> 'a list
```

where the first argument represents the number of available seats, the second argument the list of running candidates and the third argument the list of ballots.

Stateful Representation. Some assumptions about the internal operation of the function are needed to capture the stateful or procedural nature of the legislation. It is necessary to assume that COUNT_HCT possesses some form of state, and that the state changes over time. Moreover the state must take a particular structure, so we can reason formally about its various components.

In a strictly functional programming language there is no implicit concept of time or state. The closest thing to a state is the set of values of all of the variables at a given level of recursion. In this conceptual representation of state, the "time" is given by the level of recursion. Naturally, a proper representation of time must be strictly monotonic. That is, with each recursion the time must increase. In other words, backtracking back up the recursion cannot be permitted until the final result is ascertained (and it becomes possible to backtrack all the way to the surface tail-recursively). Ultimately, within the Hare-Clark context, our concept of time need only capture the temporal difference between the stages of the count, not the assignment of individual variables or other small differences. Bundling the requisite variables into a "state" represented by a tuple allows us to recurse on the tuple and treat it as a close approximation of a mutable state.

Based on the properties referred to by the legislation, it is assumed that the state of the count is represented by a tuple of the following structure:

```
(time, seats, quota, elected, excluded, rem, surps, groups)
```

where...

time is a parameter representing temporality (the level of recursion). It increases
by one with each recursion;

seats is the number of seats to be filled. Note that this value is not intended
to change over the course of the count;

quota is the number of votes required by candidates in order to be declared
elected. It is calculated at the beginning and remains unchanged throughout;

elected is a list of candidates who have been elected. Declaring a candidate
elected (as specified in the legislation) means placing a candidate in this list;

excluded is the list of excluded candidates. Excluding a candidate is interpreted
as placing a candidate in this list;

rem is the list of continuing candidates, along with their current vote counts and
their transfer history. Each candidate in this list is represented by the tuple
(**name, total, transfers**) where:

   name is the identifier of the candidate (this can be any equality type);

   total is the total value of votes assigned to the candidate;

   transfers is a list of transfers assigned to the candidate and is of the form
   (**value, ballots, clause**) where

      value is the transfer value associated with the transfer and is a tuple of
      the form (**numerator, denominator**);

      ballots is the list of ballots associated with the transfer.

      clause represents the clause responsible for the transfer of the ballots
      to the candidate concerned. This will likely be removed when the
      specification is reviewed as the implementation does not use it;

surps is a list of pending transfers of surplus votes from elected candidate;

groups is a list of transfers pending from the exclusion of a candidate. Each
member of both **surps** and **groups** is of the form (**value, ballots**) where
value is a tuple (**numerator, denominator**) for the transfer value and
ballots is the list of ballots awaiting transfer.

Assuming the function performing the recursion on the state tuple is called
FINAL_STAGE, we have the following function type definition:

```
FINAL_STAGE: num # num # num #'a list #'a list #
  ('a # num # ((num # num) #'a list list # num) list) list #
  ((num # num) #'a list list # num) list
  -> 'a list
```

It can be argued that these assumptions are not necessary: that the functions
can be quantified in each of the clauses. This would remove any dependency on
naming conventions, but the clauses will still need to make statements relying on
what form the functions take. This has the potential to blow out the complexity
of the individual clauses as each clause will need to cover many more possibilities
in terms of functional structure. Whether or not this would actually happen is
unclear. Potentially, more experience is needed to truly take advantage of the
expressibility of higher order logic.

With the assumptions in hand, it becomes possible to translate the legislation into HOL4's formal syntax. The translation of one example clause, is given in Sect. 5.4. An example function and statements that are used by the clauses are given in Sect. 5.2 below. Sanity checks are given in Sect. 5.3. Note that the definitions, sanity checks and clausal statements will need to be revised to take into account the final form of the implementation. They will also need to be reviewed for their accuracy.

5.2   Example Definitions

The function shown in Listing 1.1 is used to simplify the clauses in Sect. 5.4. Such functions are intended to be executable and translatable into SML so that they may be used by the counting program should this be necessary.

Listing 1.1: Executable function definitions.

```
1  (* Returns list of ballots whose first preference is cand *)
2  val FIRSTS_FOR_DEF = Define '
3      FIRSTS_FOR cand ballots =
4          FILTER (($= cand) o HD) ballots';
5  (* Sums the number of ballots with a first preference for
6     each of the running candidates.  This is needed simply
7     because the legislation specifies that this is how the
8     quota should be calculated. *)
9  val SUM_FIRSTS_DEF = Define '
10    (SUM_FIRSTS []        ballots = 0)
11 /\ (SUM_FIRSTS (c::cs) ballots =
12                         LENGTH (FIRSTS_FOR c ballots)
13                         + SUM_FIRSTS cs ballots)';
```

5.3   Sanity Checks

In addition to the clauses of the Tasmanian Hare-Clark legislation, some proof obligations have been defined as sanity checks. These checks can be assumed in the clausal statements, reducing their complexity, as shown next.

Listing 1.2 specifies that it must be impossible to introduce candidates to the list of continuing candidates after the count has begun. In other words, if a candidate is in the list of continuing candidates, then that candidate must have been in the list of candidates in all preceding states of the count.

Listing 1.2: Candidates cannot be introduced partway through the count.

```
1  !seats cands ballots state state'.
2     (COUNT_HCT seats cands ballots = FINAL_STAGE state)
3     /\ (COUNT_HCT seats cands ballots = FINAL_STAGE state')
4     /\ TIME_VAR state' > TIME_VAR state
5     ==> !cand. IS_REM_CAND state' cand
6              ==> IS_REM_CAND state cand
```

5.4   Example of a Clause in Higher-Order Logic

Each of the 14 clauses in the Tasmanian Hare-Clark legislation was thus hand-translated into higher-order logic. We give just one example below.

Clause 2: First Preference Votes to Be Counted

The number of first preferences recorded for each candidate, on ballot papers which are not informal ballot papers, is to be counted.

This is somewhat abstract in the context of our counting procedure and leaves little to specify concretely. The proof obligation for this clause in HOL4 instead specifies how the counts should be incorporated into the initial state tuple. See Listing 1.3 below.

```
Listing 1.3: Clause 2
1   !seats cands ballots cand rem_cands quota.
2    (COUNT_HCT seats cands ballots =
3          FINAL_STAGE (t0,seats,quota,[],[],rem_cands,[]))
4    /\ (MEM cand cands =
5        MEM (cand,
6            LENGTH (FIRSTS_FOR cand ballots),
7            [((1,1), FIRSTS_FOR cand ballots, clause2)])
8            rem_cands)
```

Note that the "count" of the first preferences is given by `LENGTH (FIRSTS_FOR cand ballots)`. The function `LENGTH` is a predefined function in HOL4, and `FIRSTS_FOR` is defined in Listing 1.1 and `MEM` is the member predicate on lists.

6   From HOL4 to an SML Implementation

The implementation is first written in HOL4, then translated into SML. The translation is performed iteratively, ironing out any features used in one language that are not available in the other. Since the implementation is initially programmed in HOL4, the features that need removal are primarily those available in HOL4 but not SML (a lambda calculus interpreter for instance).

The semantic equivalence of these two implementations is not rigorously guaranteed. A visual comparison is still convincing for this larger case study, however, thanks to the strict functional nature of the implementations and the restricted feature set they use.

The implementation breaks ties using the lexicographical ordering interpretation (option (c) on p. X). It does this by merge-sorting the list of remaining candidates according to candidate counts at each stage of the recursion. Merge sort is stable, allowing it to maintain the lexicographical ordering discussed without further interference.

6.1   Testing the SML Implementation for Efficiency

The implementation was tested both for preliminary correctness and to ascertain whether it could handle the input sizes likely in real public elections. All of the tests were conducted using PolyML (http://www.polyml.org/) on GNU/Linux with an Intel Core i7-3740QM processor and 16 GiB of RAM.

To test for bugs, we compared this implementation against an implementation of the ACT's Hare-Clark system produced previously by Dawson. Several randomly generated examples were produced with lists of votes ranging from 50 thousand to 300 thousand in length and between 10 and 40 candidates covering a range of possible scenarios.[1] The two programs produced the same results for each example, giving preliminary indications that the program is correct.

However, there are differences between Hare-Clark ACT and Hare-Clark Tasmania. The main difference that might lead to a different outcome at an election is that the transfer value is calculated differently. Tasmanian Hare-Clark calculates the transfer value based on the total number of votes in the transfer leading to the surplus whereas the ACT calculates it based on a subset of those: the unexhausted ballots. The following small example illustrates the difference.

Imagine an election between 3 candidates (A, B and C), with two available seats and a total of 5 votes. Let's say the votes were as follows: [A,B] [A,B] [A] [A] [C] where the vote can be read from left to right in order of preference (so the first vote has A as its first preference and B as its second). In the first round, A will be elected with 4 votes and a surplus of 2 (the Droop quota is 2 votes). B and C remain unelected with counts of 0 and 1 respectively. In the second round, 2 of A's votes will be counted towards B, but the transfer value differs between the ACT and Tasmanian systems:

TAS $=$ (surplus/total votes in prev. transfer) $= 2/4 = 1/2$
ACT $=$ (surplus/total unexhaust. votes in prev. transfer) $= 2/2 = 1$.

Thus, the ACT would transfer the votes in full, whereas in Tasmania they would transfer them as half votes. So the result after round 2 would be:

TAS: 1 for C, 1 for B so B eliminated as C had more votes in previous round;
ACT: 1 for C, 2 for B so C eliminated.

The programs confirmed that this example leads to different results.

The program was tested separately for its ability to handle large numbers of ballots. The tests ranged from 250 thousand votes with 10 candidates to 15 million votes with 40 candidates. Note that every example took less than 80 seconds to count, and consumed less than 10 GiB of memory.

There are 5 electorates in Tasmania used to elect the House of Assembly using Hare-Clark, and these each have approximately 72,000 enrolled voters (as at September 2013) [21]. Our implementation is more than adequately equipped

---

[1] If a large number of ballots are generated naïvely, they become spread too evenly between the candidates. This results in no candidate being elected until the final stages of the count, which is unrealistic. The candidates were given random popularity ratings to produce uneven distributions of ballots to avoid this issue.

to handle counts of this size. The largest electorate used in any PR election in Australia is New South Wales (NSW), with an enrolment of just under 5 million voters (as at August 2014) [18]. Once again, our implementation is well able to handle counts of this size.

An initial analysis shows that our SML code has computational complexity O(num_candidates * num_candidates * num_votes), possibly worse. We are confident that we can remove at least one of these occurrences of num_candidates by using SML arrays, and setting up a HOL4 theory formalising the appropriate extra correctness properties. An alternate view is that the verified code only has to be run once, and it doesn't matter if it takes a week to run, even if the faster unverified code has already produced a result which has been announced.

We are currently investigating whether it can handle hundreds of candidates as occurred in the 2015 NSW State Election. Incidentally, being functional, and moving bits of data all over the place, it depends crucially on real memory.

7   Proving Termination of Functions and Properties of the Results of Those Functions

HOL4 requires function definitions to terminate, because the underlying logic of computable functions requires that all functions be total. So HOL4 does not actually allows us to state termination as a formula of higher-order logic: rather the evidence of it is that HOL accepts the definition of a function.

Once we input a function definition, HOL4 automatically attempts to generate a termination proof using in-built strategies based upon term-rewriting. If HOL4 cannot produce a termination proof automatically, it outputs the statement of a lemma which would allow it to complete the proof. If the user proves the lemma interactively, then HOL4 completes the proof of termination itself.

Once HOL4 accepts a function as terminating, it outputs, automatically, an induction principle which can be used to prove an arbitrary property P of the function. By instantiating this property in various ways, we can prove interesting properties of the function as illustrated next.

7.1   Properties of the Function MERGE

Definition 1 (MERGE_def). *The function* MERGE *(used to define* MERGE_SORT*) is*

```
    (MERGE R []        right    = right)
/\  (MERGE R left      []       = left)
/\  (MERGE R (l::ls)  (r::rs) = if R l r
                                then l::(MERGE R ls (r::rs))
                                else r::(MERGE R (l::ls) rs))
```

where [] *is the empty list,* x::xs *is a list with head* x *and tail* xs *and* R *is a function that returns* true *if its first argument is "less than" its second.*

Theorem 1. *The* `MERGE` *function terminates for all inputs.*

Proof. HOL4 is able to deduce termination automatically because in successive recursive calls, one list argument gets smaller while the other remains the same.

Some function definitions, however, require the user to prove a termination condition: in general, that there is some well-founded relation for which the argument(s) to the function get "smaller" in successive function calls.

HOL4 generates, automatically, an induction principle (lemma) called `MERGE_ind` for proving properties P of the result of the `MERGE` function:

Lemma 1. (MERGE_ind). *For all properties* P, *if the following conditions hold*

1. `P R left right` *holds whenever* `left` *or* `right` *is empty*
2. `P R (l::ls) (r::rs)` *holds whenever* `~ R l r` *and* `P R (l::ls) rs` *hold*
3. `P R (l::ls) (r::rs)` *holds whenever* `R l r` *and* `P R ls (r::rs)` *hold*

then `P v v1 v2` *holds for all values of* `v`, `v1` *and* `v2`:

```
!P. (!R right. P R [] right) /\ (!R v4 v5. P R (v4::v5) [])
 /\ (!R l ls r rs. ~ R l r /\ P R (l::ls) rs ==> P R (l::ls) (r::rs))
 /\ (!R l ls r rs. R l r /\ P R ls (r::rs) ==> P R (l::ls) (r::rs))
==> !v v1 v2. P v v1 v2
```

Note how HOL4 has reformulated the first clause of `MERGE_ind` to avoid overlapping cases by using `v4::v5` instead of `left` to enforce that the left argument is a non-empty list since the other part of this clause already handles the case where `left` is the empty list.

As an example of a proof by induction using `MERGE_ind`, we prove that the result of `MERGE`, viewed as a set, is the union of the lists l and r, viewed as sets.

Theorem 2. `!v v1 v2. set (MERGE v v1 v2) = (set v1) UNION (set v2)`

Proof. We instantiate P of the theorem `MERGE_ind` to

$$\texttt{\textbackslash c l r. set (MERGE c l r) = set l UNION set r}$$

HOL4 then sets out the framework for a proof by induction, where the inductive steps and their assumptions match the structure of `MERGE_def` (Definition 1). Intuitively, each step in the definition of `MERGE` preserves the desired property.

8   Proving Sanity Checks, Difficulties and Errors Found

8.1   That the List of Candidates Remains Unchanged

We showed that the list of elected, excluded and remaining candidates is unchanged. This needs to be formulated precisely, since these lists are changed by moving candidates from one list to another, and by re-ordering the remaining candidate list according to the number of votes each candidate has.

We use the built-in function `PERM`, which means that one list is a permutation of the other. The definition of `PERM` is provided by HOL. So we show that at each iteration, the concatenation of these lists is permuted.

8.2   Conditions Which Need to Be Proved

These are examples of conditions which seem obvious, and are assumed by the code (and, indeed, by the legislation), but proving that they hold requires several steps of reasoning and tracing through the code. Their proof is a lower priority since whenever they are not satisfied, the code as written will not complete without error, but for completeness, we intend to prove all such conditions.

The Condition that There Be "Remaining" Candidates. Since the counting program chooses the lowest ranking candidate to be eliminated, it requires that the list of "remaining" candidates be non-empty. We found that to prove this from the code as written would be very convoluted, since the part of the code which excludes a candidate requires that there be a candidate to exclude, and will have an undefined effect otherwise. That is, to avoid reasoning about an undefined effect, we have to prove that the list of remaining candidates is non-empty: leading us back to where we started!

We "solved" this problem by adding an extra termination condition: stop if the list of remaining candidates becomes empty. This avoids having to reason about undefined effects, but defers the problem since we now need to prove that this extra termination condition never has effect. However, doing so is significantly simpler since we never have to reason about undefined effects.

That Transfer Values Do Not Have Denominator Zero. The code requires the denominator of a fractional transfer value to be non-zero. This in turn requires that the final parcel of votes which elects a candidate is non-empty and that a candidate can get only one new parcel of votes in each iteration of the algorithm.

8.3   Errors Discovered

We found some errors where conditions (expressed in HOL4), which we set out to prove, were in fact not provable. We have not yet found cases where this was due to errors in the code (that is, the specification, in HOL4, of the program's behaviour). Rather, the errors were all in the expression of the conditions which were to be proved. We surmise that this is because the "program" specification, in HOL4, was translated into Standard ML, and tested. No doubt there were errors which were found in the course of this testing. On the other hand, the correctness conditions were not tested in this way.

Taking the nth Member of a Shorter List. The condition that the list of remaining candidates are distinct utilises the function EL n list which returns the nth member of list but is undefined when list has fewer than n members.

Need to Assume Candidates Distinct Initially. To prove that the list of remaining candidates are distinct at any stage, it is necessary to assume that the list of candidates provided initially is distinct. This assumption was omitted.

Acknowledgements. We are extremely grateful to the many suggestions for improvement from the reviewers of VoteID 2015. We have tried to take every comment into account, and have even used some of the suggested prose verbatim.

References

1. AAP. AEC costs WA Senate election at $20M, February 2014. http://www.sbs.com.au/news/article/2014/02/25/aec-costs-wa-senate-election-20m

2. Abate, P., Dawson, J., Goré, R., Gray, M., Norrish, M., Slater, A.: Formal methods applied to electronic voting systems (2003). http://users.rsise.anu.edu.au/~rpg/EVoting/

3. ACTEC. Hare-Clark electoral system (2015). http://www.elections.act.gov.au

4. Arrow, K.J.: A difficulty in the concept of social welfare. J. Polit. Econ. **58**(4), 328–346 (1950)

5. Beckert, B., Börmer, T., Goré, R., Kirsten, M., Meumann, T.: Reasoning about vote counting schemes using light-weight and heavy-weight methods. In: VERIFY 2014: Workshop Associated with IJCAR 2014 (2014)

6. Beckert, B., Goré, R., Schürmann, C., Bormer, T., Wang, J.: Verifying voting schemes. J. Inf. Sec. Appl. **19**(2), 115–129 (2014)

7. Benaloh, J., Moran, T., Naish, L., Ramchen, K., Teague, V.: Shuffle-sum: coercion-resistant verifiable tallying for STV voting. IEEE Trans. Inf. Forensics Secur. **4**(4), 685–698 (2009)

8. Bennett, S.: Inglis Clark's other contribution: a critical analysis of the Hare-Clark voting system. http://samuelgriffith.org.au/docs/vol23/vol23chap5.pdf

9. Cochran, D.: Formal specification and analysis of danish and irish ballot counting algorithms. Ph.D. thesis, ITU (2012)

10. Cochran, D., Kiniry, J.R.: Formal model-based validation for tally systems. In: Heather, J., Schneider, S., Teague, V. (eds.) Vote-ID 2013. LNCS, vol. 7985, pp. 41–60. Springer, Heidelberg (2013)

11. DeYoung, H., Schürmann, C.: Linear logical voting protocols. In: Kiayias, A., Lipmaa, H. (eds.) VoteID 2011. LNCS, vol. 7187, pp. 53–70. Springer, Heidelberg (2012)

12. Farrell, D.M., McAllister, I.: The Australian Electoral System: Origins, Variations and Consequences. University of New South Wales Press, Sydney (2006)

13. Gordon, M.J.C., Melham, T.F.: Introduction to HOL: a theorem proving environment for higher order logic. CUP (1993)

14. Goré, R., Meumann, T.: Proving the monotonicity criterion for a plurality vote-counting program as a step towards verified vote-counting. In: 6th International Conference on Electronic Voting: Verifying the Vote, pp. 1–7 (2014)

15. Hill, I.D., Wichmann, B.A., Woodall, D.R.: Algorithm 123: single transferable vote by Meek's method. Comput. J. **30**, 277–281 (1987)

16. Kumar, R., Myreen, M.O., Norrish, M., Owens, S.: CakeML: a verified implementation of ML. In: POPL, pp. 179–192 (2014)

17. Newman, T.: Hare-Clark system (2004). http://www.utas.edu.au/library/companion_to_tasmanian_history/H/Hare-Clark%20system.htm

18. NSWEC. Enrolment statistics. New South Wales Electoral Commission (2014). http://www.elections.nsw.gov.au/enrol_to_vote/enrolment_statistics
19. Poppleton, M.: The single transferable voting system: functional decomposition in formal specification. In: IWFM (1997)
20. Community Z tools. http://czt.sourceforge.net/. Accessed 2 June 2015
21. TEC. Annual report 2013–2014. Tasmanian Electoral Commission (2013)
22. Teague, V., Halderman, J.A.: Thousands of NSW election online votes open to tampering (2015). http://theconversation.com
23. Wen, R.: Online elections in Terra Australis. Ph.D. thesis, University of New South Wales (2010)

Experience Reports

Challenging an E-voting System in Court:

An Experience Report

Richard Hill(✉)

Hill & Associates, Geneva, Switzerland
rhill@hill-a.ch

Abstract. The Swiss political system is decentralized, and this includes voting operations. Several cantons have implemented Internet-based e-voting systems. The system used until recently in Geneva was a simple Internet voting system which assumed that the voter's personal computer had not been compromised. This was considered risky already at the time and various counter-measures were considered. The one that was implemented in practice was to limit the proportion of voters that could vote via Internet. At present, there is consensus amongst experts that such systems are unsafe and should be improved, in particular by implementing verification. In order to stimulate improvements in the system, the author challenged the use of the Geneva system in court, arguing that it was not compliant with constitutional principles and cantonal law on voting rights. At the end of a long and complex legal process, the Swiss Federal Tribunal (supreme court) ruled that the complaints could not be heard on their merits, because they did not allege that weaknesses had actually been exploited in a specific vote. This decision differs from those taken in other jurisdictions and highlights the difficulties of bringing scientific arguments into the court system.

Keywords: E-voting · Internet voting · Court challenges to e-voting

1 Introduction and Background

Switzerland is a federal state: the subdivisions are called cantons and communes. Although most laws in Switzerland are federal and apply throughout the country, that is not the case for many administrative matters such as taxation and voting. Fundamental voting principles are specified in the Federal Constitution and in the federal act on political rights. Lower level measures are included in the federal ordinance on political rights. Federal provisions apply throughout the country. But, within the limits specified by those principles, cantons are free to organize and administer elections as they think best. A detailed explanation of this complex situation is given in [1].

E-voting was introduced gradually and in a controlled manner (that is, with restrictions on its use), since the early 2000's. Internet voting has been used for federal votes since 2003. A comprehensive overview is given in [2]. The proportion of Internet voters is limited to 30 % of the cantonal electorate and 10 % of the federal electorate. About half of the 26 cantons use Internet voting systems and most of them are not close to reaching the authorized limits [1]. In Geneva, about 20 % of the voters who have the

© Springer International Publishing Switzerland 2015
R. Haenni et al. (Eds.): VoteID 2015, LNCS 9269, pp. 161–171, 2015.
DOI: 10.1007/978-3-319-22270-7_10

possibility to use Internet voting do so and the introduction of Internet voting did not increase the rate of participation [3].

The introduction of Internet voting was greatly facilitated by the fact that correspondence voting is widely used in Switzerland, and Internet voting was viewed as a natural extension of correspondence voting [1, 4].

The canton of Geneva started to use Internet voting in 2003 in trials at the communal level, and used it for a federal vote in 2004 [1]. During the early stages of the development process, computer experts identified the risks associated with Internet voting and recommended measures such as the development of a dedicated operating system that would be distributed on CD ROMs and uploaded by voters on their personal computers for the vote, but such measures were rejected as being too complex: it was felt that they would discourage use of the Internet voting system [4]. For similar reasons, solutions involving coded voting [5] were not implemented.

The system that was implemented was basically an electronic version of the correspondence voting procedure. The system is not fully electronic: the voter needs the very same paper material used for correspondence voting. The identification codes that prevent voters from casting multiple votes are provided in the correspondence voting material. Proxy voting is not allowed in Geneva. In order to prevent (or at least discourage) proxy voting, the voter must sign the identification card used for correspondence voting: this card must be sent to the voting authorities, but it is of course separate from the actual ballot, so anonymity of the vote is preserved. In the case of Internet voting, voters must provide their birth date and commune of origin (each Swiss citizen is associated with one or more commune of origin). In families, family members typically know the birth date and commune of origin of other family members.

When a voter accessed the Geneva Internet voting system that the author challenged, Java applets were downloaded to the voter's PC (the system has been modified and continues to evolve). Various sophisticated encryption measures are used for the communications between the user's personal computer and the state's servers. A detailed description is given in [6]. But the system used in 2011 did not have any provisions for verifiability (see [7–9] for a discussion of that technique) nor were any particular measures foreseen to check whether a user's personal computer had been compromised by malware [5, 7, 10]. In June 2013 a computer engineer demonstrated that it was relatively easy to insert in the voter's personal computer malware that could modify the voter's vote before it was encrypted and sent to the state's servers, and this without the voter being aware of the change [11].

Geneva cantonal law does not limit the proportion of Internet voters, but this has no practical effect for most votes, because cantonal votes are held in conjunction with federal votes, so the federal limits apply. That is, when there is a vote that concerns both federal and cantonal matters, the federal rules apply, and the proportion of Internet voters is limited.

However, the limits do not necessarily apply if a vote concerns only cantonal matters. The schedule of federal voting is fixed in advance by the government and there are usually four votes per year, each involving several separate questions (typically a yes or no vote on a constitutional amendment or on a federal law).

In May 2011, there was no federal question. The Geneva government decided to allow 100 % of the Geneva voters to use Internet voting for the cantonal questions. The same happened in November 2011.

The purpose of this paper is to present the outcome of an attempt to challenge the Geneva system in court. A comparative analysis of the case law regarding electronic voting in several countries, and also of the respective laws, is given in [13]. As we will see, the approach taken by the courts in Switzerland differs from that taken by the courts in other countries.

2   What the Appellant Did

The author of the present paper filed court challenges (called appeals in Switzerland) against the use of the Geneva system by all voters for the May and September 2011 votes. He requested the courts to find that the Geneva system did not conform to cantonal law and the Federal Constitution.

The reasons being that there was no guarantee that the vote sent to the state's server accurately reflects the voter's choices, that a family members can vote for another family member without that member's knowledge, and that the secrecy of the vote was not guaranteed.

The appeals were filed only against the votes where 100 % of the Geneva voters were offered the possibility of voting via Internet because, as explained below, an appeal can only be successful if the appellant can show that an irregularity could have affected the outcome. It is highly unlikely that the federal outcome can be affected by an irregularity in an Internet voting system that is offered only to 30 % of the voters. So an appeal against the use of the Internet voting system in a federal vote had lesser chance of being successful.

As we will see, the appeal was unsuccessful and this colors the present paper.

3   Why the Appellant Did It

The motivation behind the appeals was to stimulate improvements to the Geneva system, in particular the implementation of verifiability. In the author's view, the Geneva government (who had put into place the challenged Internet voting system) and the Geneva parliament (who had passed the law allowing the challenged system to be offered to all voters) did not know or understand that there has long been consensus amongst computer scientists that e-voting is risky [5, 12], that the rather simple Geneva system was inadequate, and that appropriate systems can be put into place.

4   The Appellant's Background

The appellant in these cases is not a lawyer and he did not mandate or consult lawyers regarding the cases. The complainant has degrees in mathematics and statistics from MIT and Harvard University, but he has mostly worked as a programmer, information systems manager, and telecommunications manager.

5   The Legal Process

Legal challenges to cantonal votes in Geneva must be filed with the cantonal court. The decision of the cantonal court can be appealed to the Federal Tribunal, which is the Swiss supreme court.

The deadline for filing the appeal at the cantonal level is rather short, 6 days. The deadline for filing the federal appeal is 30 days. At the cantonal level, the court will consider the receivability of the appeal before considering the arguments on the merits; it will consider both cantonal law and federal law, in particular the provisions of the Federal Constitution.

At the federal level the court will consider the receivability of the federal appeal, and the receivability of the cantonal appeal (but it will only consider whether the cantonal decision on receivability was arbitrary). Regarding the merits, it will freely review the application of both cantonal and federal law, but it will rely on the facts established by the cantonal court, unless the appelant can prove that the cantonal court established the facts in an arbitrary manner.

As we will see below, these technical legal procedural niceties were significant to the cases.

5.1   Receivability

In order to be receivable, an appeal must be filed within the deadline, by a person who has the right to file the appeal (in this case any voter). And it must respect formal rules regarding the format of the appeal, the language in which it is written, the number of copies to be submitted, etc.

There were no receivability issues at the federal level (even if the Geneva government did attempt to challenge the receivability of the federal appeals). On the other hand, there were significant issues regarding the receivability at the cantonal level. On the one hand, this might appear surprising: why should the court try to avoid considering the merits of the case? On the other hand, it is understandable: courts are not comfortable evaluating what is primarily a technical dispute [13].

5.2   Merits

The Law Applicable to the Merits. According to federal law (art. 34 of the Swiss Constitution and the resulting case law of the Federal Tribunal), the results of a vote must faithfully reflect the voter's intent, the vote must be secret (with some exceptions which are not relevant for the cases at hand), and one person can vote only once. It is not necessary for a complainant to prove that irregularities actually affected the result of a vote: it suffices to show that irregularities could have affected the result [14].

According to cantonal law (art. 60 of the Loi sur l'exercise des droits politiques), a voter must use equipment that is sufficiently secure, the government publishes security rules, and the government can suspend the use of e-voting systems if it believes that security is insufficient. In this context, "security" does not refer merely to security of the information technology used in the e-voting systems, it also refers to the reliability and security of all other aspects of the e-voting system, including manual operations.

The Substantive Arguments. The appellant alleged that the Geneva system did not comply with the law because the personal computers used by voters are vulnerable to malware that can change a vote without the voter's knowledge (for example, man-in-the-browser attack), that a man-in-the-middle attack was possible, that the state's server could also be compromised, that massive fraud could not be detected, that the secrecy of the vote could not be guaranteed, and that a family member could – easily and without risk of detection – impersonate and vote in place of another family member (also a risk in old persons' homes).

Further, the appelant alleged that the Geneva government had not produced the security requirements called for by cantonal law, and that the government should suspend the use of Internet voting until those security requirements were published.

The appeal was directed against the specific system (software) implemented and used in Geneva and the allegedly missing detailed regulation of security, and not against the principle of e-voting, nor against the provisions of the Geneva Constitution or of the cantonal law authorizing Internet voting. Indeed, appeals against those provisions per se would have been time-barred: an explicit challenge of the provisions of the Constitution or the cantonal law would have had to be filed within 30 days of their promulgation. On the other hand, the provisions can be challenged implicitly in the context of an appeal against a specific vote. The appellant attempted to do this but, as we will see below, the appeal was not accepted because the appellant could not present evidence showing that specific weaknesses had been exploited in a specific vote.

The appeal included the following figures. Figure 1 shows how malware could be introduced so as to change what the voter entered and send the falsified vote to the state's server. Figure 2 shows how a man-in-the-middle attack would be possible if the voter's personal computer were compromised, for example by replacing its X.509 certificates. Figure 3 shows the results of the Internet vote compared to the correspondence vote for the May 2011 vote for each of the five questions considered in that vote. As can be seen, the Internet vote differed systematically from the correspondence vote, which is not usually the case [15]. And the difference for question 5 was statistically significant and it actually affected the result of the vote for that particular question.

The appeals pointed out that a computer engineer had actually shown how easy it was to insert malware that would modify a vote, without the voter being aware of it [11]. And it stressed the fact that the 2013 report of the Federal government called for not allowing more than 30 % of voters to use the existing systems, and for the development

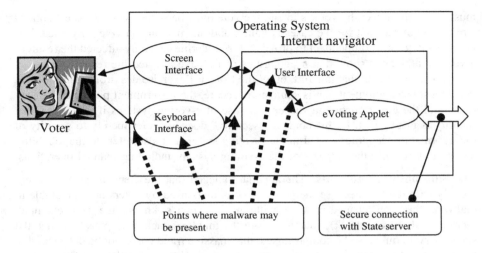

Fig. 1. Vulnerabilities to malware

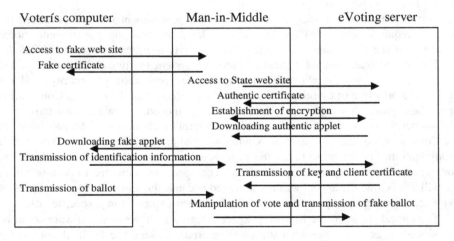

Fig. 2. Vulnerabilities to man-in-the-middle

and implementation of verifiable systems [2]. The appellant argued that the federal restriction of 30 % on the proportion of voters allowed to use the Geneva Internet voting system should apply also to cantonal votes.

The cantonal court's judgment provided a good summary of all the arguments outlined above [16].

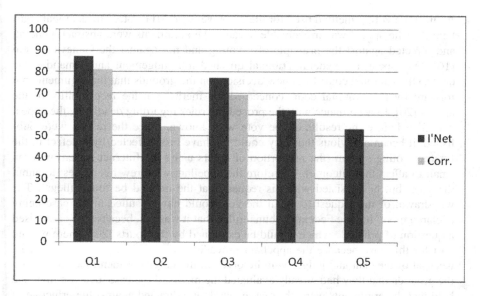

Fig. 3. Differences between Internet vote and correspondence vote for May 2011 vote

6 The Actual Procedures

The complainant filed six separate legal actions. In four of them he appealed to the Federal Tribunal against the cantonal decision. The six separate actions were:

1. Against the voting method used for the May 2011 vote. This complaint was mistakenly filed too late, so it was irreceivable. There was no appeal to the Federal Tribunal. The total cost of this action was CHF 500.
2. Against the result of the May 2011 vote. This was declared time barred and thus irreceivable at the cantonal level because the cantonal court held that the complaint was in reality directed against the voting method, not against the result of the vote [17]. The complainant appealed to the Federal Tribunal: the appeal was rejected [18]. It should be noted here that, with respect to cantonal procedural law (in this case the deadline for filing the cantonal complaint), the Federal Tribunal will only overturn the cantonal decision if it finds it to be arbitrary. The Federal Tribunal's judgment did not explicitly deal with the fact, put forward in both the cantonal complaint and the federal appeal, that there was an unusual difference between the results of the correspondence vote and the Internet vote, see Fig. 3 above. So the complainant filed a request for revision, on the grounds that the Federal Tribunal had overlooked a significant fact. The Federal Tribunal rejected this request [19]. The cost for this action was CHF 500 at the cantonal level, and CHF 1000 for each stage at the federal level, so the total was CHF 2500.
3. Against the refusal of the Geneva government to suspend e-voting as requested by letter. The cantonal court held that there was no appealable decision: the mere refusal to comply with the request in a letter was not a formal decision. There was no appeal to the Federal Tribunal. The total cost of this action was CHF 500.

4. Against the voting method used for the 27 November 2011 vote. The cantonal court held that the appeal was irreceivable because the arguments were abstract, general, and directed against the principle of e-voting and not against the Geneva system [16]. On appeal, the Federal Tribunal quashed this judgement and remanded the case to the cantonal court for a new decision, on the grounds that the arguments put forward by the cantonal court concerned the merits, not the receivability of the appeal [20]. In accordance with the procedural rules regarding deadlines, the appeal was filed before the results of the vote were known. Once the results were published, it became obvious that they could not have been affected by a defect in the Internet voting system (the proportion of voters using the Internet system was too small to affect the outcome). Therefore the appellant withdrew his request to annul the vote, but he persisted with his request that the method be found illegal. The withdrawal of the request to annul the vote could have resulted in the case being declared moot, but the Federal Tribunal ruled that it was not, because the case raised a question of principle which should be examined by the courts [20]. There was no cost for this case because the appellant prevailed.
5. Recusal of the cantonal judges who involved in the judgment mentioned above, on the grounds that they had already evaluated the merits of the case, because they had held that the arguments were abstract, general, and directed against the principle of e-voting and not against the Geneva system. The request was refused both by the cantonal court and by the Federal Tribunal [21]. The cost was CHF 350 at the cantonal level and CHF 2000 at the federal level, so the total cost was CHF 2350.
6. Second cantonal judgment regarding the 27 November 2011, the case having been declared receivable by the Federal Tribunal. The cantonal court rejected the appeal on the grounds that the arguments were abstract, general, and directed against the principle of e-voting and not against the Geneva system [22]. On appeal, the Federal Tribunal agreed [23]. Since this judgment ended the process, it will be discussed in more detail below. The cost was CHF 1500 at the cantonal level and CHF 1000 at the federal level, so the total was CHF 2500.

7   The Federal Court's Reasons

In essence, the Federal Tribunal [23] held that an appeal can only be lodged if weaknesses have been actually exploited during a specific vote. The fact that a weakness exists, and that it could be exploited in a way that cannot be detected, is not sufficient, and this even if the appeal is directed against the procedures used and not against the outcome of the vote. According to the Tribunal, arguments of that nature must be decided at the political level. Thus in practice one cannot appeal to the courts against the characteristics of an electronic voting system. The Tribunal, in so ruling, distances itself from the case law of other jurisdictions.

It should be noted that the Tribunal rejected (for the reasons mentioned above), the following claims regarding the Geneva system:

1. A voter can vote more than once using the electronic system, and this in a way that cannot be detected. This is not due to the computerized system properly speaking:

the weakness is in the method used to identify voters when they are voting electronically.

2. A virus or other malware could have changed the results of the vote.
3. The secrecy of the vote cannot be guaranteed, because malware could compromise the secrecy.
4. The regulations at the cantonal level are not consistent with cantonal law because they do not contain the required level of detailed requirements regarding the security of the voters' computers.
5. Because the federal law does not allow use of a system such as the Geneva system for all voters, and this precisely for the reasons set forth by the appellant, making such a system available to all voters for cantonal votes violates the Federal Constitution.

Regarding the case law of other jurisdictions, claims similar to those put forward by the appellant have been evaluated on their merits by courts in Austria, Germany and India [13]. In those cases the courts ruled that the electronic systems in question did not conform to the law and could not be used without changes. The German judgment is particularly broad and some commentators are of the view that it essentially prohibits e-voting [26].

A case judged in Estonia is worth mentioning because it creates a catch-22, that is, a situation from which an individual cannot escape because of contradictory rules [24]. At the time, Estonia was using an Internet voting scheme that shared the main characteristics of the Geneva system described above: it assumed that the voter's personal computer had not been compromised. A computer specialist deliberately infected his own personal computer with a virus that tampered with his vote, and then challenged the voting process in court, using as evidence what had happened in his own personal computer. The court dismissed the case, holding that the situation was analogous to that of a user who deliberately casts an invalid ballot. But the computer specialist would have committed a criminal offense if he had tampered with the computer of another voter without that voter's consent. So, in effect, there was no legal way for the computer specialist to present to the court evidence regarding how easy it was to tamper with the Internet voting system by tampering with voters' personal computers [27].

As Driza Maurer and Barrat put the matter [28], absence of proof of tampering is not proof of absence of tampering. We will discuss this point in more detail in the next section.

8   Next Steps

On the one hand, the judgment of the Federal Tribunal might seem surprising because, having first ruled that the appellant raised matters of principle that should be evaluated by the courts, it subsequently ruled that the matters in question were better left to the political system. On the other hand, the judgment must be seen in light of the evolution of the Swiss federal rules regarding e-voting systems. While the case was progressing through the courts, the Federal Council tightened the requirements for e-voting significantly, mandating the use of verifiable systems if more than 30 % of the voters are allowed to use an e-voting system [25]. While this change in federal law does not directly prevent the use of non-verifiable systems for cantonal-only votes, in practice it has resulted in the implementation of verifiable systems in the cantons. Thus the court cases discussed above may have influenced the actual implementation of e-voting systems in Switzerland, even if they were thrown out by the courts [28, 29].

Nevertheless, one might take the view that the situation in Switzerland is not satisfactory, because there is no way to ask for judicial review of a cantonal government's implementation of the federal rules regarding e-voting systems. For sure the systems are subject to review and approval by the federal government, but that is not the same as review and approval by an impartial and independent judiciary.

And indeed a group of federal parliamentarians has proposed to change the federal law so that the courts would have to evaluate on their merits arguments such as the ones outlined above [30]. That is, courts would evaluate whether a specific implementation of an e-voting system complies with the applicable federal and cantonal laws and regulations, and this independently of whether or not an appellant can prove that specific weaknesses were exploited in the course of a specific vote.

Further, it seems reasonable to conclude that parliaments need to take greater responsibility for the security of the systems that are actually implemented, and that they should be more involved in the tradeoffs between verifiability versus secrecy, usability versus coded voting or dedicated operating systems, and low costs versus dedicated hardware. All those topics warrant considerable further inter-disciplinary discussions, because they relate to legal, technical, and social matters [28].

References

1. Maurer, A.D.: Internet Voting and Federalism: The Swiss Case. Revista General de Derecho Público Comparado, No. 13, 2013. In: Barrat, J. (ed.) El voto electronico y sus dimensiones juridicas: entre la ingenua complacencia y el rechazo precipitado, Iustel, Madrid, Spain (2015)
2. Swiss Federal Chancellery: Vote électronique. http://www.bk.admin.ch/themen/pore/evoting/index.html?lang=fr
3. Commission externe d'évaluation des politiques publiques: Voter par Internet: évaluation des effets du vote électronique à Genève, Geneva, Switzerland (2013). http://goo.gl/BZpFn4
4. Chevalier, M.: Internet Voting: Status, Perspectives, and Issues, Chancellery of the canton of Geneva, ITU-T Workshop on e-Government (2003). http://www.itu.int/itudoc/itu-t/workshop/e-gov/e-gov010.html
5. Oppliger, R.: Traitement du problème de la sécurité des plate-formes pour le vote par Internet à Genève, Chancellerie du canton de Genève, Geneva, Switzerland (2002). http://goo.gl/t8o9gG
6. Chevalier, M.: La solution genevoise de vote électronique à cœur ouvert, Direcktdemokratie, Flash Informatique No. 6 (2011). http://goo.gl/9HUZXx
7. Dubuis, E., Haenni, R., Koenig, R.: Konzept und implicationen eines verifizierbaren Vote Eletronique Systems. Berner Fachhochschule, Bern, Switzerland (2012). http://goo.gl/pj7Gyl
8. Dubuis, E., Fischli, S., Haenni, R., Serdült, U., Spycher, O.: A verifiable internet voting system. In: CeDEM 2011, Conference for E-Democracy and Open Government, Krems, Austria, pp. 301–312 (2011)

9. Barrat, J., Chevallier, M., Goldsmith, B., Jandura, D., Turner, J., Sharma, R.: Internet voting and individual verifiability: the Norwegian return codes. In: EVOTE2012, Bregenz, Austria, pp. 35–45 (2012)
10. Swiss Federal Council: Rapport sur le vote électronique (2013). http://www.admin.ch/opc/fr/federal-gazette/2013/4519.pdf
11. Andrivet, S.: Attacking E-Voting: A Concrete Case, in Nuit du Hack 2013, Advtools (2013). http://goo.gl/1FamYU
12. Jones, Douglas W., Simons, Barbara: Broken Ballots: Will Your Vote Count?. University of Chicago Press, Chicago (2012)
13. Maurer, A.D., Barrat, J. (eds.): E-Voting Case Law: A Comparative Analysis. Ashgate, Farnham (2015)
14. Auer, A., Malinverni, G., Hottelier, M.: Droit constitutionnel suisse. Staempfli, Bern (2006)
15. Christin, T., Trechsel, A.S.: Analyse du scrutin du 26 septembre 2004 dans quatre communes genevoises. E-Democracy Center, University of Geneva, Geneva, Swittzerland (2005). http://goo.gl/4YqhFz
16. Chambre administrative, Cour de Justice de Genève: ATA/533/2012, 21 August 2012. http://justice.geneve.ch/tdb/Decis/TA/ata.tdb?F=ATA/533/2012
17. Chambre administrative, Cour de Justice de Genève, ATA/414/2011, 28 June 2011. http://justice.geneve.ch/tdb/Decis/TA/ata.tdb?F=ATA/414/2011
18. Federal Tribunal: 1C_329/2014, 22 July 2014. http://relevancy.bger.ch/php/aza/http/index.php?type=highlight_simple_query&highlight_docid=aza%3A%2F%2F22-12-2011-1C_329-2011
19. Federal Tribunal: 1F_5/2012, 19 March 2012. http://relevancy.bger.ch/php/aza/http/index.php?type=highlight_simple_query&highlight_docid=aza%3A%2F%2F19-04-2012-1F_5-2012
20. Federal Tribunal: 1C_477/2012, 27 March 2013. http://relevancy.bger.ch/php/aza/http/index.php?type=highlight_simple_query&highlight_docid=aza%3A%2F%2F27-03-2013-1C_477-2012
21. Federal Tribunal: ATF 1C_563, 29 August 2013. http://relevancy.bger.ch/php/aza/http/index.php?type=highlight_simple_query&highlight_docid=aza%3A%2F%2F29-08-2013-1C_563-2013
22. Chambre administrative, Cour de Justice de Genève, ATA 118/2014, 25 February 2014. http://justice.geneve.ch/tdb/Decis/TA/FichierWord/2014/0001/ATA_000118_2014_A_3506_2011.pdf
23. Federal Tribunal: 1C_136, 22 July 2014. http://relevancy.bger.ch/php/aza/http/index.php?type=highlight_simple_query&highlight_docid=aza%3A%2F%2F22-07-2014-1C_136-2014
24. Wikipedia: Catch-22 (logic). http://en.wikipedia.org/wiki/Catch-22_(logic)
25. Swiss Federal Chancellery: Des nouvelles dispositions régissent le vote électronique. http://www.bk.admin.ch/themen/pore/evoting/index.html?lang=fr
26. Seedorf, S.: Germany: the public nature of elections and its consequences on e-voting. In: [13]
27. Madise, U., Vinkel, P.: A judicial approach to internet voting in Estonia. In: [13]
28. Driza Mauer, A., Barrat, J.: Conclusions. In: [13]
29. Kuoni, B.: Case Law on e-voting – a swiss perspective. In: [13]
30. Swiss Parliament: Zulassung einer rechtlichen Prüfung der Modalitäten der elektronischen Stimmabgabe, Curia Vista 15.412. http://www.parlament.ch/d/suche/Seiten/geschaefte.aspx?gesch_id=20150412

Author Index

Printed in the United States
By Bookmasters